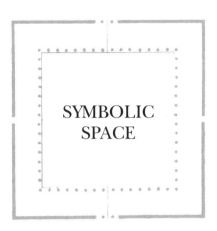

SYMBOLIC SPACE

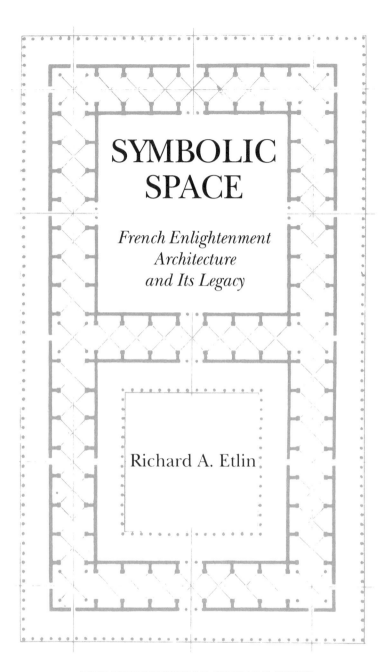

SYMBOLIC
SPACE

*French Enlightenment
Architecture
and Its Legacy*

Richard A. Etlin

THE UNIVERSITY OF CHICAGO PRESS

Chicago and London

RICHARD A. ETLIN is a professor in the School of Architecture, University of Maryland. He is the author of *The Architecture of Death: The Transformation of the Cemetery in Eighteenth-Century Paris* (1984); *Modernism in Italian Architecture, 1890–1940* (1991); and *Frank Lloyd Wright and Le Corbusier: The Romantic Legacy* (1994).

The University of Chicago Press, Chicago 60637
The University of Chicago Press, Ltd., London
© 1994 by The University of Chicago
All rights reserved. Published 1994
Printed in the United States of America
03 02 01 00 99 98 97 96 95 94 1 2 3 4 5

ISBN: 0-226-22084-2 (cloth)

Library of Congress Cataloging-in-Publication Data

Etlin, Richard A.
    Symbolic space : French Enlightenment architecture and its legacy
/ Richard A. Etlin.
        p. cm.
    Includes bibliographical references and index.
    1. Neoclassicism (Architecture)—France. 2. Architecture,
Modern—17th–18th centuries—France. 3. Signs and symbols in
architecture—France. 4. Neoclassicism (Architecture)—Influence.
I. Title.
NA1046.5.N4E84   1994
720′.944′09033—dc20   93-50194
                                                               CIP

For Mildred Leon Etlin
and in memory of Ben Etlin

CONTENTS

ILLUSTRATIONS

ILLUSTRATION CREDITS

Numbers refer to figures, not to pages.

American Competitions 1 (Philadelphia: T-Square Club, 1970): 29.

Anice Hoachlander, Hoachlander Photography: 25, 48

Architectural Archives of the University of Pennsylvania: 24, 33, 43, 94 (Photo: Eric E. Mitchell), 96

Archives Nationales, Paris. Photo: R. Lalance: 79

Artists Rights Society (ARS), New York/SPADEM, Paris © 1994: 1, 17, 67, 80, 100, 107

Artemis Verlags AG: 99

Associated University Presses: 32, 34, 38, 39

Avery Architectural and Fine Arts Library, Columbia University in the City of New York: 76, 113

Bibliothèque Mazarine, Paris: 68–71

Bibliothèque Nationale, Paris: 2–13, 15, 36, 51–56, 81, 82, 88–90

Caisse Nationale des Monuments Historiques et des Sites, Paris. © CNMHS/ SPADEM: 107 (Photo: J. J. Hautefeuille)

Carnegie Library of Pittsburgh: 103

The Detroit Institute of Arts ©: 40–42, 44, 45

Dumbarton Oaks, Trustees for Harvard University: 83–86

Fondazione Giuseppe Terragni (Per concessione della Fondazione Terragni): 102, 105

The Frank Lloyd Wright Foundation © 1985, 1988, 1993: 97, 98, 104, 108–112

Inventaire Général de la Documentation et de la Protection du Patrimoine, Paris: 1 (Photo: Bernard Emmanuelli), 17 (Collection Jacques Lebel), 80 (Photo: Bernard Emmanuelli), 100 (Photo: Bernard Emmanuelli)

The MIT Press: 94

Musée Carnavalet, Paris: 16 (Photo: Vaysse), 35 (Photo: Vaysse), 87, 91 (Photo: Vaysse), 92 (Photo: Vaysse), 93 (Photo: R. A. Etlin)

Musée du Louvre, Département des Arts Graphiques. © Photo R.M.N.: 101

Paul P. Cret Architect (and successor firm H2L2 Architects/Planners): 24, 26– 28, 30–34, 38–47, 49, 95, 96

Richard A. Etlin: 106

PREFACE

The eighteenth century saw radical changes in the world of architecture. The classical vocabulary that had dominated the field since the Renaissance was transformed through neoclassicism into a new type of aesthetics and a new mode of composition whose underlying logic subverted the major tenets of the Renaissance and Baroque styles. At the same time the Académie Royale d'Architecture, through a felicitous combination of institutional rigor and focused talent, created a body of student and pedagogical work that laid the foundations for the architectural education of the next century and even beyond throughout the Western world. The conceptual basis of the modern house, as a system of public and private spaces with specific functions organized with respect to the dual poles of ceremony and comfort, was formulated at this time. The supremacy of the formal mode of gardening that had reigned since the Renaissance was changed and to a large extent replaced by a new vision of nature organized as a picturesque or landscape garden. This was accompanied by a revolution in Western attitudes toward death that sought to overturn burial practices a thousand years old. Finally, the physical image of the city, while profiting from the legacy of Renaissance and baroque urban design, was crystallized into a coherent pattern that became the basis for modern urbanism.

In France each of these changes acquired special significance for the world of architecture. Although neoclassicism was an international phenomenon, the architects who combined the greatest theoretical insights with the most audacious and breathtaking buildings were the Frenchmen Etienne-Louis Boullée and Claude-Nicolas Ledoux. The radical quality of their architecture offered a relationship between compositional elements that would be taken up again nearly a century and a half later in the pioneering phases of what is known today as the "International Style." In the realm of architectural education, it was Boullée's student, J.-N.-L. Durand, who transformed the work of the late eighteenth-century academy into the pedagogical method that through the institution of the Ecole des Beaux-Arts would dominate the West until after World War I. With respect to domestic architecture, one of the principal, most enduring, and most widely copied or emulated house types created in the eighteenth century was the French *hôtel*. As for the landscape garden, whereas it arose initially in Great Britain, it was in France, center of the cemetery reform movement, that the garden became the ideal for a new type of burial ground. It was the Parisian Cemetery of Père Lachaise that was the first Western burial ground of this type and the model for the others that would follow. By giving voice to a clear vision of the well-ordered, commodious, beautiful, urbane, and salubrious city, eighteenth-century architects and other enthusiasts created the intellectual model that would be realized piecemeal over the course of the next century until, through concerted action, it crystallized into the Paris of the Second Empire, the Vienna of the Ringstrasse, and the City Beautiful movement in the United States.

This book studies each of these issues by devoting successive chapters to a different component of the field—urbanism, architecture, gardening, and funerary architecture. Whereas the importance of the subject matter would justify such a work merely on its own account, I have attempted to point out still another issue that seems to pervade all aspects of this period. I call this symbolic space.

Architecture is concerned primarily with the creation of domains for human activity. It is a truism to say that to achieve this goal architecture organizes and even creates spatial realms. Yet the space that architecture uses cannot simply be described as a function of its measurements. Architectural space is not merely the geometer's space. It is never neutral. It is always infused with qualities that affect the viewer and the user. On the most direct level these qualities derive from the physical nature of the place, seen under differing conditions of light and shade. Architects, though, also invest their buildings, their spaces—both the void and the container—with other types of meaning. All of these intellectual and subjective considerations about space, which reach beyond the mere measurement of height, width, and depth, and beyond the mere description of geometric features, are aspects of symbolic space.

Symbolic space runs the entire gamut from the most primal to the most intellectual. On the primal level, we must remember that our very sense of being in this world is irrevocably linked with a sense of body space. The anthropologist Edward T. Hall has taught us to recognize that we carry a kind of space bubble around us that expands and contracts according to the nature of our relationships with other people. We physically distance ourselves from people according to the degree of intimacy or formality in our relationships.[1]

This insight into our essential body self can be extended into a more general sense of existential space whereby we fill a room with our presence as we enter it. Although many of us deaden our responses to such experience by blocking it out of consciousness in favor of other emotional and intellectual concerns, we have only to read Marcel Proust's *A la Recherche du temps perdu* to remind ourselves about the degree to which we insert ourselves into rooms and make them our own through a sense of our body space. Whereas the narrator in Proust's novel is primarily concerned with feelings of intimacy and security within a domestic setting, the other side of the spectrum involves feelings of exhilaration related to grand religious spaces. With respect to this latter issue, it would be helpful to recall that the great American architect Louis Kahn used to say that the Roman Pantheon was a perfect building except for one problem: it has a door. Kahn meant that as soon as we enter this huge, centralized, and domed building, we immediately feel as if we are occupying the center and filling the great room with our presence. We are already one with the space even before we traverse the distance from the entrance to the central spot under the opening of the dome.

Such experiences involving existential space are essential for creating what might be termed the "deep structure" of architecture. By "deep structure," I am referring to those particularly intense experiences in which sentience, the feeling of vital life, takes on a particularly intense coloring. This is sometimes achieved through what may be termed the expressive aspect of a building or place, or by the creation of a domain that seems qualitatively different from the surrounding world, an area that puts us in contact with something intangible. With Boullée's funerary architecture, for example, we find the birth of a tradition in commemorative design that utilizes such sentiments. The particular conjunction in that era of the memorial grounded in this "deep structure" of architecture and of the individual as its focus is readily understandable as a reflection of two main Enlightenment concerns—the heightened sensitivity to sentience that Jean-Jacques Rousseau popularized through his repeated references to and observations about "le sentiment de l'existence" and the new worth accorded the individual, grounded in natural law and natural right, that gave us the principles of the American and French revolutions.

I have long wondered whether this "deep structure" of architectural experience was at the basis of the foundation rites of early civilizations.[2] Thanks to studies by Mircea Eliade and Joseph Rykwert, for example, we know that the need to delimit a zone of space from the undifferentiated void of the outer world was fundamental to the establishment of a community.[3] These precincts were fashioned with rituals that made the ceremony seem a recreation on a small scale of the universe, a cosmogonic act that joined the community to the gods. Passage across the boundary between the profane world without and the sacred domain within acquired special importance. Even today the threshold, any threshold, retains a symbolic character that extends beyond its merely functional purpose. It seems likely that the basic configuration of early settlements organized according to a cosmogonic ritual, which privileges the perimeter and the center, is grounded in the human psyche's need for orientation related to our own body sense.

Yet, as the anthropologist Claude Lévi-Strauss has shown, in certain contemporary non-Western cultures the arrangement of buildings around the periphery of a precinct, as well as at its center, and the division of the precinct into sectors is also used to order social relationships.[4] When one passes beyond the simplest instances of "deep structure" in space, whether at the intimate scale of psychological shelter, as found in the houses of Frank Lloyd Wright, or at the cosmic scale, as found in the Pantheon or the Gothic cathedrals, we find that symbolic space is invariably commingled with various codes of order by which humans organize their world. There are even codes of ordering spaces and giving them meaning in Wright's houses and in Gothic cathedrals. These codes of order are also aspects of symbolic space, investing arrangements of rooms or places with meaning according to social and cultural hierarchies established by sequence, contiguity, separation, exclusion, and so forth. Since the human mind will seek different types of meaning in the same place at the same time, the simultaneous infusion of multiple intellectual and spiritual purposes into a single place or space also invests it with symbolic meaning. Therefore, it is possible to speak about three different types of symbolic space—the primal, experiential space of "deep structure"; the hierarchically organized space according to social codes; and the multiple, simultaneous layering of meaning given to a particular place.

These three types of symbolic space provide the unifying thread of this book. Chapter 1 considers the image of the eighteenth-century city as a layered mental construct, in which actual physical space was subjected to a complex mental layering of conceptual spaces—the space of magnificence, the space of hygiene, the space of clarity, and the space of emulation. The space of magnificence concerns the monumental ordering of the city, combining streets, plazas, and buildings according to the contemporary notion of *embellissement*. A consideration of the space of hygiene reveals that this same monumental network of buildings and spaces was also conceived as a guarantor of public salubrity in an age that became obsessed with urban hygiene. The space of clarity addresses the newly found need to go beyond the traditional directives of decorum and propriety in architectural expression to invest each building with a "character" that corresponded to and even revealed its purpose. Here I introduce Boullée's definition of character, which involves three components: metaphorical character, which is achieved through the narrative organization of forms and spaces; expressive character, which relies on the emotional impact on the viewer of simple geometric forms; and symbolic character, which utilizes temple-like spaces dedicated to high ideals in order to make them, in a manner of speaking, present, palpable.

With the advent of the French Revolution, it seemed to contemporaries even more urgent to realize this multifarious vision of the city while creating as well a symbolic revolutionary space. In Chapter 2, I discuss the concept of revolutionary space under the rubrics of narrative space, expressive space, and numinous space. These correspond to the three aspects of architectural character—metaphorical, expressive, and symbolic—briefly introduced in Chapter 1 and the subject of further discussion in Chapter 3.

Chapter 3 examines the interplay between the richly symbolic aspects of architectural character epitomized in Boullée's designs and the rationalized code of ordering architectural elements for teaching architecture devised by Durand. By concentrating on the twentieth-century civic architecture of Paul Philippe Cret, I have attempted to show how the greatest of Beaux-Arts architects combined the eighteenth-century legacy of character with the nineteenth-century Beaux-Arts rationalized system of ordering form.

Chapter 4 considers other codes of architectural ordering, beginning with the one postulated by the abbé Marc-Antoine Laugier's secular parable of the primitive hut, then proceeding to the related system of ordering established by Boullée in his civic and religious architecture, and finally considering the code established by Jacques-Germain Soufflot's Church of Sainte-Geneviève. All three of these codes of ordering are juxtaposed with the new aesthetic experience so prized in the neoclassical era, which was grounded in the forest of columns and which returns the discussion to the realm of "deep structure."

Chapter 5 considers two interrelated symbolic codes of ordering— the social and architectural systems for organizing the floor plans, rooms, and facades of the town mansion or country house. Chapter 6 examines changing attitudes toward death in the eighteenth century and how they were reflected in cemetery design. This chapter traces the three successive stages in the definition of the functional and symbolic aspects of the new cemetery, while investigating the fundamental role of commemoration in the genesis and evolution of the new type of gardening, the picturesque or landscape garden. Chapter 7 focuses on one aspect of commemorative architecture, what I term the space of absence, which seems to be the most primal and most profound of the four types of "deep structure" considered in the book, the other three being expressive character, symbolic character, and numinous revolutionary space.

Throughout the book, usually at the beginning or end of each chapter, I have endeavored to suggest briefly the enduring quality of the Enlightenment legacy. Except for the consideration of Cret's architecture, it has not been my intention to develop the nature of this legacy through extended discussion or demonstration. Rather I have limited my observations to focused points and broad generalizations, ranging from the legacy of Boullée to Aldo Rossi, Leon Krier, and Louis Kahn; from the abbé Laugier and his contemporary urbanists to Baron Haussmann and Napoleon III; and from Jacques-François Blondel to Auguste Perret and Le Corbusier. To develop these ideas further would require another book. My primary concern here has been to sketch a way to consider the principal themes of French Enlightenment architecture and to think of them within the conceptual framework of symbolic space.

ACKNOWLEDGMENTS

In this book I have rewritten and gathered together under the theme of symbolic space articles and conference papers, published and unpublished, that I have prepared over the course of the last twenty years. I am pleased to acknowledge here my major debts of gratitude to people and institutions that have supported my work.

The first chapter has been adapted from a paper of the same title delivered at the symposium London and Paris in the Eighteenth Century, sponsored by the Committee on the Growth and Structure of Cities at Bryn Mawr College on October 29–30, 1976. I am grateful to Catherine Lafarge for having invited me to participate in this event. Chapter 2 was originally the last section of this symposium paper. Research for this theme of revolutionary space was supported by a summer grant from the University of Kentucky. I thank both this institution and my dean, Anthony Eardley, for their support.

I developed my study of revolutionary space into a longer essay that I presented as "1789: Revolutionary Space and Its Legacy" at the symposium Approaches to Art History of the Revolutionary Period, cosponsored by the New York University Humanities Council and the Institute of Fine Arts, February 11, 1989. Robert Rosenblum kindly invited me to participate in this event.

The nucleus to Chapter 3 is an unpublished essay first written during the second half of 1984 under a grant from the National Endowment for the Humanities to plan an exhibition of the civic architecture of Paul Philippe Cret. For facilitating my study of the Cret archives, I am grateful especially to Paul Cret Harbison at Cret's successor firm H2L2, and to Julia Moore Converse, archivist at the Architectural Archives of the University of Pennsylvania. The Van Pelt Library of the University of Pennsylvania has kindly permitted me to quote from the correspondence between Paul Cret and Albert Kelsey kept in the Cret Papers in Special Collections. Visits to Cret buildings and work at their archives was a pleasure, thanks to the assistance provided by Lawrence Downey, former associate director of the Indianapolis Public Library; Philip A. Knachel, associate director of the Folger Shakespeare Library; Mary Anne Goley, director of the Fine Arts Program at the Federal Reserve Board; and Cherryl A. Wagner, former assistant archivist, and Marilyn Ghausi, former museum archivist, at the Detroit Institute of Arts. I am grateful to the Detroit Institute of Arts for kindly permitting me to quote from documents conserved in the Museum Archives. Working with several Cret scholars on this project greatly helped my understanding of the architect's work. Carol McMichael was an excellent guide who accompanied me on a tour of the University of Texas at Austin. My appreciation of McMichael's work on Cret is expressed in the text. I am particularly indebted to the writings of Elizabeth Grossman, with whom I passed many enjoyable hours pouring over Cret's drawings in the Philadelphia archives. On October 31, 1986, at the Graduate School of Architecture, University of Pennsylvania, I delivered an earlier version of this chapter as a lecture entitled "Paul Cret and the French Academic Legacy."

Of all the articles in this book, the fourth chapter least resembles its original. I developed this chapter out of my conference paper, "The Rise and Fall of the Church of Sainte-Geneviève: A Study in Changing Aesthetic Values," read in English at the international colloquium Soufflot et l'Architecture des Lumières, Lyons, June 18–21, 1980. This paper was published in the acts of the colloquium as "Grandeur et décadence d'un modèle: L'Eglise Sainte-Geneviève et les changements de valeur esthétique au XVIIIe siècle," *Les Cahiers de la Recherche Architecturale,* supplement to numbers 6–7 (October 1980). Chapter 5 has been developed out of "'Les Dedans,' Jacques-François Blondel and the System of the Home," *Gazette des Beaux-Arts* 91 (April 1978), which has graciously allowed me to reformulate my earlier text for this book.

Chapter 6 presents in condensed form major themes from the second part of my book, *The Architecture of Death: The Transformation of the Cemetery in Eighteenth-Century Paris* (Cambridge, Mass.: MIT Press, 1984), and avails itself of material published on this theme in my articles that have appeared in *Oppositions* (1977), *Lotus International* (1983), and the *Journal of Garden History* (1984).

Chapter 7 has been reworked from my conference paper, "The Space of Absence," written for the colloquium An Architecture for Death: First International Encounter on Contemporary Cemeteries, June 4–7, 1991, in Seville, sponsored by the Department of Architecture and Housing, Ministry of Transport and Public Works, Regional Government of Andalusia. I am grateful to Francisco Javier Rodríguez Barberán for having invited me to participate in this colloquium and to the conference sponsor for permitting me to adapt this chapter from the version published in *Una Arquitectura para la Muerte. 1 Encuentro Internacional sobre los Cementerios Contemporaneos. Actas* (Seville: Consejeria de Obras Publicas y Transportes. Direccion General de Arquitectura y Vivienda, 1993).

Finally, I thank Karen Wilson, senior editor at the University of Chicago Press, as well as the two readers whom she secured, for offering penetrating suggestions and exacting requirements in response to my first draft for this book. My text benefited immeasurably from their assistance. Any shortcomings that still remain are, of course, my own.

1

Paris: The Image of the City

The image of a city has to be found in the interplay between physical appearance and mental construct. For the eighteenth-century French observer who took an active interest in the quality of the surroundings, the city was a composite of the seen and the imagined, of the real and the potential. This was the age when utopia became uchronia, where the place was not the distant but the familiar, and when the time was some future date when the full vision of a transformed habitat would have been realized.[1] The difference between a uchronia such as Louis-Sébastien Mercier's *L'An deux mille quatre cent quarante: Rêve s'il en fut jamais* (The year 2440: A dream if there ever was one) (1771) and a tract on urban design such as Poncet de la Grave's *Projet des embellissements de la ville et faubourgs de Paris* (Project for the embellishment of the city and faubourgs of Paris) (1756) resided more in the choice of literary genre than in differences between underlying philosophies.[2]

In the latter half of the eighteenth century, these two types of writings constituted the principal components of an ample body of city planning literature that sought to refashion the city. One of the most striking aspects about French culture at this time was the extent to which intellectuals—not only architects but also clergyman, doctors, lawyers, scientists, and writers as different as Voltaire and Mercier—took an active and public interest in the physical aspect of the city. Their books, pamphlets, and letters to the editor, as well as architectural drawings, offered new projects, generally unsolicited, to improve the commodity, salubrity, order, and beauty of the city as well as to promote virtue and merit.

The contemporary image of the city, then, included an anticipated alteration of the physical fabric for symbolic and aesthetic as well as functional purposes; it was informed by the moral and intellectual ends that the built world could serve. The result was a richly layered mental construct, with these layered perceptions often lacking clearly demarcated divisions. For the purpose of analysis, though, they might be classified under four separate headings: the space of magnificence, of hygiene, of

1

clarity, and of emulation. Together these overlapping conceptual realms constituted the Enlightenment ideal of *embellissement,* whose English-language rendering as "embellishment" must be understood to include cultural aspirations and functional amenities as well as aesthetic pleasures.

This eighteenth-century mental construct reminds us that the image of the city cannot be entirely explained by the notion of topological "legibility" outlined by Kevin Lynch, in terms of paths, edges, districts, nodes, and landmarks.[3] Eighteenth-century *embellissement* at once subsumes this idea and extends beyond it to include the full flavor of urban goals that can make the city, as Donald J. Olsen has reminded us, into a "work of art": a "treasure to be preserved, an achievement of and monument to Western civilization, economically flourishing, culturally active, a joy to visit and a privilege to inhabit."[4] If Louis Napoleon and Baron Georges-Eugène Haussmann were able to transform Paris in this manner in the third quarter of the nineteenth century, it was because they were heirs to the Enlightenment urban ideal that envisaged the city holistically according to overlapping symbolic dimensions.

The Space of Magnificence

The first and perhaps foremost category that Donald J. Olsen articulates and explores in his study of nineteenth-century London, Vienna, and Paris as works of art is "the city as monument." The eighteenth century had a term for this notion as well as a full program that would be left to future times to implement. Viewing the city both in its specific features and in its entirety, it furnished a conceptual reading of the city according to what might be termed a space of magnificence. I adapt this term from the title to the preface of John Gwynn's *London and Westminster Improved* (1766), "A Discourse on Publick Magnificence."

As a capital city, Paris had to have a physical magnificence worthy of its importance. In this case, the seen was an outward sign of the unseen; the physical, a manifestation of the cultural. It was believed that the buildings and spaces of the city could make manifest the character of the people who lived and worked there. As the neoclassical architect Louis Combes explained, "It is [architecture] that has given that magnificence to our cities which astonishes the enlightened traveler, which elevates his soul, and, from his first view of the city, which teaches him about the genius and the grandeur of the people whom he is visiting."[5] The architect François-Joseph Belanger continued this thought when he explained that architectural monuments provided an ever-present, open book of a nation's history. "These various monuments," he wrote, "delineate the major points of a nation's history, of its civilization, its tastes, its mores, its character, its sensibility, its ideas, and even its opinions. . . . [These monuments] are the honor, glory, and pride of the cities that possess them."[6]

The first requirement for a city's magnificence was to present the approaching visitor with the image of a distinct physical entity. Paris could not be allowed to spread haphazardly into the surrounding countryside but rather had to have discrete limits. At mid-century, the abbé Marc-Antoine Laugier suggested establishing numerous *barrières* around Paris. These gateways would be placed at regular distances to transform the perimeter of the city into a regular polygon. Beyond this boundary, the city would not be permitted to extend.[7] Toward the same time, Poncet de la Grave envisaged a more elaborate project that included not only completing the ring of boulevards around Paris but also surrounding them with a canal for the dual purpose of providing water for the city and ports for the *faubourgs* and enhancing their visual splendor.[8]

The principal component of the city's exterior limits was the entryway itself. We have only to follow Babouc's arrival at Persepolis to appreciate Voltaire's thinly disguised critique of the undistinguished gateways into Paris.[9] Such "pitiful" wooden *barrières* met by crooked streets made one wonder whether he or she was truly entering, in the words of Poncet de la Grave, "that famous city where the nobility of all nations and the great majority of Frenchmen come to develop good taste and the sciences."[10]

Paris, then, had to present a magnificent entrance, for the gateway to the city announced and, in some manner, summarized in a single image the city's cultural achievements. For Laugier and Poncet de la Grave, the suitable entrance was to be found in the magnificent triumphal arch, as typified by François Blondel's Porte Saint-Denis, built in 1671 as part of the new monumental entrances to Paris after the city's ramparts were demolished.[11] Toward the end of the century, Claude-Nicolas Ledoux was to build the famous tax wall for the Ferme Générale, with its tree-lined boulevards and its forty-five monumental *barrières*. In response to criticism directed against the wall and its monuments, Legrand, in his *Description de Paris* (1809), argued that "one cannot deny that it was appropriate to construct edifices of a grand character for the embellishment of a city such as Paris and for the honor of the arts that the government causes to flourish there."[12]

Ledoux's *barrières* redefined the nature of the city gateway for the late eighteenth and early nineteenth centuries. He called them "Propylaea" after the magnificent Greek entrance pavilions to the Acropolis of Athens.[13] From Carl Langhans's Brandenburg Gate (1789–1794), welcoming the visitor to Berlin at the magnificent promenade of Unter den Linden, to Rodolfo Vantini's paired cubical buildings (1827–1833) at Porta Venezia in Milan, the freestanding entrance pavilion, often a creative adaptation of the Athenian Propylaea, provided an even more impressive alternative to the triumphal arch that Laugier and his contemporaries had envisaged.[14] After mid-century, as rail travel revolutionized European culture and commerce, the railroad station assumed the function previously held by the neoclassical and Greek Revival *barrières* and by their classical predecessors in the form of the triumphal arch gateway. Mid-nineteenth-century Paris helped to pioneer the symbolic purpose of this new building type through the monumental architecture of the new railroad stations that now ringed the city.

This cultural charge has remained active in the West even if the businessmen and bureaucrats who oversee these buildings have, at times, forgotten it. It is ironic that in 1992, thirty years after the demolition of New York City's Pennsylvania Station (1902–1911), a grandiose Beaux-Arts building that took its cue from the Parisian Gare du Nord (1858–1866) and its later counterpart, the Gare d'Orsay (1898–1900), a spokesman for Amtrak echoed the sentiments of Voltaire and Laugier while bemoaning the company's and the city's ill-conceived loss: "A station is the gateway to the rail service and the city it serves. We feel urban stations such as in Chicago, Philadelphia and Washington, all of which have been renovated, have been tremendous successes because they exhibit a sense of optimism and grandeur, an esthetic beauty which we feel is very important." Regretting the destruction of New York City's Pennsylvania Station, Amtrak was now hoping to acquire and transform into a train station the monumental Beaux-Arts post office across the street.[15]

In the century preceding the railroad, though, the perfect city, even if contained within a bounded area, would nevertheless have to announce itself to the traveler long before its actual limits. From Colbert to Laugier to Durand at the turn of the nineteenth century, Paris was to be preceded by broad, tree-lined avenues that would shelter the traveler from the sun and would herald the magnificence of the capital city.[16] At the gateway, the architectural entry would be set within an elaborate design of public squares and streets. The projects for a *porte de ville* that won the first three prizes in the 1738 *Grand Prix* competition displayed the prevalent values of the period and could have been used to illustrate Laugier's *Essai* published nearly two decades later.[17]

Viewed as a whole, Paris had two privileged axes that could give coherence to the city's organization as well as grandeur to the promenade which began beyond the city's gates. When fully developed, these axes would form perpendicular spines through the city. As is well known, this arrangement had to await the urban transformation of the Second Empire when it was completed as the "great crossing" of Paris.[18] Yet the concept dates back to Enlightenment schemes for the embellishment of Paris.

In the eighteenth-century vision of the city, the west-east axis would extend from the Pont de Neuilly to the hill of the Etoile, down the Champs-Elysées to the place Louis XV (now place de la Concorde), then through the Tuileries Garden to the Louvre, across the city to the Bastille, on to place du Trône (now place de la Nation), and out along the avenue de Vincennes. Long before Napoleon's triumphal arch was raised on the hill at the Etoile, this eminence had been the subject of numerous proposals for colossal monuments, including a triumphal arch, an amphitheater, an obelisk, a giant elephant, and an immense fountain.[19] The arid gardens between the Etoile and the Tuileries Palace were the subject of numerous projects of embellishment, which ranged from André Le Nôtre's plan to dig a canal through the middle of the Tuileries Garden to Pierre Chaussard's proposal for an Elysium to dead military heroes beside a meandering stream that would be added to the Champs-Elysées.[20]

The completion of the Louvre, as is well known, was a popular subject that had to await first Napoleon Bonaparte and then Louis Napoleon for its realization. Finally, from Claude Perrault to Charles de Wailly, the east facade of the Louvre was envisaged as the point of departure for a street extending to the barrière du Trône. Thus, as de Wailly explained, "one would be able to cross Paris along its longest diameter on a straight line, passing all the while its most beautiful monuments and public promenades."[21]

Not only was this vision realized by Louis Napoleon and Baron Haussmann, but even to this day Paris has remained true to this scheme through the development of the so-called *grands projets* of the 1980s, which reorganized the circulation within the Louvre around the new glass pyramid entrance pavilion built in its courtyard; which focused the development at La Défense, while extending the vista of the monumental axis from the triumphal arch of the Etoile to its new counterpart, the *Grande Arche* at La Défense three miles away; which transformed the former train station of the Gare d'Orsay into a museum for nineteenth-century art; and which added an additional monument to the place de la Bastille, the imposing building that houses the new Opéra de la Bastille.[22]

The other principal axis would have extended from the Porte Saint-Martin to the Porte Saint-Jacques. In considering the organization of Paris neighborhoods, Laugier preferred this north-south alignment as a hinge to the city's future development. According to this scheme, the two entries would be connected by a straight thoroughfare. At each end, streets would branch outward in a radiating fashion to communicate with different quarters.[23] Under the Second Empire, this axis was completed with the opening of the boulevard Sébastopol and the boulevard Saint-Michel just to the west and parallel to the rue Saint-Martin and the rue Saint-Jacques. Through this realization, the north-south axis had its inception in the monumental facade of the gare de l'Est and the new boulevard de Strasbourg, both the product of the Second Republic, which now extended southward along the Boulevard Sébastopol.

Within the city, a variety of design techniques could be employed to enhance the magnificence of individual monuments and, as a result, to augment the grandeur of the whole. The square, for example, provided the preferred location for a major edifice. Charles Villette was speaking for half a century when he announced that, if appointed as magistrate of public buildings, he would construct nothing new but rather would merely tear down. Paris had so many majestic buildings which were crowded into a tight urban fabric that did not permit a satisfactory view.[24]

The square, moreover, was thought to impart dignity to the sculptural monument placed at its center. Hence, when in 1748 the City of Paris announced its intention to erect a statue of Louis XV, the directeur général des bâtiments opened a competition to locate and design a suitable square.[25] Many of the numerous competition entries provided not only a geometrically regular space, often a circle, lined with regular and symmetrical facades, but also extended the building fronts into the neighboring side streets. The result would have been to create a totally controlled visual world within which the monument would have appeared. Long before Baron Haussmann earned the sobriquet of the great *démolisseur,* Viel de Saint-Maux ridiculed the enthusiasm of those eighteenth-century would-be *niveleurs* (levelers) when he suggested that one way to satisfy the current mania for adjusting street alignments would be to place the houses of Paris on rollers. Then, whenever an architect wished to create some new perspective, the buildings could easily be shifted about.[26] With respect to the competition for a statue honoring Louis XV, the king, as is well known, chose to donate his own prop-

Figure 1. Le Febvre, "Triumphal bridge leading to place Louis XV [today place de la Corcorde]," *prix d'émulation,* May 1786.

erty just outside the city beyond the Tuileries Garden rather than "devastate commercial neighborhoods and sacrifice the commodity and interests of a great number of his subjects by the destruction of innumerable houses."[27]

In fashioning the urban squares that would embellish the city while simultaneously augmenting the value of adjacent properties, architects paid particular attention to the aesthetic shaping of this outdoor room. Embroidering upon the example of the place Vendôme, with its beveled corners, Charles-François Bailleul won a second prize in the 1733 *Grand Prix* competition for the design of a square that emphasized the sculptural volume of the open urban space to the detriment of regular and functional rooms to the other side.[28] The circular square especially was faulted for disrupting the shape of rooms in the surrounding buildings.[29]

The urban bridge was the complement to the urban square as a means for focusing attention on a monumental edifice. Louis Combes's prizewinning design for the *Grand Prix* of 1781, which stipulated a "cathedral for a capital like Paris," featured not only a monumental building but also set it within a grand *place,* after the manner of Bernini's Saint Peter's square, which in turn is preceded by a bridge in this French sequel.[30] This bridge isolates the spectator far more effectively than a street, for it focuses his or her movement and attention on the object at

7

the end of the perspective. In its ideal form, the eighteenth-century bridge (fig. 1) would become a triumphal passageway with covered walkways, colonnades, statues, triumphal arches, and obelisks. However, first the bridges of Paris had to be freed of the houses that had covered several of them for centuries. This traditional extension of the urban fabric across the Seine was to the contemporary observer an eyesore, which no longer had to be suffered after the demolition effected according to the edict of 1786.

Although Paris was not to know the colonnaded bridges envisaged by the academy's students, it was soon to enjoy the realization of a monumental complex of spaces reminiscent of Combes's vision. The sequence extended from the neoclassical facade to the Chambre des Députés (1806–1807) across the Pont de la Concorde (1787–1791) to the place de la Concorde (1755), with its two monumental facades framing the view to Eglise de la Madeleine (begun 1763, finished with a new design between 1806–1842).

The facades of the major eighteenth-century public buildings of Paris, both real and ideal, generally displayed a monumental character that the great academic teacher Jacques-François Blondel termed "une grande architecture."[31] As Etienne-Louis Boullée would explain, "To appear grand . . . is to announce superior qualities."[32] Buildings that exhibited a "grand architecture" had vast dimensions and proportions. Rather than reflecting the scale of the human figure by showing many floors, they presented an imposing mass with few horizontal divisions. This approach to architectural composition, in large part stimulated by the aspect of the east facade of the Louvre (1667), would become the determining characteristic of nineteenth-century Beaux-Arts monumental design throughout the West.

Finally, the space of magnificence was also that of festive gaiety and of nocturnal magic. Between the permanent architecture and the temporary decoration ensued a collaboration in which each assisted the other. Long before the modern architects of the 1930s learned to design with artificial nighttime illumination in mind, the architects of the French Enlightenment covered the facades of public buildings with temporary illumination. Building on the traditions of the previous century especially, the City and the Court between 1763 and 1790 offered a "profusion of festivals with sumptuous decor."[33]

The ephemeral structures for the festival could do more than just decorate and enhance a noble architecture; they could also rapidly, if only temporarily, effectuate urban transformations that only time, money, power, and skillful administration might realize. The false facade could hide a Gothic style or correct an asymmetrical arrangement. A wood and canvas triumphal arch could transform the space for an antici-pated procession. And with the assistance of a dissembling darkness, a nighttime illumination could establish entire vistas, correcting irregular-ities of street alignments and building heights in a transformation whose facility certainly left contemporary observers wistful about the difficult-ies of effecting permanent change.

The Space of Hygiene

While eighteenth-century Parisians were exulted by the space of mag-nificence, they were also haunted by the absence of a space of salubrity. One cannot overemphasize the degree to which the contemporary ob-session with public hygiene influenced the image of the city. When re-formers wrote about the space of hygiene, they usually explained their views in terms of the quality of the air. In this age of prebacteriological science, the air was understood as the "fluid" vital to life, capable of undergoing noxious alterations. Without movement, the air, like water, would stagnate and become unwholesome. Mere living corrupted the air through breathing and transpiration. The ill were thought to produce a putrid or fetid air considered to be the agent of disease. And the dead gave off particularly noxious emanations that could suffocate, cause ill-ness, or slowly undermine health.[34]

Paris, then, appeared as a city of multiple pollutions. Within the space of the living, slaughterhouses, prisons, the various crafts and trades, the cemeteries, and even the churches themselves where the priv-ileged were buried—all were deemed to contribute to the corruption of the air. In addition, the city itself, by gathering together so many people who gave off wastes through respiration, transpiration, and excretion, posed a problem to the salubrity of the air.

The doctors, scientists, and architects who addressed themselves to the problems of public hygiene believed that through the proper distri-bution of activities in space, through the improved design of buildings and open spaces, seconded by mechanical and chemical agents, and by new municipal services, the city could be transformed into a salubrious habitat. The smells that had plagued the city in previous ages were now so worrisome that one wonders whether a commonsense concern for hygiene can fully explain the intensity of the contemporary response. Although eminently rational in its program, the space of hygiene, none-theless, in this Age of Reason, also appears to have furnished a symbolic space that banished a fear of the unseen and the unknown that foul-smelling air portended. It offered an illusion of certainty within the midst of constant reminders about the ambiguities of mortal existence. It presented the most secure symbolic replacement of the temperamental goddess Fortuna by the self-styled Siècle des Lumières, the Age of Enlightenment whose favorite symbol was light chasing out the clouds and the obscurity of darkness.

The goal of this reform movement, which dominated the contemporary psyche from the 1740s onward, was the constant provision of a renewed and pure air. "One of the principal parts of the salubrity of a large city like Paris," explained Dr. Jacques Dehorne, "is to favor the free circulation of the air that we breathe, by destroying . . . all obstacles that would intercept it . . . [and] by removing from the midst of our habitations, all foyers of uncleanliness and of corruption."[35]

In its very nature as a physical entity, the city placed impediments to the free flow of air. The conditions that contributed to a healthy or unhealthy environment were, in either case, multiple and mutually reinforcing. Thus, the medieval quarters of Paris with narrow, crooked streets bordered by tall buildings were decried for retaining their foul air and for blocking out both the sun and a new, refreshing atmosphere. These conditions were aggravated by high density of rooms and people, poor construction, few and small windows, stagnating puddles in poorly paved streets and in small courtyards, inadequate systems of street and roof drainage, the stench of latrines, etc.

The remedy to this physical obstacle was a city of long, straight, and wide streets, without dead ends and bordered by buildings of low height. A Royal Declaration of 1783 established regulations that promised to provide a fresh and renewed air to the lower floors and to the people in the street itself. Uniform facades and uniform building heights were proposed as a suitable means of avoiding all pockets of space that would entrap a portion of the air.

Laugier saw an excellent opportunity to create salubrious housing in the extensive private gardens spread throughout Paris. He proposed eliminating the typical apartment building with its crowded courtyard in favor of rearranging the urban fabric around superblocks with a ring of buildings facing the street and freestanding homes in the middle. That way all dwellings would have adequate ventilation.[36] Within the dwelling itself, reformers foresaw improvements in sanitation and even of mechanical ventilation, the latter to be adapted from contemporary practices in mines and ships.[37]

The public square was seen as important for introducing sun and air into the dense urban fabric. The larger the city, the more squares were needed. Furthermore, to be most effective, the square had to be placed at the intersection of several streets.[38] A spacious urban square was thought to serve as a "reservoir" for pure air, which when pushed by the wind would renew the air within the streets.[39] To Laugier, the only square in Paris that satisfied these conditions was the place des Victoires. All the others were too enclosed and therefore too isolated from the surrounding neighborhoods.[40]

Public gardens too, as well as squares planted with trees, were to be distributed throughout the city. There the artisan and the convalescent would be able to breath healthy air not far from their homes.[41] At the turn of the century, the architect Goulet proposed new embankments along the Seine built with wide, planted terraces made pleasant for a promenade.[42]

Under the Second Empire, Louis Napoleon and Baron Haussmann, heirs to this tradition and spurred by the mortality caused by recent cholera epidemics, realized their "surgical" cuts through the city with wide, tree-lined boulevards that they and their contemporaries hoped would make the city more salubrious. The citizens of Paris were provided with a series of new public parks and neighborhood squares.[43] After that time, when the discovery of bacteria eliminated the imperative to create uniform facades, architects attempted to perfect hygienic modern street design with arrangements that ranged from Eugène Hénard's *à redans* housing and his expanded Haussmannian park system to Sauvage and Sarazin's terraced "hygienic" housing. The ultimate extension of this impulse was Le Corbusier's radically anti-urban solution to the problem found in his Radiant City, a so-called city within a park.

The ground was an important source of corruption to the air. Both Patte and Tournon published cross-sections of suggested improvements depicting well-paved and properly drained streets with underground channels to collect wastes from the home into covered sewers. These new evacuation systems were to be seconded by an abundant flow of water to wash streets and thereby refresh the air. Although the street cleaners who crossed Paris with their water in a regular fashion from mid-century onward became "a European celebrity,"[44] and although the beginnings of a sewer system were adumbrated in the early nineteenth century, the city had to await the Second Empire until the Enlightenment vision of underground sewers was finally realized.[45]

This vision included the provision of underground conduits of water to supply new public fountains, which would contribute to the salubrity of the air. Eighteenth-century architects looked forward to the opportu-

nity to decorate Paris's public squares with "isolated, shooting fountains," which would purify the air before cleansing the streets.[46]

As for the siting of the city, the land around Paris furnished "no
foyer from which the air as wind could bring harmful exhalations."[47]
Straddling a river that flowed toward the west, the city was also favored
with ideal conditions for a healthy atmosphere.[48] Through human intervention, though, eighteenth-century Paris seemed threatened by obstacles to the air from both within and without. Several bridges—Pont-au-
Change, Pont Notre-Dame, Pont Saint-Michel—for centuries had been
covered with houses, which now were repeatedly denounced not only
as an eyesore but also as an intolerable menace to urban hygiene. By
constituting a "barrier" that "opposed the free action of the winds,"
these houses obstructed the principal means for renewing the city's air.[49]
The destruction of these impediments, along with the construction of
new embankments toward the end of the century, was applauded for
facilitating the rapid current of air that moved along with the Seine.
These transformations were considered especially important because
the lowest layers of the atmosphere were thought to be the most infected
and the most difficult to renew.[50]

While Paris was being cleared of its obstructions to the air at the
center of the city, the Ferme Générale was constructing a wall, which to
some observers threatened to block the free exchange of air between
the city and the country along the periphery. Since Paris was located in
a basin and was surrounded by hills, even the modest height of the new
wall, it was argued, would significantly reduce the quantity of fresh air
that would reach the city.[51]

All of these reforms, which were to refashion the physical fabric of
Paris, were accompanied by a complementary program that proposed
excluding the cemeteries, hospitals, prisons, and slaughterhouses from
the city. The danger posed by their continued presence within the realm
of the living was by no means one-sided. Just as these foyers of putrefaction and disease were a threat to the city, so too did the city constitute an
obstacle to the proper functioning of these institutions. The offending
institutions needed expansive sites where the building or grounds could
be properly designed with the requisite internal ventilation as well as a
generous isolation that would allow the winds to sweep away the corrupted air.

For cemeteries, the absence of trees was initially seen as promoting
good ventilation. Later, trees were envisaged as a means to purify the air
of the "miasmata" that were thought to rise from the graves. Prisons had
to be designed with cross-ventilated cells arranged around exercise

courts, whose differentiated spaces offered the further virtue of separating hardened criminals from youthful and minor offenders as well as keeping men and women apart. Hospitals were to be given long rows of wards with cross-ventilation, arranged either in parallel wings that were connected with covered walkways or in a circle. Furnaces, either at the center of a wheel of radiating wings or underneath the long wards arranged in parallel lines, were proposed to facilitate ventilation by creating strong convection currents. Architects and doctors even considered circular or funnel-shaped wards that would present no dead space to capture pockets of stagnant air.[52] The desire to create a space of hygiene for these building types through rational design gave birth to a functionalism in architecture, whose successor buildings in the nineteenth and then the early twentieth century formed the basis for what is known today as the twentieth-century Modern Movement or International Style.

The city, then, which was both commodious and magnificent, would also be salubrious. Since all three readings of the city were mutually reinforcing, it is difficult to assess the respective importance of any one factor. If the space of magnificence appealed to the Parisians' loftier feelings, the space of hygiene appears to have been rooted in their deepest fears.

The Space of Clarity

Public buildings for the eighteenth-century observer could not simply be monumental or hygienic. They also had to display an intelligibility achieved through appropriate architectural expression. This expression was termed *caractère,* or character. When considered together, the ensemble of public and even private buildings of a city would constitute a space of clarity.

The legacy of this Enlightenment concept was far-reaching and is still with us today. In the nineteenth century, architects continued to seek appropriate expression, while then using the pluralism of different historical and cultural styles so popular in the Romantic era. A style was chosen through its "association" with a particular era that was seen as incarnating values appropriate to the building type.[53] One of the most complete examples of this phenomenon can be found along the major thoroughfare that made late nineteenth-century Vienna into a "work of art," the Ringstrasse. As Olsen explains, here "the Gothic of the Votivkirche evoked the piety of the High Middle Ages, the Greek of the Parliament buildings Athenian democracy, the Northern Gothic of the Rathaus the independence of the medieval commune, the Renaissance of the University humanistic scholarship."[54]

The eighteenth-century architect, unwilling to use this panoply of historical and cultural styles, sought appropriate "character" within the parameters of the neoclassical aesthetic. He was assisted in large part by Vitruvius who, as Quatremère de Quincy reminded his readers, explained that the ancients distinguished between the temples dedicated to different gods by differing their form. Gods or goddesses associated with the sky ("Jupiter Lightning, the Heaven, the Sun, or the Moon") were to have hypaethral temples, that is, open to the sky; those known for "virile strength" ("Minerva, Mars, and Hercules") were to be designed with the Doric order, which was considered to be modeled after the proportions of the male body; those in honor of "delicate divinities" ("Venus, Flora, Proserpine, Spring-Water, and the Nymphs") were given the Corinthian order, whose proportions evoked a slender feminine body and whose ornamentation was consistent with this purpose; and, finally, gods such as "Juno, Diana, Father Bacchus," etc., were given the Ionic order, which expressed a "middle position" between "the severity of the Doric and the delicacy of the Corinthian."[55]

In the hands of Jacques-François Blondel, this Vitruvian synopsis became the basis upon which to found not only the legibility of each building but also a radically new approach to architectural composition, known today as "neoclassicism." Blondel required that every building express some degree of force or grace appropriate to the building type. Whereas this idea of architectural expression was rooted in the long-standing view of the architectural orders—Doric, Ionic, and Corinthian—as metaphors of male strength or female grace, Blondel departed from tradition by insisting on the primacy of massing in building design and architectural expression: "I have said it more than once, a beautiful architecture suffices to itself. The architect should begin with the naked mass and be content with this, before trying to add ornamentation. This must be born within the very bosom of architecture. Otherwise it will appear as a misplaced accessory."[56] Blondel's enthusiasm for subtle distinctions in expressive character prompted him to articulate a highly differentiated gamut of nuanced possibilities, which he discussed under headings such as "male, firm, and virile character in architecture" and "on the difference that must be kept in mind between light, elegant, and delicate architecture." The key to his theory, though, resided in his insistence on the massing of the building as the carrier of meaning, with the orders reduced to a supplementary and even superfluous feature.[57]

In the hands of the most avant-garde neoclassical architects, this approach to architectural expression through appropriate character yielded what Emil Kaufmann has termed an "autonomous architecture,"[58] largely freed of the conventions of Renaissance and Baroque classicism, which had been based upon an expression of a successive channeling of the forces of gravity down to the ground through either one of two models or through their combination. One model consisted of a building sitting on a rusticated and hence heavy base, with a *piano nobile* and possibly another floor above to constitute together the main body, and sometimes a diminutive attic at the top; the other used a succession of floors expressed with the stacked orders, from bottom to top, Doric, Ionic, and Corinthian, or, if the orders were absent, a modulation in the stone surface according to a progressively lighter degree of rustication as one leaves the ground.

The masters of the new neoclassical style, Etienne-Louis Boullée and Claude-Nicolas Ledoux, revolutionized architectural composition through their use of simple, unadorned, prismatic volumes that took Blondel's teachings to their ultimate conclusions. It is not surprising that Boullée, himself a teacher in the manner of his master Blondel, further developed the idea of "character." Drawing upon the writings of Germain Boffrand and Nicolas Le Camus de Mézières, Boullée transformed Blondel's emphasis on merely identifying a building's purpose when considering its character, to evoking an appropriate feeling. "Let's look at an object!," Boullée exclaimed. "The feeling that we first experience obviously comes from the way in which the object affects us. I call character the effect that results from this object, which causes in us some impression."[59]

Reaching into the depths of the human psyche, Boullée anticipated that viewers would be primed for the aesthetic experience that a simple prismatic volume can occasion. Through his intense involvement with architectural sensation, Boullée believed that the general public would react on a similar level. He found tall forms inspirational, low forms saddening, and horizontal forms ennobling.[60]

Character, at this time, was understood in two complementary ways. On the one hand, the exterior aspect of an edifice was supposed to inform the viewer about its destination. This requirement, as members of the Jury des Arts discovered in Brumaire, year II (1793),* of the French Revolution, was often difficult to satisfy. Thus, the painter Neveu re-

---

*On September 21, 1792, at its first session, the National Convention unanimously abolished the monarchy. In October 1793, the Revolutionary Calendar was adopted, with year II backdated as having started on September 22, 1793.

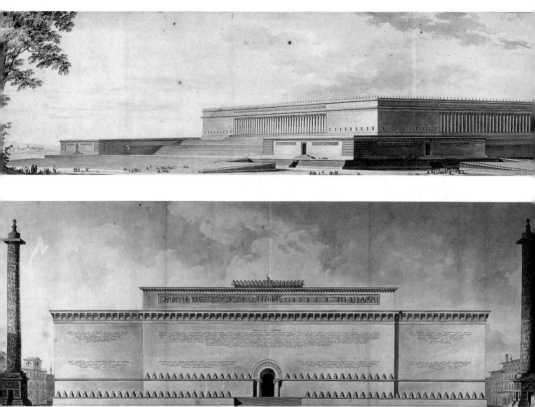

Figure 3. Etienne-Louis Boullée, Palais National (project), Paris, c. 1792.

jected all the competition entries for a barracks with the observation that "none of these buildings shows on the exterior the use to which it is destined." "Upon inspection of their form," he continued, "I could take them to be a munitions plant or a mint or a large national farm, and so forth."[61] Neveu's list of building types reveals that all the designs belonged to one of those general groupings associated with varying degrees of force or grace and of sobriety or gaiety articulated by Vitruvius and Blondel. In this case, it was a question of buildings with a sober or severe character. Yet the difficulty in identifying the particular building type within the group still remained. It was far easier to satisfy the complementary notion of character, which was to recognize the appropriateness of visual expression once the destination was known.

To clarify the ambiguities inherent in this situation, Boullée went beyond what might be called the expressive role of character to add still

Figure 2. Etienne-Louis
Boullée, Palais de Justice
(project), Paris, 1780s.

another dimension, what could be called metaphorical or allegorical character. This condition was especially important for civic buildings that used horizontal prisms as the primary means for establishing their expressive character. As Boullée explained when considering one such design,

> The decoration of this civic building must be majestic and imposing. This effect falls within the domain of architecture. But since there is more than one monument that requires a similar character, I thought it necessary to seek a way to designate this building by suitable means that are particular to its destination.[62]

To this end, Boullée designed each of his civic buildings according to an appropriate metaphor or allegory. His project for the ministry of justice (fig. 2) presents that allegory of virtue triumphing over vice, with the courthouse placed on top of the prison, whose low, rusticated form appears to be sinking into the ground, a metaphor suggesting that incarceration is tantamount to premature death. Boullée's project for the Paris city hall, conceived at a moment during the French Revolution when great emphasis was being placed on popular assemblies, was designed according to the metaphor of a human beehive.[63] The building was given extensive openings and wide, unencumbered passageways for easy access by the citizenry. Similarly, Boullée's proposed Palais National for the revolutionary government (fig. 3) presented a blank facade inscribed with the Constitution after the manner of the biblical tablets brought down from Mt. Sinai by Moses. His Royal Library project (fig. 4) became an architectural rendition of Raphael's *School of Athens,* his Paris opera project (fig. 5) a temple of Venus where women would display the latest finery, his museum project (figs. 6, 7) a temple of Parnassus, his stadium (fig. 8) a French Colosseum, and his cemeteries for Paris

Figure 4. Etienne-Louis Boullée, Royal Library (project), Paris, 1785.

Figure 5. Etienne-Louis Boullée, Opera (project), Paris, 1781.

Figure 6. Etienne-Louis Boullée, "Project for a Museum at the center of which is a Temple of Fame containing the statues of great men," 1783.

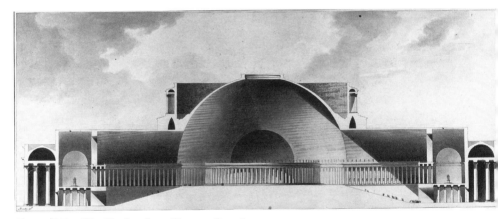

Figure 7. Boullée, "Project for a Museum," section.

(fig. 9) vast Egyptian-like wastelands.

In the ideal city of the late French Enlightenment, each building would tell its purpose through its expressive and possibly metaphorical character; each would move the viewer with an appropriate feeling prompted by its aspect. Whether one considers the ensemble of Boullée's unexecuted projects for civic buildings, the collection of the *Grands Prix* and other competition designs by the students of the Académie Royale d'Architecture, or the totality of buildings both real and ideal that Claude-Nicolas Ledoux assembled for the salt works of Chaux, one finds the built world imbued with such a space of clarity. Ledoux took the

19

Figure 8. Etienne-Louis Boullée, Colisée (project), Paris.

notion of metaphorical character to such an extreme that an exasperated nineteenth-century critic dubbed it *l'architecture parlante* (speaking architecture).[64]

To these two categories of expressive and metaphorical character, Boullée added a third, what might be called "symbolic character." As a true child of the Enlightenment, Boullée provided each of his civic buildings with a temple-like space consecrated to the idea of the institution housed there. In his public library project (figs. 10, 11), the building is preceded by a semicircular outdoor temple that focuses thought on the essence of what a library is, which in Enlightenment terms meant the repository of humankind's knowledge about the universe.[65] The interior itself of Boullée's Royal Library project was such a symbolic space, created by a giant amphitheater of books where the shades of the past's great minds would commune, so to speak, among themselves and with the readers. In the museum project, semicircular temples around the exterior are a prelude to the central interior motif, conceived as an artificial mountain crowned with a circular temple of Fame, whose columns would carry statues of great men sculpted by the greatest artists. This artificial Parnassus was effectively dedicated to the dual concepts of art and achievement. The ultimate example of a space consecrated to a lofty idea can be found in Boullée's cenotaph to Sir Isaac Newton (figs. 12, 13), whose sarcophagus is placed at the center of a spherical cavity, symbolic of the globe on the exterior and of the universe on the interior. As the architect explained,

> Oh Newton! Since by the magnitude of your wisdom and sublimity of your genius, you have determined the [initial] shape of the earth [as a perfect sphere], I, in turn, have conceived the project of enveloping you within your discovery. . . . I wanted to characterize your sepulcher with the figure of the earth. . . . The interior of this sepulcher is conceived in this same spirit. Utilizing your divine system [of the unifying cosmic principle of gravity], . . . the form of the monument is a vast sphere [with the

Figure 9. Etienne-Louis Boullée, cemetery project, variant I, Paris, c. 1785.

> tomb at] its center of gravity [and the surface like] a clear night, produced by the stars that ornament the dome of the sky.[66]

In all of these buildings, Boullée joined together expressive, metaphorical, and symbolic character. Newton's tomb, for example, achieves expressive character on the outside through the combination of horizontal and spherical forms with vertical massing and on the inside by using the vast spherical cavity to convey the sensation of the immensity of Nature. It exhibits metaphorical character by depicting the earth to the exterior and the universe inside. It achieves symbolic character through the temple-like space of its interior, an eighteenth-century Pantheistic reinterpretation of the ancient Roman Pantheon. If there is a hierarchical order among these three types of character, then it would appear that symbolic character provides the raison d'être for the two others.

Although Boullée gave memorable expression to the concept of symbolic character in both his writings and his designs, he was not the

Figure 10. Etienne-Louis Boullée, "Project for a Public Library on the land of the Capucines with an entrance in the form of a Temple to Apollo and with central galleries containing the statues of great men," c. 1785.

Figure 11.
Boullée, Public
Library (project), plan.

Figure 12. Etienne-Louis Boullée, Cenotaph to Sir Isaac Newton (project), Paris, 1784.

Figure 13. Boullée, Cenotaph to Newton, interior view with starlit sky created by sun shining through openings in the dome.

only French academic architect to conceive buildings in this manner. We can find other examples of temple-like spaces consecrated to an idea in the *Grand Prix* competitions of his time. One of these projects, in particular, J.-N.-L. Durand's second prize in the *Grand Prix* of 1779, a museum, served as the model for the symbolic spaces of Boullée's public library project, with its symbolic portico as well as its central temple-like room.[67] In effect, under the Académie Royale d'Architecture, the central symbolic room was a recurrent feature of the annual *Grand Prix* and the monthly *prix d'émulation* designs from the 1770s onward. We can see how powerful and longstanding this tradition has been merely by looking at John Russell Pope's National Gallery of Art (1937) and National Archives Building (1933–1935), both in Washington, D.C. The former is organized around a symbolic rotunda dedicated to the ideal of great art and culture; the latter uses a hemispherically domed rotunda to house the Declaration of Independence, the Constitution, and the Bill of Rights. It would be difficult to find a more appropriate match between the ideas expounded in these documents, the idea of a symbolic space not only to house them but also to make them manifest, and the mentality that could conceive both, a mentality convinced about the correctness and naturalness of such abstract ideas as the rights of man and the legitimacy of democracy in the human community and in relation to the cosmic order.

The Space of Emulation

Eighteenth-century Paris, then, as dreamed by the enthusiasts for *embellissement,* would have been a city ordered according to the imperatives of magnificence, commodity and hygiene, and clarity. We have seen that this last category was to be achieved through architectural character, understood as possibly combining expressive, metaphorical, and symbolic components. This last aspect, symbolic character, had a corollary in the contemporary mind, in the idea of emulation, that is, the desire to equal or surpass the admirable deeds of others. The same mental outlook that reveled in symbolic, temple-like spaces consecrated to high ideals also believed that public honors and commemorative monuments were powerful spurs to exemplary behavior. "I am convinced," explained Voltaire, "that the mere view of these glorious monuments [of outstanding British citizens at Westminster Abbey] has inspired more than one soul and has formed more than one great man."[68] The cult of statues to great men and women, which spread throughout the West in the nineteenth century, and which acquired such a significant place within the city at least until World War I, had its origins in the Enlightenment space of emulation. As June Hargrove has observed in her study of such monuments in the French Third Republic, the "concept of recognizing individuals for accomplishment rather than birth sprang from the same egalitarian philosophy of the Age of Enlightenment that had fostered the revolution."[69]

Although Voltaire had found Westminster Abbey an exemplary source for commemorative monuments, the space of emulation was not to be limited to the interior of a city's churches. Rather, it was to be sought everywhere within the realm of the living and then too as an integral feature in the new burial grounds to be constructed beyond the city. The statues that were to decorate the sheltering peristyles along the streets, squares, and bridges of Paris would present sources of inspiration at every step. One author, wishing to assure the proper effect of a public statue on passersby, attempted to calculate the ideal size of the public square relative to the piece of sculpture. The goal would be to oblige the pedestrian to pass by the statue at the optimum distance to register strongly the "useful effect that this object can have on the senses."[70]

The task of spurring emulation might profitably employ the abstract language of geometry. To this end, the architect and set designer Servandoni proposed decorating a vast amphitheater to be constructed just outside Paris with the statue of the king at the center and with statues of illustrious Frenchmen around the circumference. The royal figure, then, "would have appeared as the source from which all issues and the center to which all leads."[71] The spacing of the statues themselves could be designed to promote emulation. Servandoni envisaged leaving several places unfilled. This idea was taken up again by Ramel in a plan for a museum of great art.[72] In both cases, the eloquence of this empty space was to promote a deed or an accomplishment worthy of the anticipated honors.

Prompted by the example of several provincial capitals, which had a room in their city hall with busts of great men of the city or province, the abbé Laugier proposed that each public building in Paris be given its hall of "illustrious men."[73] Dussausoy offered a similar proposal when he outlined his plan for transforming the Louvre into a type of civic center, which would house the Royal Library and the academies, each to be decorated with the "busts of the men who had distinguished themselves in the arts and letters and sciences." The gallery along the Seine would be destined for public festivals and decorated accordingly with marble statues of the "illustrious men who have contributed to the glory of the monarchy."[74] Several years later in 1774, the comte d'Angiviller, in his capacity as the newly appointed directeur général of the Académie Royale de Peinture et de Sculpture, initiated a project to fill this long gallery of the Louvre with busts of France's great men.[75]

Paris did acquire its own counterpart to Westminster Abbey through the conversion of the Eglise Sainte-Geneviève into the French Panthéon in 1791. While some patriots wished to transform this church into a temple of Liberty, Quatremère de Quincy insisted that it be dedicated to *la Renommée* or Fame, whose statue he hoped would crown the exterior dome, where it would preside over figures of the virtues that would decorate the thirty-two columns around the drum. Although none of these statues was erected, the side windows of the church were walled up so as to create a more sober atmosphere deemed appropriate for the building's new destination.[76]

In many respects, the ideal place for promoting virtue was at the cemetery. From the beginning of the reform movement in the 1740s to abolish the thousand-year-old custom of interring the dead inside parish churches and in adjacent or neighboring burial grounds, the cemetery was seen as providing the space of emulation par excellence. For citizens imbued with the new Enlightenment belief in the importance of the individual, the cemetery would furnish honors to meritorious ordinary people. In one of the early texts in this cemetery reform movement, the abbé Porée explained that "since there are different orders in society and a merit that is relative to each, people of all stations would find a model, all virtues would receive a type of recompense."[77]

The new cemeteries that were envisaged over the course of this sixty-year-long reform movement were conceived as enhancements to the *embellissement* of Paris. As one enthusiast argued, "Since it is a question of public and permanent buildings, these new cemeteries can be made into veritable monuments of a funerary genre worthy of decorating the capital."[78] The cemetery, then, was to belong to the space of magnificence, and, as we have seen, to the space of hygiene. For reformers such as the abbé Porée, it would also serve as a space of emulation.

This was the vision of the cemetery adopted by the Académie Royale d'Architecture, whose architects and students impressed into service all the appropriate means of monumental design to this end. In 1765, just two months after the Parlement of Paris ordered, albeit ineffectually, all the cemeteries of the city closed by the end of the year, the academy offered a *prix d'émulation* for a cenotaph to Henry IV, symbol of the exemplary ruler, where the "empty tomb of this prince would be surrounded by vast peripheral galleries for the tombs of the famous men who had made France illustrious."[79] Then, in 1766, Louis-Jean Desprez

26

won a *prix d'émulation* for a cemetery, destined for one of the city's largest parishes, which was no mere burial ground but rather a space of emulation. The young architect dedicated this burial ground to Voltaire not only as a great writer but also as the champion of funerary honors accorded to merit.[80] The central chapel in this unexecuted design was destined for royal sepulchers and the circumferential galleries for the tombs and statues of great men. The chapels that gave additional splendor to this peripheral arcade also served to demarcate zones to honor different virtues. The even more magnificent corner chapels were not only traditional Baroque compositional devices to impart monumentality but also were used in this design to honor great men who were not Catholics and hence who could not be buried in the other parts of the cemetery. The space of emulation prompted by these Enlightenment ideals spurred architects to honor the merits of individual citizens even more elaborately in subsequent competitions that reached beyond the closing of the academy and into the Revolution under its successor institutions. It should be stressed that the academy's vision of the cemetery as a space of emulation contrasted vividly with those designs promoted by private entrepreneurs who reified the current practice of funerary distinctions according to wealth and social status.[81]

The most elaborate development of a space of emulation can be found in the *Grand Prix* competition of 1799 for a public cemetery to be located just outside of Paris. Whereas the program only stipulated that monuments to the "illustrious men" of the republic would be placed under the galleries around the central edifice,[82] the winning entries transformed the burial ground into a highly differentiated realm of immortality. In Grandjean de Montigny's first-prize design, the visitor would encounter a circumferential canal, bordered by trees to either side and decorated with exedras in which "monuments to the memory of illustrious men" were to be placed. After crossing this canal, the visitor would enter the central chapel crowned with a "temple of memory" by passing through a row of statues dedicated to the various virtues by which one might be honored. Across the base of the terrace one would read: "Here in the bosom of glory rest the small number of those who have lived for posterity. Traveler, stop for a moment, and learn from the venerable ashes of these illustrious men to become worthy of the rewards due to their talents." At either end of the terrace, visitors would pass through a cypress grove to a row of more monuments to the illustrious dead. Then, moving along the central axis, they would encounter the amphitheater in which the populace would judge whether the deceased merited the honors of the temple of virtues. This amphitheater was extended by a larger semicircular zone for the burial of ordinary citizens whose presence, so to speak, added moral weight to the decisions made by the living. On a diagonal to either side of the communal burial grounds were tiered exedras surrounded by laurel trees "under whose shade" the country's military heroes would be buried. A "temple of virtues," preceded by a large square, terminated the central axis. Over half the space in this cemetery was destined for honoring virtue and achievement and spurring emulation. With even the space for ordinary interments organized symbolically to second this end, the entire cemetery became a space of emulation.[83]

Whereas emulation constituted the bright side of inspiration, constraint was its darker partner. If the statue could incite enthusiasm, it could also instill "respect" and "fear."[84] As a counterpart to the space of emulation, the Age of Enlightenment also envisaged a space of constraint. The full potential of the space of constraint was not developed until the Revolution. Nurtured by their knowledge of ancient Egyptian and Roman practices of judging the dead and even sometimes depriving the unworthy of a grave, several authors imagined comparable schemes for the new French republic. These projects date from a time when numerous texts expressed horror at the thought and image of man's ultimate physical decomposition. In the year IV (1795–1796), two authors sought to mobilize the fear of death into the service of promoting virtue and deterring crime. For the "virtuous," Pierre-Louis Roederer envisaged a cemetery designed according to the current preference for the "Elysium" garden, fashioned in a "sacred" woods replete with flowers, birds, fresh air, and sunlight. The criminal, though, would be relegated to adjacent "sepulchral caverns" cut into "terrifying, arid rocks" over which vultures, "symbols of remorse," would hover.[85] Pierre Giraud, architect of prisons for the Département de la Seine, also proposed paired cemeteries. In no less fantastic a scheme, he designed a verdant "field of rest" in which the deceased would be rescued from decay through the vitrification of his or her skeleton into an imperishable bust or urn of diaphanous glass. The "mere view" of this honored ancestor would deter youth from the "route of crime and even of dissipation." Those "degenerate beings whom justice banished from society," though, would be denied the honors of vitrification. Their remains would be sent across the way to be burned in a large cauldron at the center of a cemetery sunken into the ground, which was filled with mass graves. The door of this space of perpetual banishment, this "shameful lair," would teach all inquiring onlookers that here was the "'criminals' burial ground."[86]

These dual spaces to honor virtue and to stigmatize vice were popular with authors who participated in the competition on funerary institutions sponsored by the Institut National in 1800.[87] With the formula that Roederer and Giraud envisaged, the Enlightenment space of virtue was effectively forgotten. The space of ignominy became the touchstone by which all were to be judged. No longer the worthy but the reprobates were singled out from the undifferentiated masses. Virtue became the condition of each individual as his descendants would remember him. In Giraud's project, the central chapel, formerly the space par excellence for the recognition of superior accomplishment, became the way to an apotheosis through vitrification for all but the excluded few.

As the physical aspect of Paris changed in the nineteenth century when the new cemeteries opened during the Consulate became populated with majestic sepulchral monuments, the ideal of emulation contributed to a corresponding transformation in the image of the city. An entire, new literary genre emerged, which complemented the traditional guidebooks to the city of the living now with itineraries through the cities of the dead. Much as the pre-Revolutionary pilgrim to Rousseau's tomb at Ermenonville had once sought out the diverse *fabriques* scattered throughout the park, now the visitor to the cemetery would progress from tomb to tomb. At the Cemetery of Père Lachaise, especially, whose funerary monuments presented a "biographical dictionary" of France's illustrious citizens, visitors were held "spellbound" as they entered into an "immediate communion" with the works, deeds, and character of the famous people buried there.[88]

With the coming of the Revolution, it became even more imperative in the contemporary mind to realize the space of magnificence, of hygiene, of clarity, and of emulation. Each was deemed especially worthy of the new nation. And the Ancien Régime was faulted for not having achieved the reforms in these fields that enlightened thought had been demanding. At the same time, there arose an understanding of still another type of symbolic space, a space of revolution. Paris, in particular, and France, in general, required not only a new architecture but also a new type of space that incarnated the values of the revolution and of the new republic. The mental construct of the city acquired still another layer of symbolic meaning.

2

Revolutionary Space

It was a commonplace of French revolutionary thought that laws alone could not fashion the mentality and habits required for a free people to live successfully in a republic that now replaced centuries of monarchic and aristocratic rule. Institutions too had to be impressed into this service. The physical world, as controlled by human endeavor that fashioned it into a built environment with edifices, open spaces, gardens, parks, cemeteries, etc., would also serve this purpose. The outpouring of projects for *embellissement,* which had characterized the decades preceding the events of 1789, continued not only with a renewed vigor but also with this new end in mind. The transition was not difficult for a culture in which space and place were readily imbued with multiple symbolic purposes and readings.

In reviewing the numerous proposals for the creation of a spatial realm imbued with the values of the Revolution, one finds the equivalent to the three types of character—metaphorical, expressive, and symbolic—achieved in the neoclassical architecture by Etienne-Louis Boullée discussed in the previous chapter. In the creation of revolutionary space, the equivalent to metaphorical character is to be found in the narrative arrangement of space. Expressive character has its counterpart in the expressive qualities of space thought to reflect or violate revolutionary values. Symbolic character, achieved through the creation of temple-like spaces, was not only reiterated under the Revolution but also, at times, seemed to have achieved a deeply rooted emotive response. I designate this latter type "numinous" space.[1] Finally, in all three types of revolutionary space—narrative, expressive, and numinous—the process of ritualized actions often played a significant role.

The material used in this chapter is a sampling of the projects, proposals, and realizations from this period. To continue the theme of the multiple readings of the city begun in Chapter 1, I give precedence in the selection of sources to Paris, which, as the nation's capital and the heart of revolutionary activity, was readily favored by contemporaries.[2]

Narrative Revolutionary Space

The possibilities for narrative revolutionary space ranged from buildings, to vast urban sites, to the entire city, and even the nation. Revolutionary enthusiasts addressed virtually all scales of the built environment
with narrative projects to celebrate the Revolution and to teach its values. Old projects for *embellissement* under the Ancien Régime as well as
new schemes particular to the era were favored subjects.

The unresolved dilemma of how to join the Louvre with the Tuileries Palace was from the early years of the Revolution onward invested
with still another task, that of creating a monumental complex of
squares, statuary, and buildings to convey spatially the meaning of the
Revolution. The overall geometrical irregularity of the site, especially
with its lack of parallel alignment between the Louvre and the Tuileries
Palace, had preoccupied designers from at least the late seventeenth
century when Claude Perrault had envisaged using a round outdoor
space to disguise irregularities and to create imperceptible transitions
between nonparallel facades.[3] This was precisely the approach that the
architect Bernard Poyet employed in March 1790, when he proposed
solving the old problem of joining the Louvre with the Tuileries Palace
(fig. 14), while also providing for a number of institutional needs. It had
long been thought that Paris could use a new city hall, the old one being
considered both too small in size and too irregular in form. The new
National Assembly would also require a building for its deliberations.
Consequently, Poyet proposed converting the Louvre into the Paris city
hall and building a new Palais National for the government in the courtyard. A slight shift in orientation reduced the lack of alignment with the
Tuileries Palace, which was further mitigated by the creation of a circular
public square, a place Louis XVI. To these functional and aesthetic ends,
Poyet joined a symbolic purpose that transformed the entire site into a
civics lesson. With the statue of Louis XVI at the center of the circular
square, whose peristyles joined the Tuileries Palace with the Palais National, Louis XVI was shown as the king who united the monarchy to the
nation through his adherence to the Constitution, a narrative message
also made explicit through the sculptural program of the central statue
of the king.[4]

Such a civics lesson might be extended to the entire city. The very
network of the streets and squares could be arranged to school the citizen so that merely by walking across town he or she would imbibe a
republican message. A certain Chamoulaud offered proposals that included, for example, reaching a place de la Justice from streets named

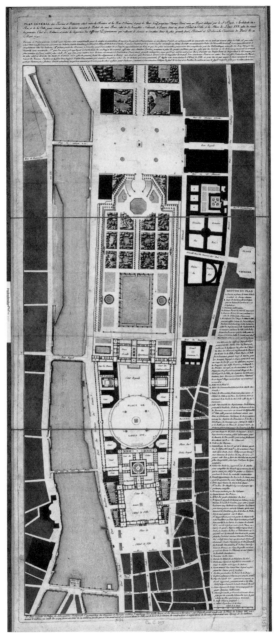

Figure 14. Bernard Poyet, project for joining the
Louvre to the Tuileries Palace, March 1790.

Severity, Impartiality, and Law. Reporting on this and other proposals for the Comité de l'Instruction Publique in year II (1794), Grégoire asked rhetorically, "Isn't it natural that from the Place de la Révolution one goes down Rue de la Constitution, which would lead to Rue du Bonheur."[5]

In Messidor, year II (July 1794), Barère, in the name of the Comité de Salut Public, proposed to the National Convention that the former toll gates be transformed into monuments to republican victories. Henceforth Paris would be called the "city of one hundred gates," with each gateway signaling "a triumph or a revolutionary epoch."[6] The Administration Centrale du Département de la Seine sought to create a similar civic message in Vendémiaire, year VII (October 1798), when it decided to dedicate one former church in each *arrondissement* of Paris to a moral or civic virtue most closely related to its history. The name engraved on the front facade would transform each building into a community center dedicated to Concord, Genius, Agriculture, Thanksgiving, Old Age, Marriage, Commerce, Liberty and Equality, Youth, Supreme Being, Peace, Victory, *Bienfaisance,* Work, or Filial Piety. "These new names," it was written, "will give a noble and true idea of the people of Paris. From whatever road the visitor enters, he will encounter authentic testimonials of this people's virtues."[7]

During the Revolution, hardly an urban design project could escape the appeal of a symbolic civics lesson. No doubt, in some cases, the expression of patriotic fervor reflected in part the hope that this would make the unsolicited scheme more attractive to the authorities. In April 1790, Mouillefarine the Younger of Troyes submitted a project of *embellissement* that would create a proposed square, place Royale Nationale de la Liberté, on the site of the former Bastille. Four broad thoroughfares would issue forth from this new square: rue du Faubourg Saint-Antoine, leading to the existing Barrière du Trône; rue Saint-Antoine, proceeding in the other direction; boulevard Saint-Antoine; and a new boulevard de la Liberté, reaching to the Seine where it would cross the river with a new Pont de la Réunion. This bridge would not only join the two banks of the Seine, it would provide a point of unity for three pleasurable views down the proposed tree-lined boulevard de la Liberté on the Right Bank and the boulevard Neuf on the Left Bank as well as across the plantings of the Jardin du Roi.

In this scheme, the theme of reunion referred not only to the physical joining of the two sides of Paris and to the aesthetic pleasures of multiple views across the city, but also to the political union of the French people, further symbolized by the three-sided obelisk located on the Pont de la Réunion at the point of convergence for the principal views. The triangular obelisk, rising above a circular base, symbolized the coming together of the three estates. The theme of union was further symbolized by the circular shape of the urban square.[8] In this project for narrative revolutionary space, the Pont de la Réunion, with its triangular obelisk, not only commemorated an event, it also offered an object lesson of unity and concord to guide a citizen's behavior.

The city of the dead, as well as the city for the living, provided great potential for narrative revolutionary space. "At the height of the Revolution," writes Robert Darnton, "from mid-1792 to mid-1794, virtue was not merely a fashion but the central ingredient of a new political culture."[9] The cemetery proposed by the Administration des Travaux Publics in January 1794 would certainly have served such pedagogical ends. At the central monument, citizens were to be honored for the virtues of Filial Piety, *Bienfaisance,* Heroic Courage, Devotion to Country, Humanity, Arts, Sciences, Literature, Great Talents, and Legislature. The corpses would be taken from depositories around the city in coffins draped with colored cloths symbolic of the "three political ages of life" and with inscriptions proclaiming that "he was born for the country," "he lived for the country," and "he died for the country." The report further envisaged the erection of tribunes and amphitheaters throughout the city's squares where patriots would instruct the populace. These same tribunes would then be taken to the cemetery, or "field of rest" as it was to be called, where the dead patriot would be praised for the "single act of his life that made him dear to the Country."[10] From this time onward, cemeteries proposed under the Revolution either favored the image of equality through identical burial, as in a project of 1800 by Athanase Détournelle in which the carpenter's level over the entrance tells all, or in the hierarchical organization of space according to different types of virtue and achievement, as in Grandjean de Montigny's prize-winning "Elysium or Public Cemetery" for the *Grand Prix* competition of 1799, discussed in Chapter 1.[11]

Expressive Revolutionary Space

Expressive revolutionary space relied on the perceived meaning of spatial characteristics. For example, it was popular to call for the elimination of spatial configurations that were understood to impart a lesson of oppression. The *barrières* or toll gates that Ledoux had constructed for the Ferme Générale between 1784 and 1789 had been unpopular since the time of their erection, as a contemporary rhyme reminds us: "Ce mur murant Paris rend Paris mumurant" (This wall enclosing Paris has all of Paris grumbling).[12] We should not forget that the *barrières* were attacked on July 12, 1789, two days before the storming of the Bastille.[13] On May 1, 1791, Charles Villette noted that the function of the toll gates had just been suppressed. Speculating on the future of the tax wall and its *barrières*, Villette asserted: "Six leagues of wall are enclosing a million people penned in like a flock of sheep. Paris will never have the air of the Metropolis of Liberty as long as it is dishonored by this remainder of servitude."[14]

The space of liberty could even be extended to the design of a zoo. For Lacépède, the *ménagerie* reflected in microcosm the politics of the human world. Throughout Europe, the zoo gave the image of a space of oppression in which animals were confined in constricting cells. Paris, though, had to have a zoo worthy of its political ideals, in which the animals would not be imprisoned but rather allowed to roam freely across spacious grounds subtly circumscribed by waterways and changes in the level of the land. "Images of constraint and the appearance of slavery," asserted Lacépède, "should not appear before the eyes of a free people."[15]

In the creation of exemplary space whose geometrical characteristics would help form the soul and guide the behavior of the new citizen, the cemetery offered a privileged opportunity for revolutionary pedagogy. Social and economic distinctions among the living traditionally had followed them into the grave through the nature of the funeral, place of burial, and existence and type of memorial. The Arrêté of 28 Germinal, year VII (April 17, 1799), issued by the Département de la Seine, explained that before the Revolution the "pomp of the funeral insulted the poor; and it is well known that this difference in Paris greatly contributed to embitter the indigent against the wealthy. At the time when the National Assembly began to deal with religion, people were saying out loud, 'Now the rich will be buried like the poor without any difference.'"[16] Under the Terror, the cemetery became a "Garden of Equality."[17] On October 19, 1793, Chaumette, the *procureur-syndic* of Paris, proclaimed that henceforth the funerals of the rich and the poor would be the same.[18] The second report on the burial grounds of Paris submitted by the Administration des Travaux Publics on 21 Nivôse, year II (January 10, 1794), suggested not constructing the customary wall with a covered walkway around the cemetery not only because new attitudes toward death and burial developing since the 1780s favored throwing open the grounds to the surrounding countryside, but also because in the future families might use the space under the arcade for funerary distinctions that would be detrimental to the egalitarianism of the Republic.[19]

The entire city itself could appear as an image of oppression. Here the prerevolutionary space of hygiene acquired new meaning as the lack of its realization seemed to be a special affront to a newly acquired dignity and freedom. When, in the year II (1793–1794), C. P. Le Sueur submitted his proposals for the "cleanliness of Paris," he followed an opening three-page paean to liberty with the declaration, "Down with the gothic monuments of superstition. Up with monuments dedicated to republican virtues placed everywhere. Out with the infectious filthy holes with their misery, sickness, and death!" "It should be noted," he continued, "that in the more than one century that people have been concerned with beautifying the city, the means of making it healthy have been neglected." "The lack of cleanliness in Paris has several causes," explained Le Sueur, as he repeated the litany of the prerevolutionary hygienic reform movement: "the narrowness of the streets and the height of the houses that prevent the free circulation of the air; the pavement always covered with water, which keeps the streets muddy; the way in which Paris is paved; the lack of public water; . . . the way in which the streets are cleaned."[20] Not only did the republican city have to be the salubrious city, its places of political assembly had to enjoy the advantages of the most healthy sites. One citizen warned against locating the new Palais National at the low-lying Tuileries Garden, where the ground was said to be damp often and the air to be filled with harmful mists. Rather, he proposed the elevated site of the Luxembourg Garden: "An honorable member of the august National Assembly, after having given flight to his thoughts and after having spent hours expressing them with as much force as energy, needs to breath a good air. For such valuable men there cannot be an air too pure."[21] Finally, a free people not only deserved a healthy environment; it was deemed a sign of its emancipation. Lanthenas argued that the degree of a people's servitude was reflected in its personal, domestic, and public cleanliness.[22]

The expressive nature of revolutionary architecture could be found most forcefully in either the "simple" or the "colossal." The simple signified a primitive grace not yet corrupted. The colossal reflected the grandeur of the idea or achievement. Thus, memorials and buildings proposed, for example, for the site of the Bastille were conceived according to these polar opposites. One government committee suggested a "modest" obelisk built with the stones of the former fortress. Free men, it was explained, needed neither luxury nor magnificence to inspire them.

This project was greeted with approval by one citizen who suggested limiting the inscription to the laconic phrase, "Ici fut la Bastille" (Here stood the Bastille).[23] Others preferred a colossal column resting upon a civic altar and crowned by a statue of Liberty, the entire monument rising hundreds of feet.[24] The anonymous *Songe patriotique*—patriotic dream—would have nothing less than an immense pyramid here rising three hundred feet high. The stones of the Bastille were to be used in the construction not only for practical but also for ritual ends. Only the base of the pyramid would be built with stones from the prison, the remainder using materials freely donated from all parts of the nation to realize a monument of national unity.[25]

Numinous Revolutionary Space

When expressive revolutionary space was invested with the ability to evoke an unseen presence, a spirit or numen, or a divinity, it became transformed into another category of symbolic activity that might be termed numinous revolutionary space. Once again, the site of the Bastille as well as its stones were a favorite subject for such purposes, which often involved a ritualized purification. The place de la Bastille is not merely the location of the hated fortress, symbol of the repression of the Ancien Régime, but an empty space that has been cleansed of its former contamination. In proposing the erection of a building to house the National Assembly on the former site of the Bastille, the architect Louis Combes of Bordeaux proclaimed on November 6, 1789, "All of France seems to want the same soil that was burdened for so long by the frightful den of despotism to undergo a felicitous expiation and henceforth become ennobled by serving as the base for a Temple of Liberty."[26]

This goal was accomplished, however momentarily, at the festivities that accompanied the celebration of the epoch-making Fête de la Fédération, begun in Paris on July 14, 1790. A *bosquet* (fig. 15) bedecked with strings of colored lights traced the outline of the destroyed fortress of the Bastille. This open-air construction became a temple of liberty that replaced the somber stone prison, whose presence it evoked only to emphasize its disappearance. A central mast, flying the tricolor flag announcing *liberté*, rose to the height of the former Bastille to reinforce this message. Constructed of eighty-three trees, one for each of the new and equal departments that had recently replaced the traditional jurisdictions of provinces, this festival pavilion was also a temple of equality and confraternity.[27] In this manner, a narrative ensemble seconded the meaning of the numinous revolutionary space.

Figure 15. Festival pavilion built along the contours of the former Bastille, July 1790.

The entire national territory could also be the subject of a ritual purification to reconstitute the entire country into a vast and unified symbolic space. For one patriot no existing French city could attain the purity requisite for a virtuous republic. All were soiled by the "emblems of the former oppression of the French people." To remedy this situation, it was proposed that a new city "dedicated to Liberty" be founded at the geographic center of France. At the center of the new city would rise a "colossal pyramid," with as many sides as there were victorious French armies. The pyramid would be covered with captured flags and inscribed with accounts of heroic exploits. The space of the city itself would be defined and consecrated by a surrounding "National Woods." Beyond this city, a series of concentric monuments and squares intended to sanctify all space issuing outward from the center would transform the entire country into a spatial civics lesson.[28]

The consecration of the entirety of the national domain and of its people that this project envisaged had been enacted ritually during the first national festival of the Revolution, the Festival of Federation in Paris on July 14, 1790. At the moment of the oath of confederation, cannon sounded in Paris to provide the first salvo that was to be echoed from village to village in an ever-expanding circle extending to the outer bounds of the French territory. The festival itself also offered repeated opportunities for the ritual reenactment of a communion between French people from all regions enclosed within a precinct of space on the Champ de Mars that contemporaries themselves termed the *enceinte*.

Both the civic festival on the Champ de Mars and the subsequent festivities on the Champs-Elysées and at the site of the Bastille were experienced as a reunion of a large human family within a consecrated space.[29] As Bernard Poyet expressed it, under the preceding "reign of despotism" the people had been kept apart and hence suffered from a harmful egotism that now the act of assembly could reverse. Poyet's architectural project for the civic festival would have reinforced the symbolism of the confederation and union within the precinct (*enceinte*) of the Champ de Mars by preceding the grounds with two triumphal arches and a Temple of Liberty composed of eighty-three *faisceaux d'armes*, each with the name of a department. A chain of tents, alternating the *troupes de ligne* and the *gardes nationales* along the raised outer perimeter of the amphitheater at the Champ de Mars, would have formed a chain of national unity.[30] Once again a narrative ensemble seconded the numinous revolutionary space.

Undoubtedly the most important ritual transformation of a symbolic space occurred at the center of the place Louis XV where the guillotine was erected on the former site of the royal statue. This public square, renamed place de la Révolution, underwent still another ritual transformation when the revolutionary violence perpetrated here, as well as all the other bloodshed elsewhere that it symbolized, was expiated by making this into the place de la Concorde. From place de la Bastille to place de la Concorde, the forceful actions and symbolic gestures of the Revolution invested the prerevolutionary space of magnificence with a resonance that continues to this day.

The expressive qualities also of revolutionary architecture could reinforce the sense of a numinous space. The pyramid, for example, that the *Songe Patriotique* had favored as a monument to national unity on the site of the Bastille, was not merely a splendid example of monumental architecture. In this age of Pantheistic fervor, it also provided the architectural equivalent to the mountain, with both seen as the incarnation of that manifestation of deity known as Nature with a capital "N." Indeed, at the Festival of Federation in Lyons on May 30, 1790, the central altar to the country (fig. 16) was an artificial mountain constructed in a pyramidal shape with a Temple of Concord at its center and a statue of Liberty standing on a civic altar at the summit. Perhaps the most famous moun-

Figure 16. Fête de la Fédération, Lyons, May 30, 1790.

tain of the revolutionary festivals was the one constructed by Jacques-Louis David for the Festival of the Supreme Being on 20 Prairial, year II (June 8, 1794).[31]

The pyramid or mountain found its counterpart in the dome, which was favored in projects for a Palais National. Mouillefarine, Combes, Florentin Gilbert, Molinos and Legrand, Boullée, and others all

Figure 17. Claude-Louis Chatelet, *Le Rocher, Folie Sainte-James, Neuilly.*

crowned their central space of gathering and, in many cases, the exterior of the building, with a giant hemispherical dome whose imagery was as cosmic as the mountain or pyramid.[32] Mouillefarine rendered his exterior dome as a globe carried upon a drum, surrounded in turn by a colonnade that formed a hypaethral temple. Combes conceived the interior of his dome as "representing the state of the sky over our horizon on July 15, 1789, memorable moment of our liberty." "This," he explained, "will be the astronomical date that will transmit with the greatest certainty to posterity this fortunate revolution. The stars and planets that were visible then will be exactly depicted here. . . . The signs of the zodiac are represented on the frieze of the colonnade that encircles the room."[33] The cosmic and universal significance of the mountain, the pyramid, and the dome was joined with the metaphor of biblical tablets, a popular revolutionary image used to convey the importance of the Constitution and the Rights of Man. Several architects used this image in their designs for civic buildings. We have seen in Chapter 1 that Boullée abstracted the idea of biblical tablets in the design of the neoclassical facade for his proposed Palais National (fig. 3). The view of the drawing of this facade was very exciting to the wife of the architect Alexandre-Théodore Brongniart. "This has a certain *je ne sais quoi* that is so grand," she wrote her husband, "that I felt goose bumps."[34]

The austerity of Boullée's facade was intentional, for it provided the architectural equivalent of virtue that was depicted in a variety of ways in revolutionary architecture. The monument at the Festival of Federation of Lyons is instructive on this account. As Robert Rosenblum has observed, it adapts the architectural vocabulary "of rugged nature and classical *fabriques* enjoyed privately by pre-Revolutionary aristocrats. . . . Thus," continues Rosenblum, "the rude simplicity of the little Doric temple enjoyed by the wealthy banker Claude Bernard de Sainte-James in the rocky picturesqueness of his Folie at Neuilly [fig. 17] produced such politically alien heirs as the design" for this revolutionary festival. "Here the type of classical *fabrique* designed for private delectation is transformed into a symbol of Republican freedom and political unity."[35] To continue this thought, it is precisely the way in which the forms have been transformed that reveals the republican spirit that the designer sought to convey. The grotto scene at the Folie Sainte-James, where a diminutive Doric temple is nestled within the arched opening and where the entire ensemble is graced with water that makes it into a nymphaeum, has remained for two centuries an image of pastoral repose. Indeed, in the mid-1920s, Le Corbusier used this scene to this end in his unrealized project for the Villa Meyer, which would have faced the park. His sketch of the view from the roof garden captures the essential aspect.[36]

At Lyons, however, the values have been reversed. The cozy grotto nymphaeum is now a majestic mountain. The slender proportions of the baseless Doric temple have been made broad and firm. The grotto no longer dominates the temple facade but rather is enclosed by it. In short, here is an image of martial valor and republican virtue that would dominate the aesthetic of revolutionary architecture. To use the analytical terminology of this chapter, in order for the numinous revolutionary space to be effective it required an appropriate expressive aspect.

The transformation in 1791 of the Eglise Sainte-Geneviève into a national pantheon, destined to house the remains of the great men of France, involved a similar use of expressive character for a numinous space. We saw in Chapter 1 that Quatremère de Quincy closed up the windows along the side walls in order to create a more sober architecture with a "mysterious" interior.[37] Although Quatremère de Quincy had hoped to isolate the Panthéon from the noise and bustle of the city by surrounding it with the "silent shadows" of a "sacred woods," which would inspire the appropriate veneration in approaching visitors, to some revolutionaries, this or any other building was inappropriate for a space of liberty, which could only be found in nature.[38] Jean-Charles Laveaux, editor of the *Journal de la Montagne,* for example, objected that the Panthéon hid the great men of France from the eyes of the multitude in underground vaults and between cold masses of stone. For Laveaux, the true pantheon belonged under trembling poplars surrounding the Champ de Mars, then rebaptized the Champ de la Fédération.[39] Whereas the site of the national Festival of Federation was a popular choice for a national pantheon, La Revellière-Lépeaux and others would settle for nothing less than a sacred woods at a rural site:

> It is a circumscribed idea to concentrate in a building and at the heart of a city a nation's glory, the fame of its best and greatest citizens. It is under the vault of the sky, in the bosom of the majesty of the forest, in its vast and somber byways, in a word, within a picturesque, varied, and tranquil precinct that those whose names are destined to be constantly present to mankind's memory should rest.[40]

With the controversy over the Panthéon, the quest for an appropriate revolutionary space coincided with prerevolutionary values about death, burial, commemoration, and the space of emulation. Once again, the desire for a revolutionary space added still another layer of perception and meaning to an already rich understanding of the physical world and of its intersection with the realms of the mind and spirit.

When one considers the far-reaching effects of major political and social changes in the twentieth century, whose institutions or regimes were viewed by some as "revolutionary," one finds the legacy of symbolic space that had characterized the French Revolution. The degree to which the architects of these later projects and constructions were aware of the French examples or were prompted by patterns of thought that had become an integral part of contemporary culture or were reaching into some primitive recess of the psyche where archetypical gestures and responses reside can never be determined.

Just as Frenchmen during the Revolution would suffer no sign of constraint in their environment, because it offered an offensive image of freedom denied, so too did building programs as varied as the League of Nations and the Fascist party headquarters, known as the Casa del Fascio, prompt analogous schemes. In their unsuccessful entry to the League of Nations competition of 1926–1927, the eminent Bauhaus architect Hannes Meyer, along with Hans Wittwer, proposed glass prisms where the physical transparency of modern plate glass would both permit and symbolize an openness to contrast with the secret diplomacy of the world that had caused the Great War. Similarly, the eminent Italian Rationalist architect Giuseppe Terragni designed the regional Fascist party headquarters in Como as a "house of glass," where the deliberations of the Fascist leaders would be visible to the populace and where the architecture would promote a unity between the leaders and the people.[41]

The proposal to use stones from the Bastille to consecrate the new civic buildings and monuments for the French Revolution was grounded in the basic human instinct that reveres relics of religious martyrs. A similar use of stone can be found in the memorial to the dead soldiers of Como from World War I erected in the early 1930s by Giuseppe Terragni, with assistance from his brother, the engineer Attilio Terragni. The memorial not only adapts a design by the avant-garde Comasco architect Antonio Sant'Elia, it is built of the stone from the Carso where Sant'Elia and his fellow soldiers fell. The side facing toward Austria is inscribed with what were believed to have been Sant'Elia's last words: "Tonight we sleep in Trieste or in Heaven with the Heroes."[42] A more recent example of this type of thought can be found in Saddam Hussein's giant "Victory Arch" (Baghdad, 1989), which commemorates Iraq's victories over Iran in the 1980–1988 war. The steel used to construct the two swords of the arch was melted down from the weapons of the "martyred" Iraqi soldiers.[43]

The unprecedented size of this Iraqi memorial—two-and-a-half times as high as the Parisian Arc de Triomphe—recalls the emphasis on grandiosity that formed one pole of expressive character in French revolutionary architecture.[44] Looking back to Nazi Germany and Fascist Italy, each of these totalitarian states made special efforts to build the world's largest edifices and building complexes whenever possible. At Nuremberg, for example, all three major structures exceeded ancient prototypes or other monumental wonders. The length of the Haupttribüne (1939) itself of the Zeppelinfeld Stadium was, as its architect Albert Speer pointed out, greater than the Baths of Caracalla. Likewise, Speer's

Deutsche Stadium (1937–1942) could contain twice as many spectators as the Circus Maximus, just as Ludwig Ruff's Kongresshalle (1934–1935) surpassed the Roman Colosseum in size.[45]

In Fascist Italy, the new university campus in Rome, the Città Universitaria (1932–1935), was conceived as the largest university complex in the world, just as the Esposizione Universale of 1941–1942 (today EUR) was to be the largest world's fair ground ever constructed, as well as the most ambitious through its program of creating a permanent monumental core for a new city outside Rome on the way to a resurrected Ostia.[46] The various arrangements of space proposed during the French Revolution that would have transformed entire districts, cities, and even the nation into symbolic renditions of revolutionary or republican values found its counterpart, for example, in the very dimensions of the site plan for the Esposizione Universale of 1941–1942, which corresponded to the size of the central area of Rome itself.[47]

The desire expressed during the French Revolution to ally the epoch-making state events with the natural order also found resonance in later revolutions. Just as Louis Combes had proposed decorating the dome of his project for a Palais National with the nighttime sky on July 15, 1789, so too did Vladimir Tatlin organize his proposed Monument to the Third International (1920) according to a cosmic metaphor. The gigantic Constructivist structure was dominated by a diagonal truss that tilted at the same angle as the earth's axis. Two intertwining helixes symbolizing the dynamism of the Russian Revolution followed the upward thrust of this diagonal truss as they created the structural framework for the meeting rooms and offices. These functional spaces, hung within the permanent scaffolding that was the structure, were each given the shape of a different geometric solid. The top one revolved daily, the middle one monthly, and the bottom one yearly. To complement the light and airy quality of the ensemble, to display a daring modern technological achievement, and, undoubtedly, to reflect the spirit of pure intentions and open deliberations, these rooms were completely enclosed by glass.

The debates over the appropriate type of space, as well as the meaningful place, to honor martyrs and the country's great men during the French Revolution found echoes in Fascist Italy and Nazi Germany. In Fascist Italy, the Martyr's Shrine (fig. 18) constructed by the leading Rationalist architect Adalberto Libera, in conjunction with Antonio Valente, for the Exhibition of the Fascist Revolution in 1932, which celebrated the tenth anniversary of Mussolini's March on Rome, became the standard by which future Fascist shrines were designed and judged. In a dark sanctuary, polished metal piers carried a circular ring covered with

Figure 18. Adalberto Libera and Antonio Valente, "Martyr's Shrine," Exhibition of the Fascist Revolution, Rome, 1932.

the word PRESENTE!, made luminous through backlighting to suggest the voices of the so-called Fascist martyrs answering the roll call both there and for eternity. At the center of the room a giant metallic cross rose above a pool of martyrs' blood, suggested by artificial red lighting, while a recording of the Fascist hymn *Giovinezza* wafted softly through the air. Under the ring of eternal glory lay the pennons of the fallen while the cross announced their immortality—"PER LA PATRIA IM-MORTALE!"

In Germany, Hitler himself took an active interest in the design of what Alex Scobie terms the first Nazi forum in Munich, the restructured neoclassical Königsplatz, where among the new buildings were erected twin *Ehrentempeln* or martyrs' temples, open to the sky. Scobie relates,

> In 1935 Hitler said that the martyrs' bodies were not to be buried out of sight in crypts, but should be placed in the open air, to act as eternal sentinels for the German nation. . . . It is interesting that later still (1940) he asked Giesler to plan his own mausoleum in Munich in such a way that his sarcophagus would be exposed to sun and rain. It is worth noting that in his will of 2 May 1938, his body was to be put in a coffin similar to that of the other martyrs and placed in the Ehrentempel next to the Führerbau.[48]

Whereas the amphitheater arranged as a symbolic space of national unity and confraternity for the first Festival of Federation on July 14, 1790, reflected the hopes for a freely engaged political and spiritual union, the Nazi counterpart created by Speer at Nuremberg had a far more sinister purpose and a much less innocent vision of mass assemblies. For Speer, *Versammlungsarchitektur* (assembly-architecture) was "a means for stabilizing the mechanism of [Hitler's] domination."[49] The vast buildings at Nuremberg "were all related in function to Hitler's interests in mass psychology and how best to influence people en masse in an en face situation (Menschenbeeinflussung im Auge)."[50] The pillars of white light created by powerful searchlights at the mass rallies there were, according to Scobie, purposeful renditions of the Church's use of somber light, candles, and incense, adapted to the ends of the Nazis' mass rallies, to the "feeling of oneness (Artgleichkeit) between 'Führer' and 'Geführte' (leader and led)."[51] It would be difficult to imagine a political ideology that differed more significantly from the ideals encapsulated in the July 14, 1790, civic festival on the Champ de Mars. The inspiration behind the space of liberty, which provided the foundation to the revolutionary space for the new French republic, would in Nazi Germany find its darkest counterpart, its ultimate perversion.

3

Character and Design Method

The ascendancy of Beaux-Arts institutional architecture throughout the West in the nineteenth and early twentieth centuries is well known. The Beaux-Arts design method and, to a large extent, style, were fostered by an educational system that not only had its center in the Ecole des Beaux-Arts in Paris, founded in 1819, but also had spread in a dominant way throughout Europe and to the United States by the turn of the century.

This system combined the three major components of eighteenth-century academic design to secure for the Enlightenment one of its most longstanding legacies to Western culture. These components were the *grande architecture* defined by Jacques-François Blondel, the idea of *caractère* or character as formulated in the competitions designs of the Académie Royale d'Architecture and as epitomized by Etienne-Louis Boullée's academic projects and teachings, and the design methodology established by J.-N.-L. Durand for the students at the Ecole Polytechnique and published in the first years of the nineteenth century.

Blondel's stipulation that civic architecture had to exhibit the qualities of *une grande architecture* achieved through grandiose spaces, colossal proportions, and massive forms with minimal horizontal divisions helped architects to focus on the ways in which institutional architecture could readily be distinguished from domestic building. The hallmarks of this "grand architecture" in Blondel's time were the east facade of the Louvre (1667) by Louis Le Vau, Charles Le Brun, and Claude Perrault, the paired buildings on what is today place de la Concorde (1755) by Ange-Jacques Gabriel, and the Eglise Sainte-Geneviève (1755–1780) by Jacques-Germain Soufflot. As Blondel explained, the east facade of the Louvre and the Eglise Sainte-Geneviève used few horizontal divisions. The former presented the appearance of two stacked floors, a base and a *piano nobile* with a colossal order; the latter eschewed the Baroque stacking of architectural orders on the facade to utilize instead a single colossal order. To achieve "grandeur" without degenerating into the merely "gigantic" was a skill that Blondel counseled his students to develop in seeking to realize a "grand architecture."[1]

In the eighteenth-century, the styles most favored in academic design were late Baroque and then neoclassical. In the nineteenth century, it became neo-Renaissance. This was stimulated largely through the Renaissance revival facade of the main building of the Ecole des Beaux-Arts itself, the Palais des Etudes (1833–1839) by Félix Duban, and consolidated through the two most influential touchstones of *une grande architecture* in the nineteenth century, the Paris Opera (1860–1875) by Charles Garnier and the completion of the Louvre (1852–1880) by Ludovico Visconti and Hector Lefuel. The profuse surface ornamentation of these two latter buildings also colored the subsequent approach to Beaux-Arts design by architects throughout the West. Beaux-Arts architecture, though, was not tied to any one style. Rather, the various styles, ranging from neo-Romanesque to neo-Renaissance to neoclassical, reflected a grounding in the classical tradition, whose elements were used to achieve what Blondel had identified as *une grande architecture.*

The notion of character, which designated an appropriate expression through architectural design that suited the building type, was seen by Blondel as some expression of force or grace achieved through a building's massing. With Boullée, as discussed above in Chapter 1, the horizontal and vertical characteristics of simple, prismatic forms played an important role in determining the effect on the viewer. In analyzing Boullée's designs and writings, we saw that he imbued his architecture with three, overlapping aspects of character—expressive, metaphorical, and symbolic.

Although symbolic character was largely particular to Boullée's time, the expressive aspect of character continued into the nineteenth century. It was so important that the architects working in the Conseil des Bâtiments Civils, the government organization that oversaw the construction and repair of public buildings, included character among its criteria of judgment. One report, dating from around 1805, which reviewed public projects for the minister of the interior, explained that in addition to considering the arrangement of the plan and the soundness of the construction, the Conseil also was assessing the building's *caractère.* Each building had to "announce on its exterior the character [corresponding to] its function." Without an appropriate character, "architecture would soon retrograde into barbarism."[2] In other words, the official national bureaucracy was requiring functionaries throughout the country to adhere to the academic standards of the Enlightenment. Within the academy itself, the idea of expressive character was passed

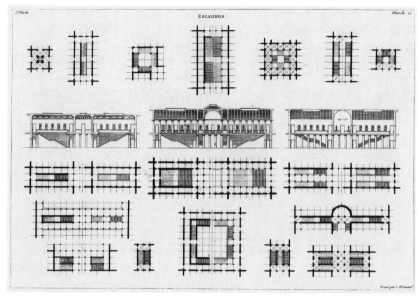

Figure 19. J.-N.-L. Durand, The "parts" of architectural composition: stairs.

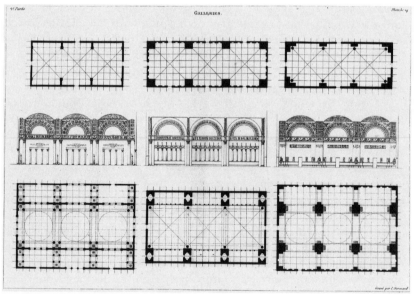

Figure 20. J.-N.-L. Durand, The "parts" of architectural composition: foyers.

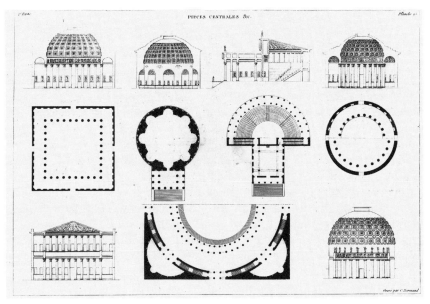

Figure 21. J.-N.-L. Durand, The "parts" of architectural composition: rooms.

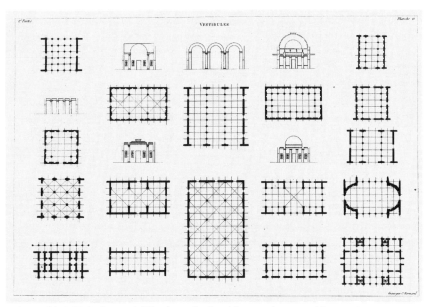

Figure 22. J.-N.-L. Durand, The "parts" of architectural composition: *galeries.*

from the generation of Boullée to that of Percier, Fontaine, and A.-L.-T. Vaudoyer, and then onto the generation of Henri Labrouste and Léon Vaudoyer.[3]

The third component of the Enlightenment legacy to future Beaux-Arts design owed its origins to the systematization of eighteenth-century academic pedagogy by Boullée's "pupil and special protégé" Durand.[4] Faced with the task of teaching architecture to engineering students in the newly created Ecole Polytechnique, Durand set about to establish a method that could be learned rapidly and applied with facility to the entire range of building types and sizes. He developed a rationalized approach to design that he presented in a series of lessons patterned after the thought process advocated by Descartes in the *Discours de la méthode* (1637), which calls for the division of any problem into smaller units, each to be handled separately, and for a progression from the simplest and easiest issues to the most complex.[5] Certainly this was an improvement on a curriculum that limited the graphic component in architecture for the engineering students to the drawings of the orders, doors and vaults, a room, and a staircase. Durand published a two-volume textbook explaining his method entitled *Précis des leçons d'architecture données à l'Ecole Polytechnique* (1802–1805). After years of teaching his rationalized design method in lecture format, Durand was successful in having the Ecole Polytechnique change the drawing component of the pedagogical program to coordinate with his teaching, which he then streamlined in a new series of lessons published as *Partie graphique des cours d'architecture faits à l'Ecole Royale Polytechnique depuis sa réorganization: Précédée d'un sommaire des leçons relatives à ce nouveau travail* (1821).[6] As Durand made abundantly clear, though, in both the *Précis* and the *Partie graphique,* his system was intended not merely for engineers but rather for all professionals in the field of architecture.

Durand's enduring contribution to the field of architecture was the way in which he defined the "parts" of architectural design. His genius was to divide a building into the most effective constituent elements for architectural design and then to demonstrate that they could be organized hierarchically on gridded paper along an armature of major and minor axes.[7] Durand's "parts" were porches, stairs (fig. 19), foyers (fig. 20), rooms (fig. 21), *galeries* (fig. 22) or galleries (longitudinal rooms that also could serve as vestibules), courtyards, and, although not explicitly named, corridors. Whereas Durand's hierarchical ordering of compositional elements along axes was firmly grounded in eighteenth-century academic teaching, his pedagogical examples helped to free

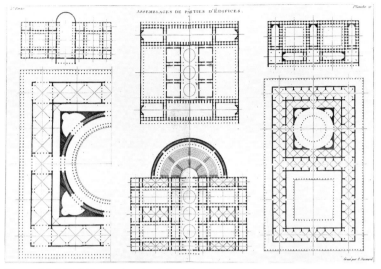

Figure 23. J.-N.-L Durand, principles of architectural composition.

architecture from the abstract rigidities of four-part symmetry, which dominated neoclassical design, in favor of the more flexible bilateral symmetry, with a major central axis and minor cross axes (fig. 23). The potential for thinking about architectural composition in this way was so rich that this method, originally conceived for engineers, was rapidly adopted by architects. As developed by the Ecole des Beaux-Arts, it became the fundamental basis for academic design throughout the West. The result was a composition in which a monumental ligature of circulation provided a clear and hierarchical organization of interior space that, in turn, complemented the *grande architecture* of the exterior facades and the grandiose proportions of interior rooms and corridors. The skillfully coordinated sequence of circulation spaces and rooms created what Le Corbusier in the 1920s would term an "architectural promenade."

The enthusiastic adoption of Durand's pedagogy for engineers by architects was only one of the ironies in the matter. It is a further irony that, in earlier years as an architecture student and subsequently as a participant in competitions for revolutionary buildings, Durand had succeeded in designing prizewinning buildings with the symbolic spaces customary to the times. Although the student and protégé of Boullée, the architect with one of the most symbolic minds and spiritual dispositions of the era, Durand in his pedagogy became the true Jeremy Bentham of his discipline. A thorough utilitarian, Durand believed that action was dominated by the desire to avoid difficulty and to secure well-being. "The goal of architecture cannot be pleasure, but rather utility." Durand ridiculed the longstanding belief that the orders were based on an imitation of the human body. He rejected Laugier's story of the primitive hut. He had no interest in the aesthetic pleasure derived from a field of columns that had dominated neoclassical sensibilities. Nor did he seem aware of the way this architecture could engage an invigorating sense of body self.[8] He believed that a building would automatically have the appropriate character as well as beauty if it were designed and constructed as economically and functionally as possible. He seems not to have believed in artistic genius, for he explained, "Talent is nothing other than the proper and skillful use of knowledge." Not only were his aphorisms trenchant, his conclusions were reductionist and uncompromising:

> Thus, all the talent of the architect amounts to resolving these two problems: 1. with a given sum of money, to make a building as functional as possible, as in private edifices; 2. the functions of a building having been given, to make this building with as little expense as possible, as in public edifices.[9]

Perhaps it required Durand's utilitarian mind to conceive his logical system of "parts" as well as its hierarchical method of combinations.

Yet, there were inherent limits to Durand's system of reasoning. Although he could define the "parts" and show how they might be combined, he had no way to determine the overall aspect of the composition. Here he had to rely on the achievements of the eighteenth-century academy. The buildings that Durand illustrates in his lessons are of two types. One type displays the compositional strategies found in the *Grands Prix* and in Boullée's designs, which had been guided by the notion of architectural character and which had been imbued with harmonious proportions. The others depart from these precedents to exhibit a lack of symbolic elements, an absence of expressive character, and an awkwardness of proportioning in the overall width to height of the building.

Even when Durand utilized earlier academic design as prototypes, he generally, as has been observed, rationalized and homogenized the features to make them fit into the gridded system along with all of the other design examples.[10] Not only were all walls made to coincide with the lines of the square grid, with columns occurring at the intersection of grid lines and doors placed in the middle of each square, but the sculpted modeling of walls, known as *poché*, was drastically reduced if not entirely eliminated. In its enthusiasm for Durand's methodology, the Ecole des Beaux-Arts in the early nineteenth century largely abandoned the use of *poché*, which had been so popular in the previous era. In many respects, the history of nineteenth-century Beaux-Arts architecture is the gradual rediscovery of the compositional and expressive potential of *poché.*

The challenge faced by Beaux-Arts architecture in the nineteenth and twentieth centuries was how to combine together these three eighteenth-century components—the *grande architecture,* character, and Durand's rationalization of academic composition—in the most effective way. To study this legacy in its fullest flowering and hence in the realization of its greatest potential, we can turn to the civic architecture of Paul Philippe Cret. Trained in the Beaux-Arts first in Lyons and then in Paris, Cret developed an illustrious career in the United States where he came by invitation in 1903 to teach architecture at the University of Pennsylvania. No Beaux-Arts architect was more skilled in applying Durand's methodology for composition than Cret. No academic architect after Boullée and Ledoux was more sensitive to the expressive, metaphorical, and symbolic aspects of character. No Beaux-Arts architect achieved a more humane and subtle rendition of the "grand architecture" that Blondel had required of the profession. To study Cret's civic works is to mine the exemplars of the legacy of the late eighteenth-century vision of architecture.

Paul Cret was a master of symbolic character. He had an uncanny ability to infuse his civic buildings with a character that seemed to capture the essence of its institution. He achieved this through fashioning the building around a great hall—arranged as an interior garden, a courtyard, or a major room—whose size and aspect as well as position gave identity to the entire building. This great hall served as a point of focus and reciprocally as a center from which the other major rooms issued. It joined an appropriate expressive and metaphorical character to the symbolic core of the design. This emphasis on symbolic character in Cret's architecture was linked directly with the academic architecture of the late eighteenth century, as epitomized in Boullée's designs and as passed on to successive generations through the publication of the *Grands Prix.*

Cret's course on architectural form at the University of Pennsylvania, whose records from around 1910 are conserved in the archives, reveals his deep sympathy with this tradition. It included at least one lesson (fig. 24) on the most symbolic spaces of late eighteenth-century academic design: the prizewinning project of 1802 by Durand and Jean-Thomas Thibault for a "temple décadaire," the central chapel of the first place *Grand Prix* of 1799 for an "Elysium or public cemetery" awarded to Louis-Sylvestre Gasse, and C. Gay's *prix d'émulation* in 1800 for a cenotaph to Sir Isaac Newton. These three buildings have no "function"; they

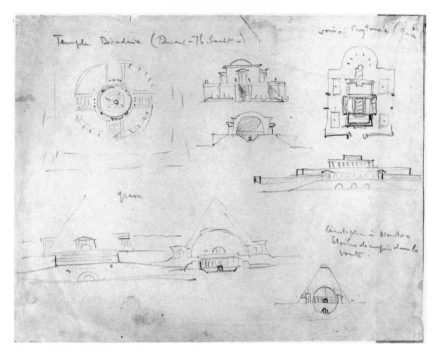

Figure 24. Paul Philippe Cret, sketch from course on architectural form, University of Pennsylvania, c. 1910. *Upper left:* J.-N.-L. Durand and Jean-Thomas Thibault, temple décadaire (project), 1802, plan. *Lower left:* Louis-Sylvestre Gasse, Elysium or Public Cemetery, elevation and section through central chapel. First *Grand Prix* of 1799. *Lower right:* C. Gay, Cenotaph to Sir Isaac Newton, section. *Prix d'émulation,* 1800.

are symbolic buildings intended for veneration or worship. The "temple décadaire" was the French Revolution's house of worship, consecrated to the "Supreme Being and the immortality of the soul." The design by Durand and Thibault, both former students of Boullée, featured a star-filled central domed room, reminiscent of Boullée's cenotaph to Sir Isaac Newton (fig. 13), a design which had both inspired the program and the designs for the *prix d'émulation* in 1800 won by Gay. As Cret noted on his sketch, Gay's design included a fully spherical central cavity covered with stars.[11] Similarly, Gasse's central chapel featured an honorific domed space, in this case with a circular temple around a sunken altar or sarcophagus. Cret's fascination with such buildings, which relied heavily on symbolic character established through a central room, would be a consistent feature of his civic architecture. In this manner, he linked his architecture directly to the academic legacy of the late eighteenth century. In 1908, Cret had articulated these values in responding to attacks on the Ecole des Beaux-Arts by stressing, "The Ecole develops in an admirable way the study of design, respect for the program, and the research of a special character proper for each building."[12]

Early Work and the Pan American Building

Cret's early interest in the symbolic potential of the great hall is evident from his extant student work. His competition design for a Museum of Archaeology (1901–1902) is organized around a glass-covered atrium whose skylight provides a crowning feature to the elevation as well. The Cret archives hold a perspective study from the same period that shows a grand interior space with mezzanine for a department store.[13] By 1906, three years after he had come to the University of Pennsylvania, Cret designed a building to house the School of Architecture.[14] This unrealized project, conceived after the manner of the building for the Ecole des Beaux-Arts in Paris, was organized around a central glass-covered atrium, designated as the Hall of Casts. This great hall would have had plaster casts and perhaps scaled models of great historical architecture, thereby doubling as a source of instruction and inspiration as well as a room that visually conveys the building's purpose.

Cret received an opportunity to realize his ideas in 1907, when he and Albert Kelsey won the competition for a building to house the Inter-

Figure 25. Paul Philippe Cret, Pan American Union (today Organization of American States), Washington, D.C., 1907. Front elevation.

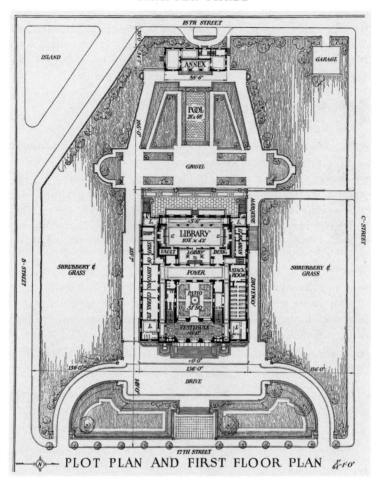

Figure 26. Cret, Pan American Union, first-floor plan.

national Bureau of the American Republics, which would become the Pan American Union in 1910.[15] Here was a building perfectly suited to Cret's symbolic frame of mind (fig. 25). As Cret later explained, the building was to be "the visible expression of the ideals of unity, solidarity, and amity to which the Union is dedicated."[16] Cret gave symbolic character to this idea by designing the building around a great central space, which in turn was given metaphorical character as a patio in a stately Latin American residence (figs. 26–28). As Elizabeth Grossman has pointed out, the residential metaphor was extended to the entire building, from the sloping tiled roof to the design of the assembly hall as a

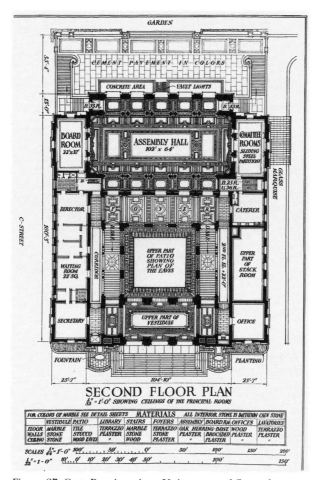

Figure 27. Cret, Pan American Union, second-floor plan.

ballroom.[17] At the time the competition was judged, Kelsey believed that Cret's idea about characterizing the building as a private residence had been largely instrumental in winning the prize. Writing to Cret about the various entries, Kelsey explained: "Your judgment in regard to making it a great house, as it were, was exactly right. Most of them had large amphitheatres with domes, and injured the appearance of their plans by showing a multitude of seats."[18]

The success of this strategy depended upon the way in which the metaphor of the central patio was realized. Cret's description of what amounts to the expressive character of the patio captures the quality of

IN THE PATIO

Figure 28. Cret, Pan American Union, central patio.

this space, whose enchanting ambience has been responsible for making the building, as Cret observed twenty years after its construction, into a place of pilgrimage for busloads of tourists:

> The patio, one of the attractions of the building, is open in summer and closed in winter by a sliding glass roof. Thus a tropical garden is maintained here throughout the year. This court was regarded as exceptionally desirable, owing to the important part which courts play in Latin American architecture. The striking original pavement of the patio is formed by hand-made tile and designed [with] . . . decorative figures in dull black on a field of red. The walls of rough white stucco support a polychrome terra-cotta frieze bearing coats-of-arms of the twenty-one republics. The strong overhanging roof, the tropical plants, the Aztec fountain, are combined to give to this part of the building a touch of exoticism which has the excuse of recalling the earliest development of American civilization.[19]

Although the building program had stipulated the inclusion of a patio, it took a conscious decision on Cret's part to place this function within the heart of the building and to make it the kernel of the design. Elizabeth Grossman, in a fascinating and pioneering study of this competition, has shown how differently the patio could have been treated.

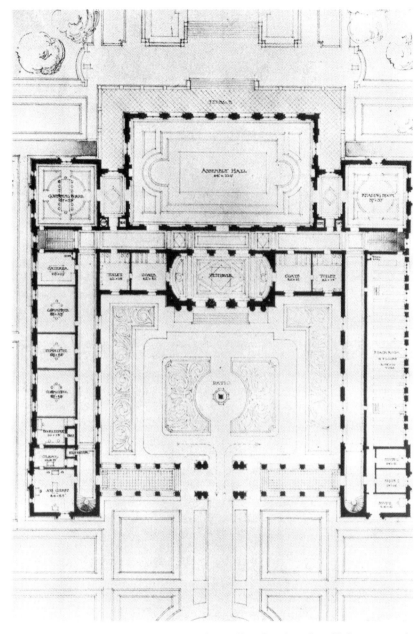

Figure 29. Edward Pearce Casey and Arthur Dillon, Pan American Union, competition design, 1907, plan.

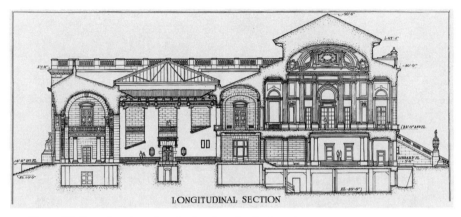

Figure 30. Cret, Pan American Union, longitudinal section.

Another team of architects, Casey and Dillon, for example, left the patio outdoors as a large forecourt (fig. 29).

Not only did Cret bring the patio inside, he wove an entire network of important spaces around it. In his design, the patio is preceded by an entrance vestibule basically of the same width and nearly the same height, whose openness permits an extensive view into the garden. The stairs that rise along both sides of the patio are also open to this interior garden (fig. 30). These stairs lead to the vestibule of the assembly hall, with the vestibule once again open to the patio below. As a result, there is the opportunity for views across, into, and out of the garden. This is a spatial composition of great visual and plastic richness with all the variety of chiaroscuro that such a configuration affords. In this way, Cret created a unified complex of the main ceremonial spaces, which was supplemented by the presence of the library and its vestibule on the ground floor to the far side of the patio and by the rear stairs leading from the assembly room to the terrace and rear garden.

The organic relationship between these main spaces, with the patio as the kernel, well illustrates the fundamental Beaux-Arts principle of composition that Cret articulated in his own later account of the building: "Architecture of merit is not to be estimated merely upon the skillful employment of forms and decoration, but upon the evidence of the architect's intelligent grasp of his problem and of his attainment of a solution that not only solves, but solves simply and directly without apparent effort and wasted motion."[20] Here the contrast between the Cret building and that by Casey and Dillon could not be more complete. In the former, not only are the library and assembly hall directly related to the central patio, they are also reached through smoothly arranged circula-

THE HALL OF THE PATRIOTS

Figure 31. Cret, Pan American Union, Hall of Flags.

tion spaces that are given the appropriate size and decorative character as well as being separated from the more utilitarian corridors which serve the administrative rooms. In the latter building, one long U-shaped corridor serves the ceremonial and functional spaces without distinction and without transition and differentiation. It also serves as a wedge between the elaborate entrance vestibule and the assembly room rather than as a gracious transition. Although both buildings used the Beaux-Arts elements codified by Durand, only the Cret building did so skillfully.

In composing the central complex of unified spaces that culminates in arrival at the assembly hall, Cret masterfully orchestrated the entire range of Durand's set pieces, which had become the basis of Beaux-Arts design. Cret's success derived from his ability to make the patio into a room of architectural distinction and then to link this room with spaces that seemed like natural appendages. The principal sequence of spaces indoors begins with an entrance hall conceived as a noble Beaux-Arts foyer. The stairs to either side of the great hall lead to a vestibule for the assembly room. This vestibule (fig. 31) was designed as a Beaux-Arts *galerie* (fig. 22), a circulation room that also served as a place in its own right. In Cret's design, this vaulted vestibule provided a passageway in the U-shaped circulation of the second floor; it also served as an anteroom to the assembly hall; and, finally, it was a room with its own identity, a Hall of Flags, decorated both with the flags of the twenty-one republics and with busts of their founders. In this way, this vestibule formed part of the symbolic space of the building consecrated to the idea of liberty and union, as it visually linked the entrance foyer and central patio to the assembly room, called the "Hall of the Americas."[21]

Finally, Cret succeeded in infusing his building with what Blondel had termed *une grande architecture,* while simultaneously imparting an engaging human scale. The size and proportions of the central patio yield a combined feeling of amplitude and intimacy. The figures drawn in the sections of this and other Cret buildings in Hoak and Church's book on American architecture document Cret's careful attention to scaling down large spaces in horizontal tiers related to the size of the human body. Certainly, the plants, fountain, and benches as well as the small-scale, highly colored ornamentation strengthen this effect.

All of these are supporting incidents to the larger scheme of rendering the great hall as a two-story space with mezzanine. We have seen that Cret used this device in his design for a department store. It is employed here again and would remain a recurrent feature of Cret's subsequent civic architecture. In the Pan American Union building, the effectiveness of the mezzanine is reinforced by opening the walls bordering the side stairs. In whatever configuration Cret would give the mezzanine within the double-story central great hall, the result would be a plastic richness and a more intimate scale imparted to the ceremonial aspect of the *grande architecture.*

Indianapolis Public Library

Cret's Indianapolis Public Library (fig. 32), the product of a competition of 1914 that the architect won in collaboration with the Philadelphia

Figure 32. Paul Philippe Cret, Indianapolis Public Library, 1914.

firm of Zantzinger, Borie, and Medary, was also designed around a symbolic central great hall. In this case, the great hall served the function of the book delivery room (figs. 33, 34). Tracing the evolution of the design, Elizabeth Grossman has pointed out that Cret took liberties with the program to provide the building with grand architectural spaces. The delivery or "circulating" room was increased in square footage by more than 50 percent, and the six stipulated reading rooms were combined into two long majestic halls.[22] This was not the first time that Cret had creatively manipulated the program to achieve a requisite generosity of effect for the main spaces. In the Pan American Union Building he had combined the three stipulated library spaces into one large room,

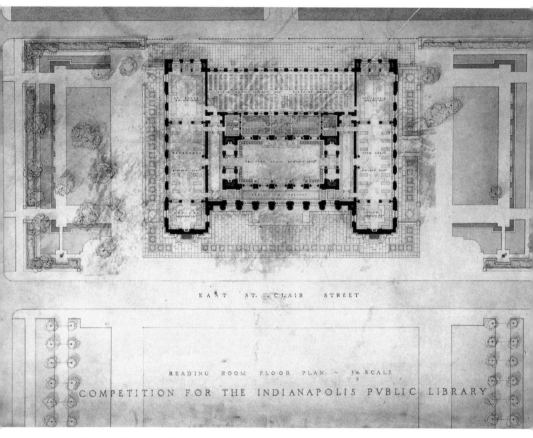

Figure 33. Cret, Indianapolis Public Library, competition plan.

thereby satisfying the program while fashioning a space adequate in size and grandeur to the neighboring central patio.[23]

As in the Pan American Union Building, the central room of the Indianapolis Public Library has been fashioned as a double-height space with a mezzanine. Here, though, the mezzanine is not a gallery at the top of the space but rather a second tier of books that lines the walls of the delivery room. In place of the central fountain of the Latin American patio, one finds the partial octagon of the delivery desk. As in the Pan American Union Building, the delivery room is opened on the sides to provide views into other spaces. True to Cret's appreciation of economy of means, the delivery room also serves the function of a *galerie* that distributes visitors to the reading rooms on either side. An appreciative *Library Journal* captured the essential nature and quality of this space:

Figure 34. Cret, Indianapolis Public Library, delivery room.

"The spacious central hall, expanding into broad galleries above de-voted to fiction while other books are open-shelved below, well lighted by high wide windows, is the characteristic feature, most inviting in friendly welcome to its store of books, and an impressive object lesson, well worth its cost in space and money."[24]

The use of a grand central room, lined with books that characterize as well as decorate the space, was a well-established tradition dating from late eighteenth-century French academic architecture. As we have seen in Chapter 1, in 1785 Boullée, with his Enlightenment outlook about the library as the repository of humankind's knowledge of the universe, had proposed a new reading room for the Royal Library as a giant am-phitheater of books, which suggested a silent and invisible assembly of the Manes or spirits of the great thinkers represented there by their writ-ten works (fig. 4). The message of this amphitheater was reinforced by

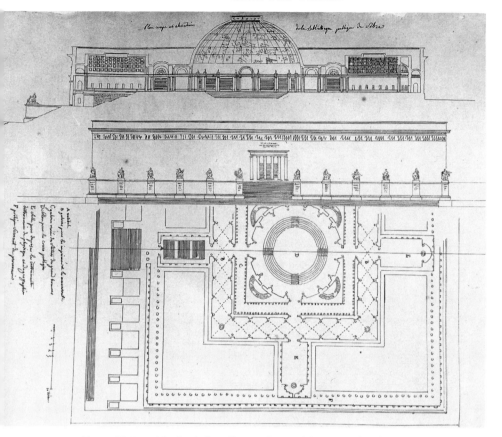

Figure 35. Jean-Nicolas Sobre, library. Competition entry for the *prix d'émulation*, November 1787.

the crowning ceremonial colonnade, covered in turn by a barrel vault with a symbolically sacred light entering from above. A statue of Minerva, goddess of arts and sciences, placed under what Boullée termed a "triumphal arch," presided over the entire scene.[25] The building's principal theme was reiterated at the entrance, which was flanked by two atlantes or giants carrying a celestial sphere.[26]

This lofty interpretation of the library as an amphitheater of books where the Manes of the great authors commune together, so to speak, was reiterated over the following decades. Jean-Nicolas Sobre, in a competition design (fig. 35) that might date from the *prix d'émulation* of November 1787, provided a central symbolic space in the form of a cylinder lined with books and roofed over by a dome covered with figures of the

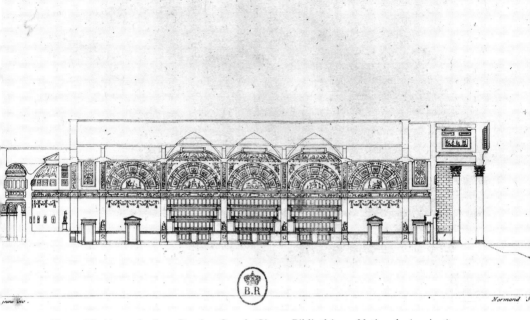

Figure 36. Alexandre-Jean-Baptiste-Guy de Gisors, Bibliothèque Nationale (project), Paris, using the unfinished Church of the Madeleine as the foundations for the design. Section. Year VIII [1799–1800].

zodiac and opened to the sky through a central oculus.[27] In the middle of the room and under this cosmic dome rose an amphitheater for assemblies of living people as well as the authors' Manes. Then, at the turn of the century, Alexandre-Jean-Baptiste-Guy de Gisors proposed to complete the unfinished Church of the Madeleine as the National Library (fig. 36) with books arranged in stepped amphitheaters, presided over by the symbolic gaze of Apollo, enshrined in a temple where he would be surrounded by statues of the Muses.[28] Thomas Jefferson's library in the upper floor of the rotunda at the head of the campus of the University of Virginia followed in this tradition. In this half-scaled rendition of the Pantheon, Jefferson placed his library under a cosmic dome, which he wanted to have painted blue with gold stars of the nighttime sky.[29] Finally, Henri Labrouste, whom Cret greatly admired, conceived his Bibliothèque Sainte-Geneviève (1838–1850) in an analogous fashion. He lined the reading room with two tiers of books, one along the floor and the other on a mezzanine backed up against the exterior walls. On the outside of these walls, Labrouste inscribed the stone with the names of the great thinkers to show, according to Neil Levine, the chain of human thought, beginning with Moses and monotheism and continuing to contemporary scientism.[30] A copy of Raphael's *School of Athens,* the painting that had inspired Boullée's metaphorical conceit for his library, was painted on the wall of the ceremonial stairwell that led to the second-floor reading room.

Labrouste's design amply demonstrates that the Enlightenment understanding of the symbolic importance of the library was still strong at the middle of the nineteenth century. As a contemporary writer in *L'Artiste* explained, "Materially speaking a library can be merely a place to store books . . . but is that all? Certainly not; for it is also a place containing the noblest of riches; the treasury where the most precious possessions of mankind are kept, the works of genius."[31] Paul Cret's delivery room at the Indianapolis Public Library, with its symbolically ample space and its two tiers of books, follows in this tradition, adjusted to reflect a twentieth-century sensibility about the library's importance to American democracy, whose local history in the state of Indiana is depicted in the decorative frieze above the piers.

Throughout his career, Cret used the architectural orders to great advantage at dramatically different scales and with varied proportions. They served various purposes, ranging from assisting in the creation of *une grande architecture* to imparting intimate human scale. Writing about the Indianapolis Public Library, Milton B. Medary explained that the "single order which is the motif of the south facade gives a scale necessary to its position at the head of the general civic composition,"[32] which was bordered to the far south side of the site by the existing Federal Building with a similar exterior columnar portico. Inside the library, the large-scale features of the exterior massing, along with the exterior giant Doric order, are echoed by the size of the delivery room with its ample piers.

Yet between the exterior portico and the interior great hall, the visitor must pass through a modest entrance foyer with narrow, delicately modeled pilasters, which creates an intimate scale. This intimacy is sustained by the short run of steps that take the visitor up into the delivery room where the space explodes, so to speak, all around. Similar flights of steps with short runs lead from either side of the delivery room to the peripheral mezzanines and into the reading rooms. Cret had already explored this technique of short flights of steps for gradual shifts in level in his student design submitted for the Labarre Prize of 1901.[33] Now he was actually realizing such a motif in the Indianapolis Public Library in a way that made gradual transitions at human scale to the next floor levels. This was a creative use of that standard element of the Beaux-Arts circulation network used here, though, to humanize the monumental space.

The two tiers of bookshelves that sweep across the grand delivery room create a second and complementary space at human scale. On the bookshelves, delicately carved pilasters with gilt capitals in the form of leaves or stylized Indian heads reinforce this effect. Most important, inside the great hall the narrowness of the mezzanine passageway in front of the piers plays an important role in reinforcing the sense of a place scaled to the human body.

These complementary scales—the grand and the more intimate—can be found in the reading rooms as well which, although made large by recasting the program, were given an intimacy by the finishings. As Medary explained:

> The same desire for intimate relation between the several departments found expression in the use of color and the choice of materials and furnishings for the interior, large scale and monumental detail being avoided as much as possible. The principal rooms are panelled in wood in domestic scale. The ceilings are rich in color and with the cork floors, leather doors and tiers of book-bindings, give an atmosphere of comfort designed to overcome the tendency of a formal architecture towards a too great austerity.[34]

Although Cret always remained true to the ideal of *une grande architecture,* he likewise combined the monumental with more intimately scaled features.

Variations on the Theme of the Great Hall

With the Pan American Union Building and the Indianapolis Public Library, Cret had established two complementary attitudes toward the great hall with mezzanine that he would apply with variations in later buildings. In 1931 at the University of Texas at Austin, he created an equivalent to the Pan American Union Building in the main floor "lobby" of the Union Building, which he fashioned as a glass-covered Spanish *cortile* (fig. 37). Carol McMichael has captured the ambience of the double-height space with its elevated gallery: "The lobby was treated as the courtyard or patio of a Spanish palace. Rising through two stories and surrounded by sheltered galleries on both levels, it was closed by an opaque skylight that bathes in filtered light the amber-tiled floor and the

Figure 37. Paul Philippe Cret, Union Building, University of Texas at Austin, 1931, lobby.

varnished surfaces of the wooden piers, the bracket capitals of Spanish derivation, and the cornices that defined the *cortile*."[35] As in the Indianapolis Public Library, this great hall is also a place of circulation that distributes visitors, in this case, into nine different places, including the vestibule to the grand ballroom and the monumental stairs down to the entrance. Serving as a *galerie,* this great hall, rendered metaphorically as a Spanish patio, becomes the physical and symbolic heart of a building consecrated to social intercourse in the university community.

Cret's library building at the University of Texas at Austin, begun in 1931, applies the lesson of the Indianapolis Public Library to present on the second floor a central great hall, which serves as the book delivery room and is conceived as a Hall of the Six Coats of Arms. This room, as McMichael explains, was "paneled in rich materials, including walnut and four different colored marbles, each from a different state. The decorative program celebrated the fact that six nations had governed Texas."[36] Grand reading rooms to either side—one for periodicals and the other for general reading—reiterate the pattern of the Indianapolis plan. To the far side of the Hall of the Six Coats of Arms, the space behind the loan desk is like a vestibule to the main book stack that rises in the form of a tower to dominate the campus as its physical and symbolic landmark, a symbol of the university's purpose after the manner of Jefferson's star-filled domed rotunda. Commanding a larger campus than Jefferson's rotunda, the tower also responds to the elevated dome of the state capitol building viewed across the city. This pairing of institutional symbols was so effective that the regents and the administration appropriated much of the first and second floors in the library for their offices and for the Academic Room, which was their meeting room.[37]

Whereas the volumetric configuration of a great hall with an upper gallery created for the Pan American Union Building was taken up again with variations in the Union Building, the alternative arrangement created at Indianapolis with the two tiers of bookshelves made possible by a low mezzanine toward the floor found expression in the reading room of the Folger Shakespeare Library (Washington, D.C., 1928–1932), fashioned as an Elizabethan Hall. Here the grandeur of the space is given intimacy as well by the three roughly equal horizontal divisions of the volume—the lightly stained wood-paneled bookshelves at the bottom that establish human scale, the light painted walls in the middle, and, finally, the deep, darkly stained wooden truss ceiling lowered along the sides over the mezzanine to complement the volumetric configuration of the lower third of the room.

Finally, to give one more example, in the Memorial Museum of the University of Texas at Austin (1935–1937), Cret returned again to the configuration of the great hall with upper gallery. This building is essentially one great hall, a funerary monument in the form of a room. Mezzanine galleries around the perimeter of the interior lower the peripheral ceiling height to define a symbolic central volume dedicated to the memory of the war dead. With this design Cret has come closest to the purity of symbolic space as conceived during the Enlightenment, in which the suggestion of mere space, centralized and focused, but unencumbered by real walls, can seem so definite and can touch so deeply.

The Great Hall and the Architectural Promenade

All of Cret's great halls belong to a hierarchically orchestrated arrangement of rooms that convey the main theme of each building. We have seen how this operates in the Pan American Union Building and the Indianapolis Public Library. Whereas the Indianapolis Public Library, the library at the University of Texas at Austin, and the Folger Shake-

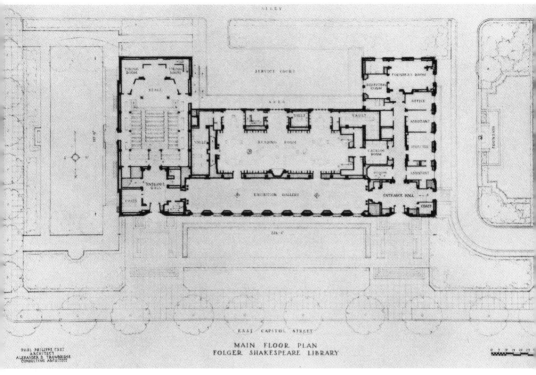

Figure 38. Paul Philippe Cret, Folger Shakespeare Library, Washington, D.C., 1928–1932, plan.

speare Library use lateral movement as an integral aspect of Cret's architectural promenade, other buildings, such as the Pan American Union Building, the Detroit Institute of Arts (1920–1927), and the Federal Reserve Board (1935) in Washington, D.C., present a predominantly linear, axial sequence.

In the Folger Shakespeare Library the great hall is the terminus of an organized sequence of movement with an important lateral shift to reach the center (fig. 38). Each front door is followed by an entrance foyer, which provides a choice of continuing forward or turning to enter a grand Exhibition Gallery (fig. 39). This room is a Beaux-Arts *galerie*, which serves as a vestibule to the great hall as well as a room with its own identity.

Carol McMichael has likened the exterior of this building to a "beautiful box, an immaculate container for precious manuscripts and books."[38] Its treasures, both literal and symbolic, are contained in and around the great hall of the reading room located at the center of the

Figure 39. Cret, Folger Shakespeare Library, Exhibition Gallery.

building. The architectural promenade required to reach this inner sanctum helps to make its characterization effective.

Whereas the more circuitous route was a positive feature in the Folger Shakespeare Library, the more complex sequencing of public rooms in the Detroit Institute of Arts required the clarity of a linear and axial arrangement of the main ceremonial spaces. Cret was initially hired in November 1919 by the Detroit Arts Commission to assist in developing a program and design for a municipal art museum. From the beginning, both client and architect concurred on the need to make the museum into a place of delight. Clyde H. Burroughs, secretary of the Detroit Institute of Arts, in a letter dated December 3, 1919, written to Cret, explained that the commissioners "are particularly anxious that [the building's] usefulness shall take precedence over its exterior form, and that there shall be about it an intimacy and warmth, if possible, such as no museum, at least on this side of the water, has as yet achieved."[39] Cret responded with a similar sentiment in his "Preliminary Report" of January 10, 1920, in which he stressed the need for a "sort of intimacy and escape from that character that has earned for museums the definition of 'cemeteries of works of art.' " This desired intimacy required investing the museum with an expressive, metaphorical, and symbolic character, for as Cret explained, "[T]he attempt to give to the museum a plan strictly adapted to its function has a tendency to make it tiresome to the visitor." The museum was not to be, as "certain rooms in German museums" had been called, a " 'machine to show pictures.' "[40]

To achieve the appropriate character, Cret stressed five necessary components. One was the creation of an "interior garden" that "acts as a rest place between two or more sections of the museum. . . . It introduces the life of plants into the dead world of glass cases and of rooms without view on the outside. The movement of running water can supplement it to great advantage." Another involved "securing of some attractive vistas through the museum" to enhance the pleasure of the visit. A "constant variety of settings" could be imparted through rooms with different appearances, as found in "museums arranged in old residences, such as many Italian museums, the Cluny or the Carnavalet museum in Paris, or the Rycks museum in Amsterdam."[41]

As for the overall conception of the plan, Cret suggested that in "the arrangement of galleries, two or three large halls seem to be desirable, the balance of the rooms being kept of a moderate size." Furthermore, the "monumental stairway" was to be eliminated in favor of reaching the main floor "by several flights of a few steps, climbed without fatigue because separated by wide level surfaces." Cret, evidently drawing on his experience with the Indianapolis Public Library, explained, "The division of the total number of steps to be climbed into two or three groups has proved to be of great advantage, as the public do not realize that they have gone to an upper floor, the small group of steps appearing to them as mere architectural features adding to the variety of treatment of the rooms."[42]

In December 1920, Cret presented a set of finished drawings to accompany his explanatory report (figs. 40–43). He had conceived the building as a cultural oasis for the enchantment of the spirit and the enhancement of the mind. At the physical center Cret placed a garden, conceived metaphorically as a Pompeian court (fig. 43). An axial sequence of related architectural elements—foyer, entrance hall fashioned as a Beaux-Arts *galerie* and serving as a hall of sculpture, garden, and hemicycle—formed an architectural promenade of great spatial va-

Figure 40. Paul Philippe Cret, Detroit Institute of Arts, project of December 1920.

riety as well as providing an exciting vista.[43]

To either side of the garden and located along its cross axis were two complementary great halls: the Hall of Sculpture and Architecture to the left, and the Hall of Modern Decorative Arts and Tapestries to the right. Through its name and decoration, each hall established the character of the exhibits in the *en suite* rooms wrapped around it: painting to the left, decorative arts to the right. Permanent exhibits of historical art were to be placed in the rooms along the side and rear of the building. The front rooms, reached directly from the entrance hall, were designated for modern painting (to the left) and temporary exhibitions (to the right).

Cret's account of the axial sequence through the central spaces is instructive, because it conveys his sense of the expressive and metaphorical character that he sought to impart to his design:

> The entrance vestibule receives abundant light from the three large bays of the main facade and provides an excellent display for sculpture. Opposite the entrance, a large opening shows the garden, its fountain and hemicycle in the distance, in an effective suite similar to the one of the Pan American Union in Washington. This garden and hemicycle complete the display of sculpture, not in the dry fashion of sculpture galleries, but

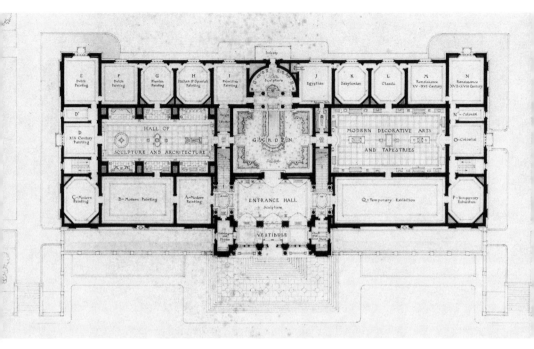

Figure 41. Cret, Detroit Institute of Arts, project of December 1920, "main floor plan."

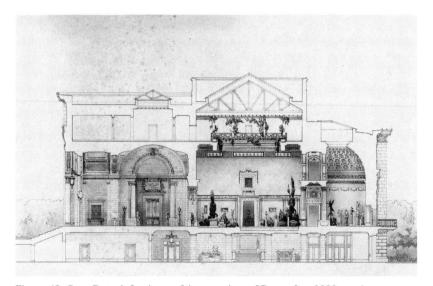

Figure 42. Cret, Detroit Institute of Arts, project of December 1920, section.

Figure 43. Cret, Detroit Institute of Arts, project of December 1920, "the garden."

among shrubs, in a picturesque setting, recalling the atrium of Pompeian houses. Seats would be provided in this garden, which is the rest place between the several sections of the museum and the heart of the whole composition.[44]

The Pompeian court, like the Latin American patio of the Pan American Union Building, would have conveyed a sense of amplitude

Figure 44. Paul Philippe Cret with Zantzinger, Borie and Medary, Detroit Institute of Arts, 1920–1927, entrance vestibule looking toward the main hall, followed by the interior garden.

and intimacy. It presents one of Cret's most complex volumetric units, with the second-story gallery made into a bridge, connecting exhibition rooms, that passes between the garden and the domed hemicycle. The ceiling of the Pompeian court is lower around the perimeter and higher at the center where a vine-covered third-floor gallery overlooks the space and romantically frames the view upward toward the sky.

Cret's report, along with his hypothetical design for the museum, earned him the commission for the actual building, which he executed in conjunction with the Philadelphia firm of Zantzinger, Borie and Medary, his collaborators at the Indianapolis Public Library. In the final design for the Detroit Institute of Arts, Cret was obliged to revise his earlier scheme to accommodate an enlarged and more complex program.[45] The hemicycle was eliminated, thereby making the anticipated bridge into a second-story loggia instead. A grand hall for displaying tapestries and monumental sculpture was introduced between the entrance hall and the garden (fig. 44). This latter space was also altered in character.

Susan Watkins, a friend of Cret's, has described the architectural

Figure 45. Cret with Zantzinger, Borie and Medary, Detroit
Institute of Arts, garden court with pool.

sequence created along the central axis as an "entrance vista" with lighting that "ascends in [a] gradual crescendo, from the cool shadow of the
entrance hall to the rich, colorful brightness of the main hall, and finally
to the sparkling, sunny glimpses of the indoor garden." This garden (fig.
45) was now conceived as a "free adaptation of the Italian baroque, with
walls of mellow-hued travertine stone, decorated with sculptural motifs
on the borders, arched niches for statuary and the colored tilework of
the drinking fountains." Provided with a fountain "with its banks of grow-
ing plants and its blue-tiled pools of gold fish," the central garden was
furnished in the corners with "little iron chairs and tables like those in
the boulevard cafes of Europe, [with] the sunlight . . . softened by an
orange-colored awning with a blue border . . . hung loosely . . . from the
cross-beams of the ceiling."[46]

Figure 46. Paul Philippe Cret, Federal Reserve Board Building, Washington, D.C., 1935.

The final design lost the clarity of the initial scheme with its parallel courtyards to either side of the central garden. Now there was only one court, which was placed to the right of the central axis. Initially open to the sky, this courtyard begins at the lower level and reaches up through two stories. Its brick walls have windows and other features that reflect the different architectural settings of the rooms around it, each fashioned as a characteristic backdrop for the periods of art on display.

The architectural distinction of the Detroit Institute of Arts, with its rich sequence of rooms along the central axis, was followed by that of the Federal Reserve Board (1935) in Washington, D.C. (fig. 46). In this later building, Cret integrated the double-height great hall with mezzanine into an architectural promenade that led from the entrance at either side of the building to the Board Room on the second floor. The compression and release of space along this sequence is probably the most complex in all of his buildings.

At the heart of the sequence, the great hall provides the building's symbolic character (figs. 47, 48). Its central skylight is inscribed with an American eagle that dominates the room, flanked on both sides of the mezzanine by the doors of the twelve regional Federal Reserve districts. This is an architecturally symbolic statement not only about the organization of the Federal Reserve system but also of the American democ-

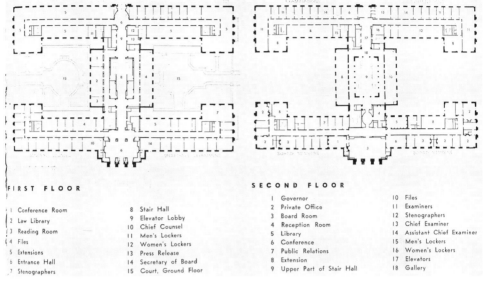

Figure 47. Cret, Federal Reserve Board Building, plans.

Figure 48. Cret, Federal Reserve Board Building, great hall.

Figure 49. Cret, Federal Reserve Board Building, foyer to the Board Room.

racy. It is a space in which symbolic character dominates in the manner of the temple-like spaces of the French Enlightenment architecture in the late eighteenth century.

It is instructive that Cret places toward the beginning and the end of his architectural sequence two oval spaces, relatively intimate in size and having the power in their form to concentrate vectors of spatial forces inward on anybody standing within them. The first occurs as the entrance foyer; the second, more intimate in size and detailing, appears in the form of an anteroom in front of the Board Room (fig. 49).[47] The centering of spatial forces that one feels in this second space encourages introspection about the gravity of the public trust invested in the governors of the Federal Reserve Board. Cret achieved a similar sense of centering in the configuration and ambience of the courtrooms in his Fort Worth Court House, designed in 1933 with Wiley G. Clarkson.

Perhaps this was the ultimate lesson of Cret's application of symbolic character. Its goal, as Boullée and the students of the Académie Royale d'Architecture and its successor bodies during the French Revolution had amply shown through their designs, was to achieve a spatial character that would seem to correspond experientially to a deeply held inner sense of a cherished religious, social, or political ideal.[48] In Cret's Federal Reserve Board Building it was the great hall and its associated sequence of rooms that conveyed the message most forcefully.

Frank Lloyd Wright and Louis Kahn

If one searches for the ongoing legacy of the late eighteenth-century concepts of symbolic character and design method, joined with a "grand architecture"—a legacy realized with both originality and clarity—then one must turn to the architecture of Frank Lloyd Wright and Louis Kahn.

Wright's seminal institutional buildings, the Larkin Administration Building (Buffalo, 1904) and the Unity Church (Oak Park, 1905), differentiate between the main spaces and the circulation in ways that directly recall the set pieces of Durand's system of design. The unity of the exterior massing is perfectly in tune with Blondel's requirements for *une grande architecture*. The affinities in aesthetic spirit between the austere massing of the Larkin Building and the austere neoclassical edifices imagined by Boullée and Ledoux reflect a similar orientation to monumental composition. And, finally, the design of each building around a "noble Room," invested with a spiritual aura, reveals an outlook analogous to the symbolic orientation of Boullée and his contemporaries.[49] Since, in the specificity of its forms, Wright's architecture was so startlingly new and modern, it might seem paradoxical that these works were imbued with the main tenets of academic thought. Yet, as recent research and criticism has shown, Wright's debt to the classical tradition was widespread and profound.[50]

The paradox first encountered in connecting Louis Kahn to the eighteenth-century academy immediately dissolves when one considers his debt to Wright, his training under Cret, and his admiration for Boullée. The distinction between the main central room and the stair towers removed to the corners of the building, which Wright had pioneered, Kahn further articulated in his work. Kahn even gave them names that helped to emphasize their identity as Durand-like set pieces—the "served" and the "servant" spaces. As one follows Kahn's development from the Richards Medical Research Building (1957–1964) at the University of Pennsylvania to the National Assembly of Bangladesh (1962–1974) in Dacca, we find Kahn developing from simple prismatic geometries set pieces which he assembles in a spirit consonant with the Beaux-Arts "parts" and their combinations that Durand bequeathed to succeeding generations. Throughout Kahn's mature period, his institutional buildings also generally were invested with compositional qualities that suited Blondel's requirements for *une grande architecture.*

Like Wright, the heart of Kahn's institutional buildings was often the great hall, whose potential for expressive, metaphorical, and symbolic character Kahn had learned especially from Paul Cret. Kahn first imbibed Cret's lessons at the University of Pennsylvania where he graduated from the architecture program in 1924 and then a few years later when he worked in Cret's office. Throughout Kahn's career he designed institutional buildings around a symbolic great hall. At Bryn Mawr College, the Erdman Hall dormitories (1960–1965) use the great hall as a communal living room and a dining room. The Phillips Exeter Academy Library (1967–1972) follows the example of Cret's Indianapolis Public Library by placing a great hall at the center and then adding symbolic circular openings in the walls that reveal the book stacks. Likewise, the Yale Center for British Art (1969–1974) uses two adjacent great halls to organize the building and invest them with symbolic character. In such a space even the cylindrical shaft of the staircase acquires a totemic aspect. John Lobell has captured the essential quality and purpose of the great halls in this building:

> Dark on the outside, the building explodes with light inside. . . .
> The courts are paneled in a luminous light oak and have balconies looking into them from the other floors of the building. One court is at the entrance. The other is near the center of the building and is Kahn's last offering to Silence, a space without function, a place for that which is not yet.[51]

Kahn's success in vesting a central space with this otherworldly quality, making it seem pregnant as a space of ideals that becomes a temple to the institution housed there, even extends to the out-of-doors. Perhaps his most powerful "offering to Silence" occurs in the courtyard of the Salk Institute (1959–1965) in La Jolla where the sight of the sky and the sound of the ocean join the silence of this exterior great hall as a perfect metaphor of the wonder of Nature and the probing creativity of the scientific mind. This is still another example of the great hall that combines expressive, metaphorical, and symbolic character according to the legacy of the French academic tradition reaching from Boullée to Cret and finally to Kahn.

Like Cret, Kahn looked back to the eighteenth-century sources of the academic ideal that inspired this shared vision of architecture. As Kahn said, "Boullée is / . . . / Thus Architecture is."[52] By temperament as well as by education and training, Kahn was perfectly attuned to the message of Boullée's work. The legacy that reaches from Boullée to Kahn is a testimony to the importance of symbolic space for fashioning architecture in the modern world.

4

The Neoclassical Interlude

The legacy of neoclassical architecture, as we have seen in the preceding chapter, reached from Boullée to Louis Kahn. Emil Kaufmann was correct in entitling his study "From Ledoux to Le Corbusier," for a similar impulse to what he called "autonomous architecture" marked both the late eighteenth-century neoclassical era and the twentieth-century modernism commonly termed the "International Style."[1] Repeatedly one finds the succeeding generation of modernists drawing not only on the lessons of their immediate predecessors but also reaching back to Boullée and Ledoux. Here Louis Kahn was not alone. Consider, for example, Aldo Rossi, whose neo-Rationalist aesthetic derives both from that particularly local brand of the International Style known as the Italian Rationalism of the 1930s and from Boullée's work, which is acknowledged through an homage paid by translating Boullée's treatise into Italian.[2]

Yet, whereas Kaufmann was insightful in the general outlines of his argument, Meyer Schapiro was also correct when reviewing the former's work by calling for an explication of neoclassical architecture on its own terms and within the context of its own times.[3] Kaufmann is not to blame if he was more interested in elucidating a common outlook between two avant-gardes separated by 150 years than in studying neoclassicism on its own terms. Rather, it is not to Kaufmann but instead to certain detractors and defenders of classicism in the nineteenth and twentieth centuries that the tendency to avoid the issue must be assigned. From the vantage point of those nineteenth-century critics of postmedieval classical architecture, such as James Fergusson, John Ruskin, and Montgomery Schuyler, who saw the entire period encompassing the fifteenth through the eighteenth centuries as one continuous era of Renaissance architecture, deemed a sorry departure from the original and creative endeavors achieved in the Gothic architecture of the Middle Ages, the particularities of the neoclassical period vis-à-vis the preceding centuries of classical building were hardly apparent and were of negligible import.

On the other hand, champions of neoclassicism, who mine the universal qualities of its outlook, as found, for example, in the provocative *Classicism Is Not a Style* (1982), edited by Demetri Porphyrios, feel no pressing need to satisfy Schapiro's charge to the architectural historian.

If neoclassical architecture is to be considered within the context of its time, then it will not be the universally powerful aura that its forms evoke across the centuries that will uniquely fix our attention but rather the specificity of its outlook, sandwiched between the Baroque and the Rococo, which preceded it, and the historicism and eclecticism that followed. Indeed, late eighteenth-century neoclassical architecture was a cultural interlude with multiple layers of meaning so specific to the era that it requires a historical study for us to understand how it was intended and perceived. I propose three ways to consider late eighteenth-century French neoclassical architecture. One involves the creation of a new grammar for architecture, a concern that in many respects parallels the narrative aspect of symbolic space considered in Chapter 2. The second addresses the articulation of a new typology for architectural form, which has similarities with metaphorical character in architecture, as discussed in Chapters 1 and 3. Finally, one finds a new aesthetic experience derived from architecture, whose experiential qualities engage the domain of sentience much as do symbolic character and numinous space, both discussed above. In short, one cannot fully understand the intentions behind French neoclassical architecture merely by looking at the drawings and buildings. The meanings they afforded contemporaries and the perceptions they prompted were inextricably tied to a multifaceted conception of symbolic space, which needs to be deciphered by considering their accompanying written texts.

Any consideration of French neoclassical architecture must begin with Jacques-Germain Soufflot's Eglise Sainte-Geneviève and proceed to consider the work of the two greatest architects of this manner, Etienne-Louis Boullée and Claude-Nicolas Ledoux. Whereas these latter men had to await the twentieth century to earn the well-deserved epithet of being "visionary architects," Soufflot, through his Church of Sainte-Geneviève, was immediately recognized as having initiated a new style.[4] Through a retrospective glance of the architecture of the preceding century, Amaury Duval summed up the sentiment of an entire half century when he credited Jacques Gondoin's Ecole de Chirurgie and Soufflot's Eglise Sainte-Geneviève as having ushered in a "revolution in architecture." With these buildings, a new "severe" style, usually called neoclassical today, began to replace the "affected taste of the old school," that is, the late French Baroque along with the Rococo.[5] In studying the transformations from one style to another one finds a curious conjunction of changing tastes along with a redefinition of the grammar of architecture, a new understanding of architectural typology, and an enthusiasm for the experiential aspect of certain components of classical architecture that might, to some observers, seem quite "unclassical" in its emotive intensity.

A New Grammar

The language of neoclassical architecture was still largely the language of classicism, based upon the orders—Doric, Ionic, Corinthian. However, the combination of the constituent elements—columns, entablatures, pediments, walls, doors, and windows—obviously has been altered. Simply by visual inspection one sees that there is a new grammar, that is, new rules that govern their ordering. Emil Kaufmann, as we have seen above in Chapter 1, termed the most innovative features of this new grammar "autonomous architecture" to designate an assemblage of geometrical prisms independent of the Renaissance and Baroque compositional hierarchies rooted in expressing the channeling of forces downward to the ground or in elevating the *piano nobile* above a rusticated base, the latter serving as a metaphor of culture and civilization created out of the raw, natural world.

Yet, the new grammar of neoclassical architecture also involved a new understanding of the meaning of the classical vocabulary and of the relationships between its elements. For the early champions of what was to become the neoclassical style, the great Baroque works of the previous decades violated what they saw as the inherent grammar of architecture. To the abbé Cordemoy, for example, the Baroque facade of Jules Hardouin-Mansart's Dôme des Invalides (c. 1680) was devoid of meaning. More precisely, the classical vocabulary of its exterior offered a message in direct contradiction to the reality of its interior. From Cordemoy and Laugier onward, classical grammar required that each level of columns with entablature signal a separate floor. The two tiers of columns under the drum and dome of Hardouin-Mansart's church falsely indicated two stories, which were not present. Such architecture was appropriate to palaces rather than churches. Furthermore, a pediment indicated a roof and hence the top of a building. Hardouin-Mansart's church sinned on this account as well by sporting a decorative pediment merely over the second story and over the central bay. Laugier praised Sainte-Geneviève for the giant portico that it featured after the manner of the Pantheon in Rome.[6]

Such criticism of Baroque architecture, for failing to adhere to a rationalized understanding of the meaning of classical elements and hence of their combinations, was accompanied by a dramatic shift in aesthetic taste. Critics such as Cordemoy and Laugier were blind to the subtle transitions of Baroque massing. They were insensitive, for example, to the ways in which Hardouin-Mansart's two-tiered portico at the Invalides provided vertical unity to the composition. A similar combination of rationalized grammar with altered aesthetic preferences can be discerned in Jacques Gondoin's praise for Sainte-Geneviève, which he compared to the latest and most notable example of a two-story church facade as found at Saint-Sulpice. "Let the public judge whether the architect of Saint-Sulpice or of Sainte-Geneviève was more successful in imparting the character of a temple; whether the colonnaded galleries [of Saint-Sulpice], which serve no purpose on a church facade, are more appropriate than the simple and noble figure of a portico crowned with a majestic pediment."[7]

Such critics also had little patience for the partially engaged columns and the pilasters that subtly modulate Hardouin-Mansart's composition at the Invalides. The visual and structural logic of the column as a vertical support required a freestanding, rounded shaft. From Cordemoy to Laugier to Boullée, to engage a column into a wall or to flatten it into a pilaster was to denature it as well as to render it visually disagreeable.[8] In the end, it was deemed that Baroque architecture offended reason and simply did not look good. Cordemoy dismissed the exterior dome of the Invalides as *effilé* and *mesquin,* thin and mean.[9]

To clarify the argument and to ground it with a legitimacy that contemporaries found in what they considered to be nature, understood as the underlying order of things and hence the basis in politics for natural law and natural right, Laugier created his story of the origins of architecture based on the natural hut:

> It is for architecture as for the other arts: its principles are founded in simple nature, and in the proceedings of nature are found clearly marked the rules of architecture. Let us consider man in his first state without any assistance, without any guide other than the natural instinct of his needs. He needs a place to rest. At the bank of a tranquil stream he spies a lawn; its young grass pleases his eyes, its softness invites him; he approaches, and languidly stretched out on this lawn, he thinks only of enjoying in peace the gifts of nature: he lacks nothing, he desires nothing. But soon the heat of the sun burns him and forces him to seek shelter. He spies a forest that offers him the freshness of its shade; he runs to hide himself in its thickness, and there he

91

is content. However, evaporating water gathers into thick clouds that cover the sky; a frightful rain falls like a torrent on this delightful forest. Man, poorly covered by the shelter of the leaves, does not know how to protect himself from this bothersome rain that completely soaks him. He finds a cave, slips inside, and finds himself out of the rain; he congratulates himself on his discovery. But new troubles bother him even in this domain. He is left in the dark, he breathes unhealthy air. He leaves resolved to rectify, through his own work, the inattention and negligence of nature. Man wants to make for himself a lodging that covers him without burying him. Several downed branches in the forest are the materials appropriate to his project. He selects four of the strongest, which he raises vertically and which he arranges in a square. Above he places four others horizontally across them; and on top of these last branches he raises still others on an incline such that the two sides meet together in a point. This type of roof is covered with leaves thick enough to keep out both sun and rain; and now man is housed. It is true that cold and heat will bother him inside his house, which is open on all sides; but he will fill in the space between the pillars and find himself secure. Such is the way of simple nature: art owes its birth to the imitation of these proceedings. The small rustic hut that I have just described is the model on which all the great creations of architecture have been conceived. It is by staying close to the simplicity of this first model that one will avoid the essential defaults and that one will achieve true perfection.

Laugier continues by explaining that his first model consists of three elements: the freestanding round column, which is a means of support; the entablature, which signifies the level of a ceiling or floor; and the pediment, which signifies a roof. He then proceeds to criticize all those Baroque departures from his idealized model: engaged columns, pilasters, broken entablatures, rounded pediments, stacked pediments, pediments placed in the center of a facade as a decorative feature, and so forth. Throughout Laugier's text it is clear that he is postulating the logic of the forms and arrangements of the parts of the Greek temple as the prototype for all future architecture and that he has used the secular parable of the creation of the primitive hut as a way to present his case.

Laugier's parable, which remains the same in both the 1753 and 1755 editions of his *Essay,* is rendered symbolically by the allegorical frontispiece in the latter edition (fig. 50). In this drawing a female figure representing Architecture (or perhaps Nature) points, for the benefit of a winged cherub (her young charge, presumably humankind), to the

Figure 50. Abbé Marc-Antoine Laugier, the "rustic
hut." Frontispiece to *Essai sur l'architecture,* 2d ed.
(Paris, 1755). Drawing by Charles Eisen.

primitive hut in which the four vertical posts are not branches that have
been erected in the ground but rather trees that grew according to Nature's direction straight upward and in a square arrangement. This hut
has not been constructed by human hands; it exists in the same imaginary world as the goddess and the cherub. It is, to reiterate, part of an
allegorical depiction of Laugier's secular parable.

Laugier's story of the natural hut was a secular parable, not an exercise in the history of primitive architecture. It belongs to the same realm
of discourse as Jean-Jacques Rousseau's account of primitive man in his

Discours sur l'origine et les fondements de l'inégalité parmi les hommes (Discourse on the origin and causes of inequality among men) (1754). Rousseau's was not an anthropological account but rather an inquiry into the basic nature of humankind undertaken by postulating a hypothetical first human. Similarly, Laugier's was an inquiry into the fundamentals of architecture presented through a fable about the conception and construction of a primitive hut. All subsequent architecture was to adhere to the principles embodied in this model. The model belonged to the world of nature in the same way the Founding Fathers of the American republic based their Declaration of Independence on the natural rights of humankind. This is the position that Alan Colquhoun has argued:

> The postulation of a common, primitive culture, which Laugier shares to some extent with Rousseau, does not involve the empirical discovery of an actual vernacular; it is an hypothesis based on what logically should have been the case, conflating the logical with the chronological. We do not know a great deal about the pre-monumental architecture of ancient Greece, but what we do know leads us to believe that it had no relation to Laugier's primitive hut. Nor is it certain what the sources of Greek monumental architecture were. Laugier was no more concerned with the "real" Mediterranean vernacular than was Rousseau with a historical primitive society. He was concerned with a distillation of classical doctrine. He was not seeking to return to the earliest hours of man, but to the pure sources of classical architecture. This process entailed, not the discovery of vernacular building, but the *revernacularization* of classicism with which to substantiate a myth of origins.[10]

Laugier's primitive hut, then, is not, as Neil Levine has argued, the "first example of built form." Levine explains what he sees as Laugier's intentions as part of his argument that Frank Lloyd Wright's architecture is an art of representation that imitates nature in the manner of this eighteenth-century model.[11] Wright's architecture certainly was a representative art that imitated nature but not through the model that Laugier established. The comparison is instructive, not because of the similarities but rather through the differences between these two men. Wright imitated primarily natural geology through visually sympathetic abstractions of natural patterns, such as the prismatic cantilevered balconies at Fallingwater, which echo the projecting rock ledges hollowed out by the water in the stream below, as well as the walls of this house built up with projecting stone courses of different thicknesses that echo the natural stratification of the local flagstone. Laugier's was not an empirical imitation of nature but rather a Platonic ideal, grounded in reason, that was invested with natural status through his mythical story.

In pursuing his argument, Levine uses the frontispiece from the second edition of Laugier's book as evidence that Laugier was suggesting an imitation of the physical characteristics of the natural world in a manner that Wright would later achieve when he made his buildings echo natural rock formations. Yet, as I have argued, this engraving is an allegorical depiction of Laugier's parable that is added to the second addition without altering the basic argument. The illustration is not to be taken as a literal depiction of Laugier's underlying concepts.

Wolfgang Herrmann, in his *Laugier and Eighteenth Century French Theory* (1962), also believes that for Laugier the "hut was the first habitation in human history." Herrmann makes this assertion, though, without adducing any evidence from Laugier's text. Rather, he seems to come to this conclusion by analogy to other contemporary and earlier writers who had perfunctorily cited the hut in this manner where it was viewed as "decidedly an object of the past." Laugier's originality, argues Herrmann, was to take the hut as the "badly needed norm by which present-day architecture should and could be guided. The aspect of the hut which in Laugier's mind really mattered was its normative function." That is the reason, I argue, that for Laugier the hut was a normative fiction. As Herrmann observes, when "ridiculed [for] his seeming preference for the savage's hut he retorted: 'If I am to be refuted, the whole line of action amounts to this: either to show that the principle is wrong or that the conclusion does not follow from it,' and in another place, wishing to justify his denigration of generally approved authorities, he exclaimed: 'I have my principle which I shall never give up.'" Note that Laugier does not appeal to the historical veracity of his hut but rather to the correctness of his principle and his reasoning. As Herrmann stresses, Laugier "rarely used the actual word 'hut' and replaced it often with the more appropriate term 'principle.'" Herrmann also notes in this discussion that in Laugier's "opinion 'to judge what should be by what is would spoil everything' and to safeguard progress 'rules [should be] founded not on what is but on what ought to be.'"[12] All of these points, culled from Herrmann's explication of Laugier's main ideas, sustain, I believe, the argument that for Laugier the story of the primitive hut was a parable through which to ground architecture in first principles. As Anthony Vidler has written, "[I]n clearly stating that his 'model' of shelter was in fact a 'principle' [Laugier] made equally clear the metaphoric, paradigmatic qualities of his artificial construct."[13]

Finally, the ideal nature of Laugier's primitive hut is indicated by its totally impractical nature. Whereas in his opening parable Laugier easily accommodates the functional inadequacies of his windswept and rain-filled "cabane rustique" by allowing the addition of walls, it should be clear from the context that this is merely a palliative. Any doubts should be dispelled when Laugier returns to this subject in his chapter on doors and windows. There Laugier explicitly lists these features as compromises to the purity of his paradigm: "A building of free-standing columns carrying an entablature needs no doors or windows: but, being open on all sides, it is uninhabitable. The need for protection from the inclemencies of the weather and other more engaging motives force us to fill in the intercolumniations and, consequently, doors and windows are needed."[14]

In rejecting what he saw as the contortions of the Baroque, Laugier advocated the use of simple geometric forms as the basis for architecture.[15] Whereas later neoclassical architects would not always adhere to the grammar that Cordemoy and Laugier required of them, neoclassical architecture generally presented clearly delineated prisms unmarked by broken entablatures or pediments, engaged columns, pilasters, and so forth. The most striking of these buildings occurred in the work of Boullée and Ledoux, whose success earned them a prominent position in our own century during a period predisposed to appreciate their achievements.

In considering Boullée's architecture, one finds that he even developed his own equivalent to the grammar outlined by Laugier. Boullée, like Laugier, kept the column as a pure form, freestanding and hence not engaged in the wall. Composing facades essentially with two elements—the uninterrupted row of columns and the unmodulated blank wall—Boullée used the columnar screen as a sign of honorific distinction in his institutional architecture. Whereas one major stand of Renaissance grammar had used the rusticated base—as a metaphor for nature—upon which the cultured work of humankind rose—shown through the piano nobile, often articulated with pilasters or engaged columns—Boullée postulated a different arrangement in which the blank wall became the foil for the columnar screen.

The visual aspect of Boullée's projects, in which the columnar screen appears as a transformation of the wall into an honorific feature, is repeatedly reinforced by Boullée's own text on the art of architecture, *L'Architecture, essai sur l'art*. In discussing his Metropolitan Church project, Boullée explains that the observer in this building experientially identifies with the freestanding columns; in the discussion of his funer-

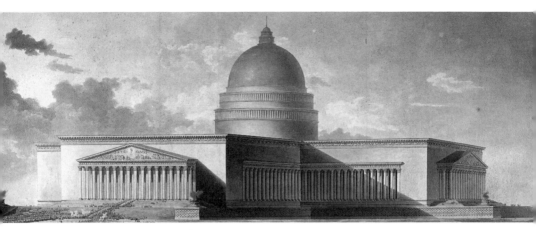

Figure 51. Etienne-Louis Boullée, Metropolitan Church (project), 1781–1782.

ary architecture, he explains that he has used the figure of the triangular pediment resting on a row of columns as a metaphor for the living person; and in his discussion of his Royal Library project, he explains that the row of columns above the amphitheater of books is an honorific crown, just as the row of columns under the arched end walls makes them into triumphal arches.[16]

In one of his earliest ideal projects, the Metropolitan Church (1781–1782) (figs. 51–53), Boullée used the columnar screen in the horizontal body of the edifice to seem as if it were emerging from the interior, where a "forest of columns" reigns, as an honorific feature.[17] It occurs in this manner at the juncture of the exterior walls to suggest an internal Greek cross purely of columns. It is found again at the end of each arm in the form of a deep portico that seems to emerge from within. Above, each of the two circular drums is crowned with an honorific ring colonnade, a feature that also is miniaturized in the lantern above the dome.

This Metropolitan Church project is the third stage in the development of a visual grammar opposing columnar screen and blank wall largely initiated by Soufflot's Sainte-Geneviève and Gondoin's Ecole de Chirurgie. The second stage can be found in Louis Combes's *Grand Prix* of 1781, whose program for a "cathedral for a capital like Paris" was an homage to Sainte-Geneviève and its architect, who had died in 1780. Combes carried the logic of Soufflot's design to the next step. His own design offered a revised Sainte-Geneviève that eliminated windows from the side walls and that ringed the arms of the cross with exterior columns, thereby further developing the theme of the columnar screen established by the portico and the ring colonnade around the drum.[18]

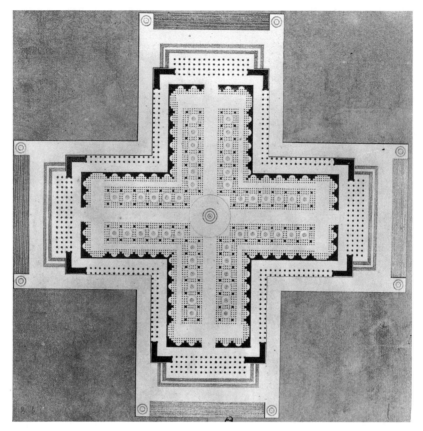

Figure 52. Boullée, Metropolitan Church (project), plan.

Boullée took this development one stage further. He eliminated the modest niches in the exterior side walls and the windows in the drum and dome as found in Combes's design to make the walls and dome pure in their surfaces. He also eliminated the cornice line from the frontispiece of each arm to make the entire surface appear as undivided wall and the entire prism as undivided volume. Then, with a tighter intercolumniation and a layering of rows of columns, Boullée arranged his peripheral columnar screens and porticoes to appear, as explained above, as an honorific transformation of wall into column and as an interior columnar church emerging from within. Above, the rings of columns no longer surround the entire body of the drum. Rather they are diminished in size and placed as crowns, once again in an honorific fashion.

The visual logic as found in Boullée's Metropolitan Church, based

Figure 53. Boullée, Metropolitan Church (project).

upon the opposition of columnar screen and blank wall and grounded in simple prisms, governs all of Boullée's ideal architecture, with special stress on the honorific columnar screen that crowns the wall, that opens the wall for entrance, or that presents the image of an interior building of columns contained within a walled precinct, like a gem within its case. As one of the few architects who designed complementary worlds for the living and the dead, Boullée used this grammar to help reinforce his message in each realm. In his funerary architecture, as Boullée explains, the view of the pediment resting on the ground (fig. 54) leads one to suppose that the columns are buried underneath it, thereby providing a metaphor for death. Boullée also placed the domes in his funerary architecture on the ground for the same purpose.[19]

To drive the message home with experiential force, Boullée used low forms that he felt prompted feelings of sadness. To heighten the effect, he followed Jacques-François Blondel's advice to lower the level of the cemetery from the surrounding land to impress into action the powerful effects of kinesthesia (figs. 9, 54). Walking down into the ground, the visitor would receive a strong reminder of his or her own mortality.[20]

Finally, Boullée altered the proportional relationship between wall and columnar screen to create claustrophobic images of relatively diminutive columns enclosed within great expanses of wall (fig. 55). In relationship to the crowning pediments, the columnar screens now

Figure 54. Etienne-Louis Boullée, cemetery project, variant II, entrance pavilion, Paris, c. 1785.

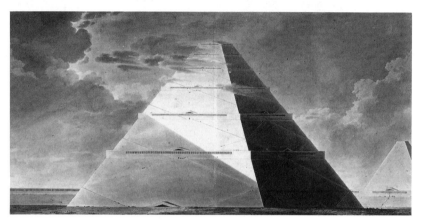

Figure 55. Etienne-Louis Boullée, cemetery project, variant III, Paris, c. 1785, the central chapel.

stretched outward in an inordinately long horizontal extension as diminutive features of even longer horizontal walls. At the lowest level, only the pediment appears, for the horizontal line here is not built architecture but rather the endless line of the earth's surface.

In certain designs, Boullée eliminated the columnar screen to have the wall architecture dominate. Yet even here one finds a substitution for the uninterrupted line of columns. In the city gate projects, there are rows of soldiers or cannons. In the tomb to honor the Spartan soldiers at Thermopylae, a frieze of warriors crowns the sarcophagus below the lid. On the library project of 1788 the wall is crowned by a continuous festoon that drapes around medallions carrying busts of the great thinkers whose books are housed within. In front of the blank-walled facade of the Palais National (fig. 3), inscribed with the Constitution, are two rows of eighty-three identical statues to symbolize the new and equal departments of France joined together as a republican nation, thereby replacing the old divisions by provinces with their separate laws and feudal relationships. Finally, outside certain funerary monuments, including the Cenotaph to Sir Isaac Newton (1784, fig. 12), rows of funerary trees take the place of rows of columns as crowning features.

The relationships between the basic elements of the classical vocabulary of architecture that Cordemoy and Laugier postulated, then, were not merely of a grammatical but also of a typological nature. If grammar defined the way columns, entablatures, and pediments could be combined, then typology governed the meaning of their forms. According to this typology, the building proper was to be defined by walls or columnar screens and the roof by a pediment or a dome. The implications of this typological approach to architecture, nascent in Laugier's parable about the primitive hut, became explicit in the work of a Boullée or a Ledoux and had important ramifications for the system of design established by Durand. To pass from Laugier to these later architects, though, required an intermediary step that can be found in Soufflot's Sainte-Geneviève and its appreciation by his contemporary, the architect Julien-David Leroy.

A New Typology

On September 6, 1764, as part of the ceremonies for laying the cornerstone of the Church of Sainte-Geneviève, the architect Julien-David Leroy presented the king with a copy of his new book, *Histoire de la disposition des formes différentes que les chrétiens ont données à leurs temples depuis Constantin le Grand jusqu'à nous* (History of the arrangement of the different forms that Christians have given to their temples from Constantine to today). Unabashedly didactic in tone, the intention here was to explain how the two new churches in construction, Sainte-Geneviève by Soufflot and the Madeleine by Contant d'Ivry, were the culminating stage in a successive chain of progressive improvements in Western architecture. The history of church architecture, according to Leroy, was a gradual unfolding of an ideal state whose culminating examples finally purified ecclesiastical design into a combination of three perfect and essential features—the regular Greek cross in plan, the field of freestanding columns in elevation, and the hemispherical dome over the crossing as the crowning feature both inside and outside. With Sainte-Geneviève, especially, the most important building type in Western society, the church, had become an exercise in typological assemblage, uniting these three excellent components as an advanced realization of Laugier's primitive hut. Since Sainte-Geneviève used the pedimented portico with colossal columns to indicate the great height of the interior nave, this church was like a sophisticated version of the primitive hut.

In comparing Sainte-Geneviève with Laugier's primitive hut, it must be remembered that Laugier was quite willing to accept architectural features other than the column, entablature, and pediment. Alan Braham's generalization about the primitive hut is misleading when it asserts, "All architecture, Laugier felt, should be based upon the use of the column, the entablature and the pediment, a ludicrous proposition which he nevertheless argued with extraordinary persuasiveness."[21] To the contrary, Laugier accepted the use of domes in churches, provided that they appeared to be adequately supported, and he even advocated the use of a barrel vault in his own ideal church design. As for walls, he recognized not only their necessity but also their aesthetic value. For the ideal church, he recommended using tall exterior side walls, as had been done at St. Peter's in Rome, to hide the buttresses.[22] All of these features would be employed in Sainte-Geneviève.

Leroy illustrated his book with a plate showing church plans and selected sections drawn with ruled scales (fig. 56). The story begins with Constantine's use of the basilica with transepts for Saint-Peter's so that this church would appear in the shape of the Latin cross. Leroy especially appreciated the extensive number of freestanding columns. The next important development occurred when Hagia Sophia was built with a vast dome carried on pendentives over the crossing. This arrangement was repeated during the reconstruction of San Marco with the added benefit of transforming the plan into a Greek cross. Other improvements here included the creation of a double dome so that the interior and exterior forms could be sized appropriately and the pyramidal effect resulting from the clustering of four smaller and lower domes around the central one.

Jumping ahead slightly in the story, we find Leroy concentrating on Sant'Agostino in Rome, which, the author argued, occupied a central role "in the chain of ideas" that marked the progressive development of ecclesiastical architecture. According to Leroy, this late fifteenth-century church was the first with a full dome raised upon a drum, which was carried in turn on pendentives by the arches of the crossing. This new

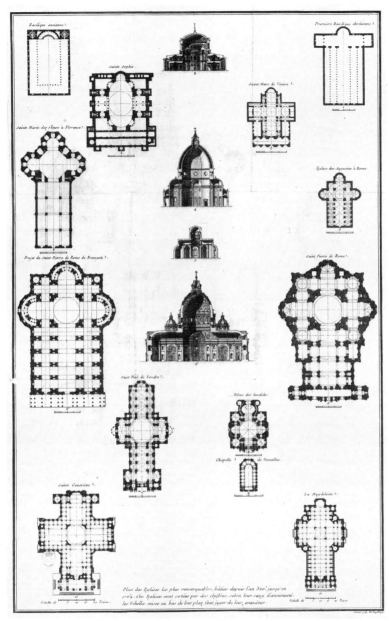

Figure 56. Julien-David Leroy, history of religious architecture, showing its historical, progressive development. From *Histoire de la disposition des formes différentes que les chrétiens ont données à leurs temples depuis Constantin le Grand jusqu'à nous* (Paris, 1764).

development in a little known and often ignored church had important consequences for the history of architecture because it was then used in the rebuilding of Saint Peter's.

With Saint Peter's, Leroy's history reaches a momentary climax. Correcting Montesquieu, Leroy informs his readers that Bramante, before Michelangelo, had the sublime idea of elevating a variant of the Pantheon, equal in size and similar in form, over the crossing. In this chapter, Leroy commended those architects who favored the regularity of the Greek cross for the floor plan instead of the Latin cross. He also applauded those unexecuted schemes that favored freestanding columns, such as Bramante's project with columnar screens at the ends of three naves and Michelangelo's proposed facade with fourteen colossal columns. Although these particular features were not realized, and although St. Peter's was built on a Latin cross plan, Leroy saw in the executed design of this church the combination of the best features of previous church design in the most perfect form to date: the concatenation of five domes, with the grand central dome over drum and pendentives beautifully proportioned in relationship to the arms of the cross, which in turn were skillfully sized relative to each other. Yet for all of its merits, Saint Peter's had two grave faults. The side aisles were too small in proportion to the other spaces and, more seriously, the massive piers that carried the dome blocked the view.

Leroy saw the next steps in church design as efforts by the architects of new churches in England and France to correct these aesthetic defects. In Saint Paul's Cathedral (begun 1675) in London, Christopher Wren reduced the thickness of the piers that supported the dome by opening transverse niches which effectively prolonged the side aisles to the end of the church. Unfortunately, this arrangement made the nave too narrow. The cross, moreover, was poorly drawn. About the same time, Jules Hardouin-Mansart at the Dome of the Invalides (begun 1679) opened the central piers to provide diagonal entry into the corner chapels. Leroy wrote appreciatively as well about the ingenious lighting at the Invalides where the upper surface of the cupola is bathed by a mysterious light coming from a hidden source. Then, with the magnificent colonnade of the east facade of the Louvre (1667) and the subsequent colonnade in the interior of Hardouin-Mansart's Chapel (1678–1689) at the Palace of Versailles, French architects seemed to have opened a new phase in perfecting Western architecture. The next stage would be to marry such splendid peristyles and colonnades with the domed church built on a Greek cross plan. This was the promise of the two new churches in construction in Paris, the Madeleine and Sainte-Geneviève.

In comparing the plans for these two French churches with Saint-Paul's and Saint Peter's, we see that both Contant d'Ivry and Soufflot attempted to reduce the massiveness of the support under the central dome in a design based on the Greek cross that is filled with freestanding columns. Soufflot's supports for Sainte-Geneviève, as is well known, caused considerable controversy. Toward 1770, before the construction of the dome, Pierre Patte initiated his vigorous and unceasing campaign to convince both the architect and the authorities that the central pillars simply would not carry the projected load. As the construction proceeded, Patte's warnings seemed more and more prescient until in 1776 the building seemed in imminent danger of collapsing. Of course the structure still stands today, albeit with the enlargements to the piers begun by Rondelet in 1806. To the exterior, the church that Leroy had praised in 1764 underwent major revisions. By 1777 Soufflot had elevated a dome of fuller profile upon a taller drum no longer executed in a Baroque taste but rather in the new neoclassical style.

With the *Grand Prix* of 1781, French architects attempted to perfect the design of Sainte-Geneviève according to the value system that Leroy had articulated. In his prize-winning project, Louis Combes regularized the geometry of the Greek cross, vastly increased the number of columns and tightened their intercolumniation, improved the open view at the crossing, and, as we have seen, augmented the continuity of wall surface and columnar screen on the exterior. Boullée's Metropolitan Church project of 1781–1782 perfected Combes's design on the exterior in ways described above and in the interior by further increasing the number of freestanding columns, by eliminating entirely any visible pier supports within the interior, by hiding even the side walls with columnar screens, and by making the interior dome seem to float miraculously above a ring colonnade, while bathing the dome in a mysterious light introduced from hidden sources. Improving upon Hardouin-Mansart's design of the drum and dome, Boullée eliminated the windows in the drum that, as he observed, vitiated the effect of the mysterious light that flooded the dome from hidden windows above.[23]

Toward the time when Boullée designed his Metropolitan Church project he withdrew from active practice to concentrate his energies on the idealized designs that he used for teaching. When considering his work as a whole, one sees that he developed his architecture by combining typological elements that paralleled the typological systems worked out by Laugier and Soufflot. I have already discussed the typological system that he created with columns, pediment, and walls that was an equivalent to Laugier's primitive hut. Earlier in this book, I also explained

Boullée's use of simple prisms as typological elements matched with different building types according to the feeling that they were to prompt in the viewer: tall forms, such as the towering dome over the tall drum of the Metropolitan Church project and the majestic pyramids in the cemetery projects were exalting; low forms, used to ring Boullée's cemetery designs, were saddening; and stable-looking horizontal blocks were deemed to be noble. There is a third type of typological architecture that Boullée developed out of the elements used in Sainte-Geneviève: the Greek cross, the freestanding columns, the circular drum, the ring colonnade, and the dome.

Let us consider first the Greek cross. Not only did it form the basis for the plan of the Metropolitan Church project, it also furnished, in the form of the Greek cross within a square, the plans for the Palace of Justice, City Hall, Museum, and Public Library. The Palais National presents a variant on this theme. In effect, the Greek cross is the basis of the plans with four-part symmetry that are so popular in late eighteenth-century French academic architecture.

The dome became the major volumetric component of most of Boullée's civic structures. In certain projects it dominates the design both inside and out, such as at the Opera (fig. 5), the Temple to Nature (figs. 57, 58), and the central temple of the Monument to the Supreme Being. In other projects, such as the Palace of Justice, the Palais National, and the Public Library, it crowns the central room without explicitly appearing on the facade. In the Museum (figs. 6, 7) and the City Hall, it occupies a position between these two poles.

The Cenotaph to Newton (fig. 13) and the Temple to Nature (fig. 58) offer an instructive point of comparison. In the former building the dome is mirrored upon itself to form a spherical cavity; In the latter building, the dome is also flipped over but now diminished in size and altered in character so as to present a complement to the dome of the sky in the form of an amphitheater of rough stone, the image of a fruitful Mother Nature, whose statue crowns the grotto at the central point.

The image of the amphitheater introduces another typological component to Boullée's civic architecture. It dominates the interior of the Opera, the Royal Library (fig. 4), and the French Colosseum (fig. 8), as well as the central rooms of the Palais National, the City Hall, and the Palace of Justice.[24] The obverse of the amphitheater, obtained by flipping it upside down, is the pyramid, which dominates the cemeteries (figs. 9, 55), the interior of the Museum (fig. 7), and, in its natural form as a mountain, the Monument to the Supreme Being.

Finally, columns, in a row or as a ring colonnade, play a crucial hon-

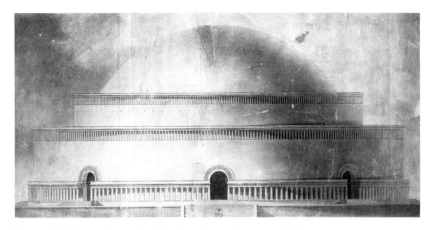

Figure 57. Etienne-Louis Boullée, Temple to Nature, c. 1793.

Figure 58. Boullée, Temple to Nature, section, c. 1793.

orific role in this architecture. The ring colonnade, especially, becomes a temple that consecrates the space contained within its precinct. This hypaethral temple crowns the amphitheater of Nature in the Temple of Nature (figs. 57–58), the interior pyramid of steps in the Museum (fig. 7), the amphitheater of the Opera, and the central assembly rooms in the Palais National, the City Hall, and the Palace of Justice. It crowns the roof of the Museum (fig. 6) and the mountaintop of the Monument to the Supreme Being. It crowns the exterior drums of the Temple to Nature (fig. 57), the French Colosseum (fig. 8), and the City Hall. It encircles the Opera (fig. 5). At the Museum (fig. 6) and the Public Library

107

(figs. 10–11), it occurs as a half circle where it doubles in function as an entrance portico. Whereas the former building offers the curved surface to the approaching visitor, the latter offers the flat side with its columnar screen. Without the semicircular entrance court, this columnar screen appears by itself at the entrance to the Palace of Justice (fig. 2) and the City Hall. In these buildings the columnar screen is read as a transformation of the wall into an honorific colonnade. Inside the Royal Library (fig. 4), as well as the library in the Palais National, the columnar screen and the barrel vault read as longitudinal transformations of the dome and the ring colonnade.

One can make a chart of Boullée's buildings which demonstrates that, within the great variety of his designs, he has used simple combinations of a limited repertory of typological elements. The buildings are listed in an order that shows not only similarities but also how a slight change in the combination of elements yielded a new design. In typological design any combination of elements can suggest a variant that appears as a transformation of a previous combination:

Round Buildings (Exterior)
Opera: ring colonnade, drum, dome
Temple to Nature: ring colonnade, drum, ring colonnade, drum, ring colonnade, dome
Cenotaph to Newton: ring colonnade (as trees), drum, ring colonnade (as trees), drum, ring colonnade (as trees), dome
French Colosseum: drum, ring colonnade, drum, ring colonnade

Round Buildings (Interior)
Opera: amphitheater, ring colonnade, dome
French Colosseum: amphitheater, ring colonnade
Temple to Nature: amphitheater (as a reversed dome), ring colonnade, dome
Cenotaph to Newton: reversed dome, dome

Squared Buildings (Exterior)
Metropolitan Church: cruciform prism with inner cruciform of columns and central columnar portico; above—drum, ring colonnade, drum, ring colonnade, drum, dome
Museum: square prism made into a cruciform with semicircular ring colonnade porticoes; above—drum, ring colonnade
Public Library: square prism with central colonnade (the face of a semicircular ring colonnade), attic above

Palace of Justice: square prism with central colonnade, attic above
City Hall: square prism with two levels of columnar screens;
    above—drum, ring colonnade
Palais National: square prism, central attic above
Royal Library: (variant 1) rectangular prism, (variant 2) rectangu-
    lar prism fronted by columnar screen with attic above, (variant
    3), rectangular prism with attic above[25]
Triumphal arch: rectangular prism with inner columnar prism, cen-
    tral attic above

Squared Buildings (Interior)
Metropolitan Church: colonnade, barrel vault with triumphal arch
    as frontispiece, drum, ring colonnade, dome
Public Library: colonnade, barrel vault, dome
Royal Library: amphitheater, colonnade with triumphal arch, bar-
    rel vault
Palais National (library): amphitheater with colonnade, barrel
    vault
Palais National (assembly hall): amphitheater, colonnade, dome

The schema of this formal typology shows the compositional approach
in Boullée's architecture. To describe the buildings, though, requires
the addition of the two other typological strategies that Boullée used—
the selection of prismatic shapes according to the feeling that they engender, and the determination of character through its expressive, metaphorical, and symbolic dimensions. Both of these features have been
discussed above.

    The same is true for Ledoux's architecture where character is largely
informed by a typological approach to design. When we consider the
salt works of Chaux, for example, we find two stages in the development
of Ledoux's "visionary" architecture. The first corresponds to the actual
constructions; the second belongs to the ideal city that Ledoux envisaged to complete his scheme. In the saltworks as built, Ledoux created
an imaginative variation on the Renaissance theme of rusticated architecture as indicative of the world of nature. After all, the saltworks were
not only out in the country, their manufacturing process involved evaporating salt from water coming from the earth. Thus, from the entrance
building with its dramatic grotto porch (fig. 59) to the director's house
with its massive rustication extending even to its front portico, to the
manufacturing buildings belching smoke through their upper windows,
the imagery of nature has been rendered as a type of nether world. The

Figure 59. Claude-Nicolas Ledoux, entrance building, saltworks of Chaux. From *L'Architecture considérée sous le rapport de l'art, des moeurs et de la législation* (1804).

conceit is not only appropriate to the building type but more specifically corresponds, as Anthony Vidler has noted, both to the saltwater issuing from the underground caves of Salins and to the grotto source of the river Loue, which irrigates the site.[26]

This narrative theme of the nether world is subsumed into a larger schema in the ideal project, which is dominated by the idea of humankind as the guardian of the earth. It is here that Ledoux designs his workers' combined houses and workshops, each characterized according to profession, through a typology of simple shapes based on the square, circle, and pyramid. Thus, the agricultural guards are housed in a spherical building (fig. 60), symbolic of the earth. The guards of the river Loue are given a house whose central form is a cylinder (fig. 61), a double abstraction of conduits for water and of the overturned urns, the typical accompaniment of the river god in garden architecture and, more specifically, the primary source of decorative imagery in the saltworks (fig. 59). The charcoal burners are housed in a pyramidal building (fig. 62) that echoes the wood piles burned to make charcoal. The coopers are given a dwelling whose facades display concentric circles (fig. 63), recalling the metal hoops for barrels and perhaps the wooden staves themselves. This image doubles as a temple of nature, for the central opening serves as an eye to the world for viewing the changing seasons just as the concentric circles lead the viewer's gaze, as Ledoux ex-

Figure 60. Claude-Nicolas Ledoux, house and workshop for the agricultural guards (project). From *L'Architecture considérée sous le rapport de l'art, des moeurs et de la législation* (1847 ed.).

Figure 61. Claude-Nicolas Ledoux, house and workshop for the guards of the river Loue (project). From *L'Architecture considérée sous le rapport de l'art, des moeurs et de la législation* (1804).

Figure 62. Claude-Nicolas Ledoux, house and workshop for the charcoal burners (project). From *L'Architecture considérée sous le rapport de l'art, des moeurs et de la législation* (1804).

Figure 63. Claude-Nicolas Ledoux, house and workshop for the coopers (project). From *L'Architecture considérée sous le rapport de l'art, des moeurs et de la législation* (1804).

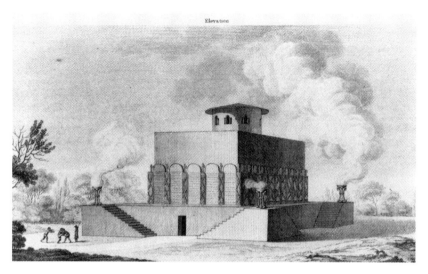

Figure 64. Claude-Nicolas Ledoux, Pacifère (House of Reconciliation) (project). From *L'Architecture considérée sous le rapport de l'art, des moeurs et de la législation* (1804).

plains, to expand increasingly outward to embrace the "vault of the sky" itself.[27] As for the forge, it is no mere shed for a blacksmith but rather, as Ledoux's narrative makes clear, Vulcan's lair, where the smith tames the forces of the underworld.[28]

In his civic buildings, Ledoux uses the cube as the basic compositional element to convey moral stability, rectitude, wisdom, and virtue. These are the themes of the Pacifère (House of Reconciliation, fig. 64), the Panarétéon (House of Morals and Wisdom), House of Union, and Temple of Memory. As for the cemetery (fig. 65) it uses the spherical cavity, actually a coupling of a dome that rises above the ground and a reversed dome buried in the earth. With the publication of the view of the planets over the heading of "elevation of the cemetery for the town of Chaux" (fig. 66), we understand that for Ledoux, as for Boullée, to be buried in the bosom of the earth is tantamount to rejoining the vast world of nature, the immensity of a nurturing cosmos.

In "Rebuilding the Primitive Hut: The Return to Origins from Lafitau to Laugier," Anthony Vidler points to the similarities that join Durand with Laugier in spite of the obvious differences in their intellectual personae:

> A reduced lexicon of structural elements, their combination and recombination according to geometrical permutations "to infinity," and the natural "variety" of the result, would become

Figure 65. Claude-Nicolas Ledoux, cemetery for the town of Chaux (project). Section. From *L'Architecture considérée sous le rapport de l'art, des moeurs et de la législation* (1804).

ÉLÉVATION DU CIMETIÈRE DE LA VILLE DE CHAUX.

Figure 66. Claude-Nicolas Ledoux, "Elevation of the cemetery for the town of Chaux." From *L'Architecture considérée sous le rapport de l'art, des moeurs et de la législation* (1804).

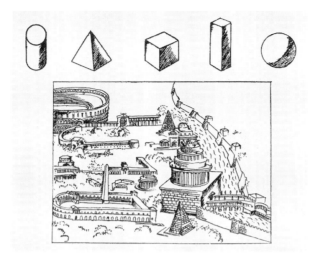

Figure 67. Le Corbusier, "The lesson of Rome," *Vers une Architecture* (1923).

the methodological and aesthetic premises of late-eighteenth-century design. Despite J.-N.-L. Durand's later scorn for the obvious impracticality of a model hut without walls, his own diagrammatic design method owed much to this combinative system, with the added influence of the posthumous publication of Condillac's own *Langue des calculs*.[29]

It is at the level of typological architecture that Durand joins Boullée and Ledoux. Yet, whereas the two older architects used simple geometrical shapes, either alone or in combination, as the basis of their typological design, Durand worked with plan elements—porches, foyers, *galeries*, corridors, courtyards, and rooms (fig. 19–22). On the one hand, it was Durand's genius to apply the typological approach to the arrangement of the plan, thereby yielding a potent pedagogical method. On the other hand, Durand's method, voided of the grammatical logic that Laugier and Boullée had established and of the typological system found in Laugier's hut, Soufflot's church, and the ideal oeuvre of Boullée and Ledoux, lacked a means to create a total volumetric image. As explained in Chapter 3, Durand was compelled to rely on the architecture of Boullée and the students of the academy to assemble his typological plan elements into coherent buildings.

If we compare Boullée's and Ledoux's attitudes toward typological design in their respective ideal cities, we find that the former was closer to the combinatory technique outlined by Laugier in the design of his primitive hut and by Leroy in his analysis of Sainte-Geneviève. Ledoux, rather, exhibited a preference for singular volumetric forms, which still read as primary even when placed within a surrounding base. This attitude toward type we find later in architectural history, by following Emil Kaufmann's advice to look from Ledoux to Le Corbusier, in the latter's reading of the "lesson of Rome" (fig. 67). Le Corbusier, though, has further ties to this era through his "Five Points for a New Architecture," which postulate a grammar for reinforced concrete buildings in the same spirit as did Laugier's primitive hut for stone architecture. And in both cases, it is not the material that drives the design decisions; rather, it is the ideal image.

Today, if we wish to find an architect working with the implications of this late eighteenth-century legacy, we should turn to Leon Krier. Krier's notion of classical composition combines a typology of set pieces in plan design similar to Durand's with a typology of volumetric elements similar to Laugier, Boullée, and Ledoux's. When considering the actual vocabulary that Krier uses, we see that reminiscences of the designs by these three eighteenth-century precursors have served as a point of departure.[30]

The New Aesthetic Experience

The third major component of the neoclassical interlude, which complemented the new grammar and the new typology that Laugier introduced, was a new aesthetic experience grounded in a feeling of spiritual transport. It manifested itself in a new enthusiasm for the vertical splendor of Gothic architecture as well as the thrill obtained along the horizontal from the field of freestanding classical columns. Eventually, in the mind and work of Boullée, it entered into the realm of the sublime.

Gothic architecture, largely ignored and disparaged by the cultural elite since the Renaissance, was rediscovered in the eighteenth century by theorists such as Cordemoy and Laugier and architects such as Soufflot and Boullée for the visible appearance of its daring construction that combined soaring naves, thin vertical supports, and largely glass walls. "I enter Notre-Dame," explained Laugier, "the most eminent of our Gothic buildings in Paris, though not by far as beautiful as certain others in the provinces. Nevertheless, at first glance my attention is captured, my imagination is struck by the size, the height, and the unobstructed view of the vast nave; for some moments I am lost in the amazement that the grand effect of the whole stirs in me."[31]

Speaking over a decade earlier to the Académie des Beaux-Arts of Lyons, Soufflot had outlined the features of Gothic cathedrals worthy of admiration. These were buildings "whose daring astonishes us so strongly." This effect resulted primarily from the light aspect of the vertical supports, the appearance of prodigious height, and the great length of the nave. With respect to the first subject, Soufflot explained that Gothic construction was "more ingenious, more daring, and even more difficult than ours." The openings in the walls "reduce [the pillars], so to speak, to nothing," even though they must carry prodigious weight. Furthermore, they appear very light in contrast to the heavy piers of modern churches. With respect to the interior volume, Gothic churches are 2.5–3 times as tall as they are wide; modern churches are only a little more than double the width. "No doubt it is this difference in proportion," concluded Soufflot, "that causes the effects which [Gothic churches] produce: if we enter a Gothic church, deceived by its proportions, we feel a pleasure that at first surprises and astonishes us and makes us say while admiring it: here is a volume of prodigious length and height. We willingly believe that we would never reach the far side."[32] While avoiding the "chimerical and bizarre ornaments of the goths," Soufflot felt that contemporary architects could learn much from the Gothic example.

The commission for the Church of Sainte-Geneviève would soon enable Soufflot to enhance the classical ethos with the lessons of Gothic architecture. In 1780 upon Soufflot's death, his assistant Maximilien Brébion, who had worked with the master for more than ten years and who had listened carefully to the explanations of his attentions, related these ideas to D'Angiviller, directeur général des Bâtiments:

> Soufflot's principal intention in building his church was to unite in one of the most beautiful forms the lightness of Gothic construction with the purity and magnificence of Greek architecture. Through the felicitous arrangement of the plan of this building he was able to produce the most beautiful effects of architecture that renew themselves at each step through variety, the elegance of all the parts, and the ingenious contrasts of the vaults. The interior peristyles present everywhere lines of columns that create the most beautiful perspectives and procure throughout the edifice a new reason for admiring the genius of this great architect.[33]

The admiration for the daring height of Gothic cathedrals and for the clustered shafts of the piers, along with their placement on a diagonal to the nave, was a manifestation of an aesthetic predilection that found comparable pleasure in the view of many freestanding columns. Whereas Cordemoy appears rigorously rational in his discussions of the new grammar of classical architecture, he displays unaccustomed enthusiasm when writing about the aesthetic effects of columns. "There is little doubt," wrote Cordemoy, "that I am for columns. It is a partiality that I share with the ancients and one that I would not know how to abandon."[34] Underneath the stolid face of reason one discovers an aesthetic predisposition grounded in the exhilarating experience of moving through a field of columns. To Cordemoy, the most majestic sight in architecture was the view through several rows of freestanding columns, especially when forming a "forest of columns"; and the most pleasing intercolumniation was the tightest. If only the interior of Val-de-Grâce, mused Cordemoy, had been built with columns rather than with heavy piers, how much more open and beautiful it would be. Likewise, if only the inside of Saint-Peter's in Rome had been fashioned after the manner of Bernini's exterior colonnade, then it would be the most beautiful piece of architecture in the world. What a pity that Michelangelo had not taken a lesson from Gothic architecture, where the prodigious number of closely spaced columnar shafts provide such intense pleasure.[35]

In Leroy's history of church architecture, the aesthetic effects of freestanding columns assumed a primary place. As with Cordemoy, the underlying impulse behind the rigor of his typological scheme is an aesthetic enthusiasm. For Leroy, architecture had three principal "qualities": *l'agrément, la force,* and *la variété des sensations.*[36] *L'agrément* was attained through harmonious proportions; *la force* derived from the grandeur conveyed by the facade and by the interior; and the "variety of sensations" involved a progressively intensifying feeling of life conveyed by the architecture. In Sainte-Geneviève, Soufflot had achieved the first quality through the proportioning of his plan as a Greek cross and through the graceful qualities of the classical language of architecture employed in the composition. He succeeded in realizing the second quality through the majesty of his front portico and through the impression of great height and expanse achieved with a light structure and abundant daylight in the interior. The third quality came from the field of columns which, as Leroy explains, also contributes greatly to architectural grandeur.

Whereas Leroy presented the two new churches under construction, Sainte-Geneviève and the Madeleine, as the culminating examples of a successive perfectioning in architecture, he also stressed the universal appeal of freestanding columns, especially in long peristyles, deep porticoes, and even in extensive clusters of support, throughout the history

of world architecture.[37] This sense of the universal approval of and interest in columns found its counterpart in contemporary architectural fan-
tasies, such as the two vignettes that Jérôme-Charles Bellicard provided
for the first volume of Jacques-François Blondel's folio edition of *Architecture françoise* (1752–1756). Each imaginary scene, purporting to capture the essence of Egyptian and Greek architecture, favors long and
multiple rows of freestanding columns.[38]

In a chapter devoted entirely to the effects of peristyles in architecture, Leroy enumerated their virtues. Addressing what he termed the
"metaphysical" dimension of architecture, Leroy expatiated on the feelings engendered by rows of freestanding columns: "Of all the freestanding bodies that one can use in architecture to form the decoration,
columns are those that with the same solidity and spacing permit from
all angles the most expansive views." Within a building filled with columns, such as Sainte-Geneviève, "the slightest movements produce the
most striking changes in the aspect" of the interior. Outside, the freestanding columns viewed under sunlight present a "rich variety" occa-
sioned by changing conditions of light and shadow over the course of
the day. Like Laugier, Leroy emphasized the lost aesthetic potential of
the pilaster and the engaged column. Contrasting the "monotonous decoration produced by columns that touch a decorated wall and the rich
variety that results from those that form a peristyle," Leroy repeatedly
stressed the "striking and varied scenes" that "multiply [the viewer's] sensations" derived from peristyles.[39] These intensifying sensations link Leroy's third aesthetic "quality" with the second, which was *la force*. Implicit
throughout Leroy's discussion of columns, this connection is made explicit in the following passage:

> The peoples who have distinguished themselves in architecture
> . . . have always preferred peristyles, which of all decorations are
> those that make us feel the most agreeable sensations. This ad-
> vantage is not the only one derived from the decoration of peri-
> styles, for they almost always without fail produce grandeur,
> which alone has the right to move us strongly, and without
> which the purest architecture hardly attracts our attention.

Leroy then continues his text with a repetition of the paean to Nature
that furnished the opening passage of his book. Now he again writes:

> All the great spectacles overawe mankind. The immensity of the
> sky, the vast expanse of the earth or of the sea, which we discover
> from mountain tops or far out at sea, seem to transport our soul
> and elevate our thoughts. The grandest of our works have the
> same effect on us. They make us feel these strong sensations, far

superior to those that only seem pleasant to us, which are the only feelings that very small edifices can give us. However, the strength of these impressions that buildings have upon us is not always proportionate to their actual size. Rather, they often depend as much on the way that the masses or surfaces are divided as upon their size.[40]

The deep peristyle to the exterior of Sainte-Geneviève, or its prototype at the Pantheon in Rome, and the field of freestanding columns in the interior of Sainte-Geneviève offered the most expansive view of space, heightened to the greatest extent the sense of grandeur, and provided the most varied and most numerous views and hence sensations, all contributing to this effect of transporting awe. With Leroy's published appreciation of Sainte-Geneviève, we encounter the sublime, that new aesthetic category promoted by Edmund Burke, which engaged the viewer in a direct communion with the awesome grandeur of Nature.[41]

Just as Combes and Boullée improved upon the typological rigor of Sainte-Geneviève in their subsequent church designs, so too did they take that "metaphysical" dimension of architecture several steps further through their use of freestanding columns. We have seen how first Combes and then Boullée successively used more columns and with a closer intercolumniation; we have seen how Boullée even employed the columns to hide the pier supports within the Metropolitan Church project (figs. 52, 53). Even more important, Boullée was more explicit than Leroy in explaining the sense of extension and expansion of a person's body sense when walking through the field of columns in his church project:

> When I remarked that a temple should offer the image of grandeur, I was not speaking only of its size. Rather, I was referring to that ingenious art by which one extends, one aggrandizes images by combining objects such that they appear to us in the fullest way through an ordering that enables us to enjoy their multiplicity, such that through the successive aspects under which they appear to us, they endlessly renew themselves to the point that they cannot be counted. Such is the effect, for example, caused by a regular and symmetrical quincunx. . . . By prolonging [its] allées such that their end point cannot be seen, the laws of optics and the effects of perspective present us with the tableau of immensity; at every step objects appearing in a new aspect renew our pleasure through the succession of varied scenes. *Thus, through a felicitous effect that is caused by our movement and that we attribute to the objects themselves, it seems that they walk along with us and that we have given them life.*[42]

Boullée then proceeded to explain that in churches this effect can be achieved with numerous long rows of freestanding columns.[43]

Like Leroy, Boullée also looked to the vast expanse of freestanding columns as a means to instilling through architecture the feeling of immensity found in what the former termed the "spectacle of the universe."[44] Like Leroy, Boullée also invoked the immensity of the sky and the sea and the vast expanse of the earth. Yet Boullée considered the degree to which that sense of body self, which was later termed "l'espace vécu,"[45] is threatened by these spectacles. Evoking the experience of the first balloonist who had begun to explore the skies in 1783, Boullée explains the sense of loss of self that can occur when high in the air or alone at sea:

> Let us imagine man in the middle of the ocean, seeing only sky and water: this scene is truly that of immensity. In this position, everything is beyond our grasp. There is no way to make comparisons. It is the same for the balloonist who, floating through the sky and having lost sight of the objects on the earth, sees in all of nature only the sky. Wandering so within immensity, in this abyss of extension, man is annihilated by this extraordinary spectacle of an inconceivable space.

The solution to this psychic annihilation is an architecture that permits viewers to anchor themselves through a sense of expanded body self to tangible objects that relate to the human figure while the scenes multiply and the view extends endlessly outward. This is the effect that Boullée attempted in the Metropolitan Church project (figs. 52, 53), and it is one that he associates with the safe but nevertheless expansive view from a mountaintop. His text continues:

> Let us return then to the pleasures attained on earth from the grand spectacles of nature. These are the ones that permit comparisons, calculations, and that will give us a clear idea of what grandeur means in order to apply it to art. Who among us has not enjoyed on a mountain the pleasure of discovering all that our sight can embrace? What do we see there? A vast expanse with a quantity of objects that their multiplicity renders incalculable. Now, do you want to present the image of grandeur in architecture? One must within a grand ensemble employ the means of the ingenious art about which we have spoken so as to multiply objects as much as possible, while achieving that just measure that we find in Greek temples, such that the objects are not multiplied excessively as in our Gothic churches nor given a colossal proportion, which provides only an image of the gigantic, as in Saint-Peter's of Rome.[46]

The reader familiar with Burke's *A Philosophical Inquiry into the Origin of Our Ideas of the Sublime and the Beautiful* (1757) will recognize here one of the two means of reaching a feeling of the sublime through what this author called the "artificial infinite." It should come as no surprise that in his later Cenotaph to Sir Isaac Newton (fig. 13) Boullée attempted to realize the other and more psychologically dangerous version of the "artificial infinite," achieved by running the eye over the continuous surface of a dome, rendered in this building with a spherical cavity.

Wishing to give the viewer an experience of the immensity of Nature, whose single unifying principle Newton was deemed to have discovered—gravity—Boullée placed the viewer at the bottom of the spherical interior to view the immense surface through an expanding sense of body self. This interior lacks the comforting and secure means of anchoring through numerous columns that the Metropolitan Church would have provided. Rather, it has only one fixed and stable point: Newton's sarcophagus. As Boullée explains, by contemplating the immense spherical cavity, the "spectator would find himself transported into the sky as if by enchantment and carried on the clouds into the immensity of space." At the same time, the viewer's sense of body self also is focused on the tomb, placed at the building's "center of gravity." While the spectator looking outward "sees only a continuous surface with neither beginning nor end" that makes him feel as if he is continuously expanding, the spectator, through the curvature of the walls, "is obliged, as if by innumerable strong forces," to remain at the center where the "tomb is the sole material object." Expanding in the mind to become one with the immensity of Nature, the viewer is saved from psychic annihilation by the anchor of the tomb with which the viewer also identifies. At the moment of epiphany the spectator becomes one with the endless circumference (Nature) and with the single tomb (Newton), thereby joining the "sublimity of [Newton's] genius," which had risen to the height of divine intelligence.[47] Through this experiential encounter with architectural space, Boullée gave new meaning to the often repeated notion, "Deus est sphæra cujus centrum ubique, circumferentia nusquam" (God is the sphere whose center is everywhere and whose circumference is nowhere).[48]

The enduring legacy of this new aesthetic branches into two directions. On the one hand, we have in our own times the tendency toward austere prismatic forms that engender either peace, as in the case of Louis Kahn, or *angst,* as with Aldo Rossi. On the other hand, there is the example of the aesthetic that Le Corbusier developed with his "Five Points for a New Architecture." These Five Points not only provide an equivalent to the grammatical and typological approaches to architecture established by Laugier's primitive hut, they also became the basis for an aesthetic of invigorating vitality that actively engages the sense of body self in relationship to space and form. From the avant-garde villas of the 1920s until the mature plastic buildings of the post–World War II period, Le Corbusier created an architecture that engaged the viewer in an experiential ballet in which the moving human body constantly redefines itself in a complex dialectical relationship with the field of freestanding columns and the freestanding walls, some straight, others curved.[49] Whenever we look to Kahn, Rossi, Le Corbusier, and others affected by this third aspect of the neoclassical interlude, we find deeply rooted sentience itself to be the artistic theme.

5

The System of the Home

The French private dwelling, whether a town mansion (*hôtel*) or a country house (*maison de plaisance*), was codified as a type toward 1730, whose compositional features persisted well into the twentieth century as a recognizable and characteristic cultural icon. In that sense the eighteenth-century French *hôtel* has entered modern culture as an enduring legacy. At the same time, the *hôtel* belongs to a particular cultural outlook or *mentalité*, which was dominated by a need to classify and then to arrange spaces with clear articulation and hierarchy. The social and architectural systems of the home codified in the French *hôtel* partook of this taxonomic mentality that saw the origins of modern functional design while simultaneously affirming the importance of symbolic organizations of space.

The Hôtel as Icon of French Cultural Identity

Julien Guadet's popular textbook from the first decade of the twentieth century written for Beaux-Arts students dated the birth of the "modern dwelling" from the period of the eighteenth-century French *hôtel*.[1] By Guadet's time, both the distribution of interior spaces and the visual aspect of the exterior had been a sign of French culture for nearly two centuries. If one looks at the new houses published by *L'Architecture Suisse* in the years preceding World War I, one finds that architects in the French-speaking part of Switzerland were still using the model of the eighteenth-century French *hôtel*, slightly modified according to local building traditions, as a sign of cultural identity. What is even more remarkable is that this new, progressive journal, which was promoting the creation of a characteristic modern architecture, found these stylistically conservative designs worthy of publication. Their appearance in this publication was a sign of the deep hold on the French imagination of the eighteenth-century *hôtel* type.

124

The eighteenth-century French *hôtel* even appealed to avant-garde designers. Our history books teach us that Auguste Perret constructed the first multistory apartment building in the world—25 bis rue Franklin (Paris, 1903)—in which reinforced concrete is used for the structure and is expressed on the exterior. Whereas the honor of this accomplishment should probably be shared with the low-cost "hygienic" apartment building (*habitation hygiénique à bon marché*) constructed that same year at 7 rue Trétaigne in Paris by Henri Sauvage and Charles Sarazin, the difference in the plans reveals the importance of the eighteenth-century *hôtel* type for the bourgeoisie at that time. As Brian Brace Taylor has pointed out, the Sauvage and Sarazin building, whose documents were submitted only two months away from Perret's, not only features an exposed reinforced concrete frame but also shows the frame itself without a ceramic covering found at 25 bis rue Franklin.[2] On the other hand, whereas Sauvage and Sarazin utilized a modern functional arrangement of rooms in the modest apartments, Perret, as Pierre Saddy has demonstrated, presented a variant on the eighteenth-century *hôtel* type.[3] To the exterior, as Peter Collins has argued, Perret adapted the traditional vertical French window to his new and modern aesthetic of reinforced concrete construction.[4]

We find another instructive comparison between Raymond Duchamp-Villon's Maison Cubiste and Le Corbusier's Maison Cook. In the Salon d'Automne of 1912, Raymond Duchamp-Villon presented a Maison Cubiste whose facade had depicted a traditional French *hôtel* modified according to the parameters of analytical Cubism. With the Maison Cook (Boulgone-sur-Seine, 1926), Le Corbusier superimposed the principles rather than the style of *hôtel* composition with those of synthetic Cubist painting to create a fully three-dimensional rendition of the eighteenth-century *hôtel* according to the aesthetics of synthetic Cubism.[5]

The comparison between the Maison Cook and the adjacent Maison Collinet constructed earlier in the same year, respectively, by Le Corbusier and Robert Mallet-Stevens, is also revealing. On the one hand, both were pioneering efforts that helped to create what became known as the International Style. Yet whereas Mallet-Stevens used the principles of the reasoned picturesque to guide his design, Le Corbusier rejected this approach in favor of the dichotomy employed by the *hôtel*, which featured a neutral "mask" on the exterior and a highly differentiated volumetric interior.[6] Repudiating both the eighteenth-century style used by his Swiss contemporaries, as well as Perret's twentieth-century rendition of the classical French window, Le Corbusier substituted the new free facade

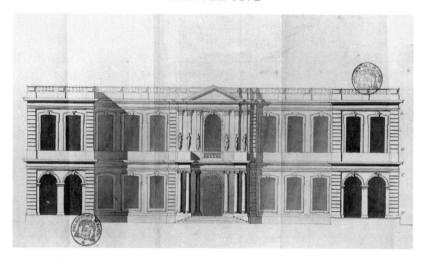

Figure 68. Jacques-François Blondel, ideal *hôtel,* courtyard facade. From "Abrégé d'architecture concernant la distribution, la décoration, et la construction des bâtiments civils."

and long horizontal strip windows of his "Five Points for a New Architecture." In place of the arrangement of rooms *en enfilade,* he fashioned his "architectural promenade." Under the transforming power of Le Corbusier's Cubist aesthetic, the interior forms of the *hôtel*—the figural rooms and their interstitial service corridors (*dégagements*)—were given new life.[7] The perenniality of the resulting aesthetic in Le Corbusier's work, grounded in the principles of Cubism, as it evolved from the prismatic villas of the 1920s to the mature plastic works in *béton brut,* the roughly finished and massive concrete forms of the post–World War II era, has become one of the most aesthetically powerful and conceptually rich contributions to the world of architecture. At times Le Corbusier would alter and even reject the exterior mask in favor of a composition organized according to the dictates of the reasoned picturesque. Yet, the initial discipline for developing the Five Points came from the dual systems of plan (*la distribution*) and facade (*la décoration*) as codified in the eighteenth-century French *hôtel.*

The Pedagogical Manual

Considering the importance, then, of this building type, it is especially helpful to have from the hand of one of the major teachers and theorists of the period, Jacques-François Blondel, a manuscript dating from

Figure 69. Blondel, ideal *hôtel,* garden facade. From "Abrégé d'architecture concernant la distribution, la décoration, et la construction des bâtiments civils."

around mid-century that succinctly explains the characteristic features of the eighteenth-century French *hôtel,* the "Abrégé d'architecture concernant la distribution, la décoration, et la construction des bâtiments civils."[8] This "Abrégé" is a manual on how to design a home, written in a period when the dwelling was organized according to extremely particular architectural and social systems with clearly articulated rules of organization and composition. As the title suggests, the "Abrégé" was an abridgment of Blondel's previous work on the home. This manuscript, however, was by no means a mere summary of earlier publications but rather a synthesis of two different approaches found in each of Blondel's major treatises on domestic architecture. The first of these studies, *De la Distribution des maisons de plaisance, et de la décoration des édifices en général* (1737–1738), provided the reader with an imaginary excursion through several country residences designed by the author. By the end of this literary voyage, the visitor would have culled the major principles by which a home should be executed. To assist the understanding of these rules, this book furnished an index that also summarized the main points. In contrast to this informal presentation of established guidelines, the "Introduction à l'architecture contenant les principes généraux de cet art," published in the first volume of Blondel's *Architecture françoise* (1752), featured a systematic exposition of principles. However, unlike the earlier text, here the theory was given independently of its application. The reader was obliged to apply the direc-

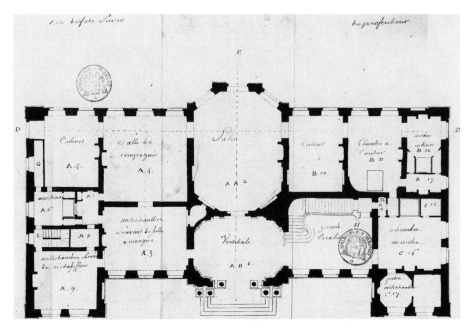

Figure 70. Blondel, ideal *hôtel*, first floor. From "Abrégé d'architecture concernant la distribution, la décoration, et la construction des bâtiments civils."

tives of the "Introduction" to the examples of noteworthy French architecture that followed. Blondel's "Abrégé," in presenting an abbreviated version of the "Introduction," which the author now applied to an illustrative ideal dwelling (figs. 68–71), permits us to follow an eighteenth-century architect through the genesis of his design for a house.[9]

Blondel, of course, was not alone in writing treatises on domestic architecture. His *De la Distribution* owes much to the example of d'Aviler's *Cours d'architecture*. In the first edition of the *Cours* (1691), the reader could find the major rules illustrated by a dwelling expressly designed for this pedagogical purpose.[10] This section was expanded and updated in successive editions. Blondel's *De la Distribution*, however, considered the principles more thoroughly than did d'Aviler's *Cours* and, in so doing, provided a model for Briseux's *L'Art de bâtir des maisons de campagne* (1743).[11]

The Rococo Hôtel: La Distribution

The *hôtel* type whose principles Blondel enunciated in his "Abrégé" is widely known now, largely thanks to Michael Dennis's *Court and Garden*

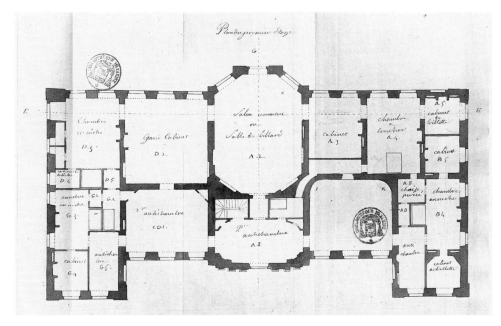

Figure 71. Blondel, ideal *hôtel,* second floor. From "Abrégé d'architecture concernant la distribution, la décoration, et la construction des bâtiments civils."

(1986), as the Rococo *hôtel.* Quoting from Talbot Hamlin's *Architecture through the Ages* (1940), Dennis sets the stage for understanding the new developments in plan design:

> For some time before the death of Louis XIV [in 1715], a revolution against the ponderous ceremonials of court life had been brewing. . . . People began again to demand private lives. . . . By the end of Louis XIV's reign this longing for personal lives and personal privacy had become universal. A complete revolution in social life occurred.[12]

The result was the Rococo *hôtel,* featuring more rooms which, in turn, were given more specific functional designations than before. As Oulmont explains, this was a period when "the architect put within the same space twice the number of rooms as in the time of Louis XIV, and besides, assigned each of them a particular use."[13] The arrangement of rooms in plan, termed *la distribution,* was a source of particular pride to French architects in the first half of the eighteenth century. They felt that contemporary French advances in *la distribution* had made their homes more comfortable than those of their immediate native seventeenth-century predecessors and of their distant colleagues of the Italian Renaissance. Whereas these earlier mansions had magnificent exteriors, the interiors were now considered wanting in basic amenities. "We have in France as well as in Italy," explained Courtonne, architect of the elegant Hôtel de Matignon (Paris, 1722–1724), palaces or *hôtels* built in the preceding centuries, whose exteriors exhibit a beautiful enough architecture, whereas the arrangement (*la distribution*) of the interior is far inferior. One finds there no amenities. It seems as if they tried on purpose to exclude daylight in favor of a feeling of dusk throughout the year. Often it is difficult to place a bed there."[14] Three decades later, Blondel would repeat Courtonne's characterization nearly word for word as he likewise celebrated the "new art" of *la distribution,* which had been developing since the early eighteenth century and even more specifically since the 1720s.[15]

To arrange and furnish the rooms of a home, then, had become a principal component of an architect's duties. As Courtonne explained, *la distribution* "is, properly speaking, the part that should be regarded as the main and the most essential, all the others being, so to speak, subordinate." This architect mocked those who would slight the interior in favor of a sumptuous or sophisticated exterior:

> In effect, when you stack columns upon columns, when your profiles are more regular and more exquisite than those by Palladio and the most famous architects of our times, and when you use the most skillful sculptors to decorate your edifice, what success do you expect if your plan is poorly arranged?[16]

The Rococo Hôtel: Display and Retreat

In explaining the rules for arranging rooms according to the latest advances in *la distribution,* Blondel revealed that the home was conceived as an organism regulated by a bipolar system of display and retreat.[17] At the core of the house was a cross-axial arrangement of public rooms, centered upon the *salon,* which was the major living room and party room. The private spaces escaped this rigor, were lower in height, and were located at a distance from the most frequented places.

The public rooms along the cross axes were organized in an *enfilade,* that is, with their doors aligned. No corridors intervened between the adjacent rooms, so they are also designated as *en suite.* From the front of the house, the *enfilade* E-E passes through the center of the vestibule and the *salon* and then, in a manner of speaking, out into the garden. In the perpendicular direction, the *enfilade* D-D runs through the length of the house as each room on the garden facade takes its place along a spine created by aligning all the doors and by providing appropriate side windows. The *enfilade,* then, had two principal requirements. It had to pass through the length of the building, and it could not be interrupted by a wall or staircase. As Blondel explained, "[T]he general laws of *la distribution* consist in maintaining the principal *enfilades* throughout the length of the building."[18] Furthermore, whenever possible, the *enfilade* had to be prolonged by windows to the exterior. If, however, the lateral *enfilade* in a town house could not be extended outside because of party walls, then mirrors were to be used to provide an artificial substitute.[19] The view along an *enfilade* across all the rooms arranged *en suite* and with their doors open was deemed a source of considerable aesthetic pleasure at this time.

Whereas all the principal rules for the *enfilade* were readily satisfied in Blondel's design, including the opening of a third *enfilade* between the *salle à manger* (A-3, dining room) and the *salle de compagnie* (A-4), the architect was not able to avail himself of the ideal position of the crossing of the axes at the middle of the *salon.* When a *salon* is given an oblong shape, explained Blondel, the lateral *enfilade* should pass through the center of the room and not to one side. In this small building, though, Blondel was faced with the prospect of making an unbecoming extension of the *salon* into the garden to achieve this, an option that he rejected. Similarly, he declined to shift the *enfilade* inward to displace the fireplace, since the chimneys could not be suitably relocated. Thus, for the crossing of the axes he was obliged to abandon the central position without availing himself of either of these alternative arrangements, which would have been possible in a larger edifice.[20]

The location of rooms along the *enfilade* had to occur according to a flexible but nonetheless prescribed order. A vestibule was de rigueur to establish the entry, which led both to the *salon* and to the *grand escalier* (H), placed preferably to the right. Conceived as an extension of the vestibule, this room, which housed the stone staircase, was purposefully opened to the entry space in a unique departure from the compartmentalization of rooms throughout the rest of the plan.[21]

Since the *grand escalier* served as part of the public domain, it led only from the ground floor to the second floor (*premier étage*) and not to the intermediary *entresol,* which was reached by hidden service stairs (L). Whereas these latter stairways were strictly for convenience, the former was a major object of display, both in its stonework and in the ceiling decoration. In connecting the ceremonial space of the *salon* to the *salon commun* (or *salle de billard*) on the second floor, this *grand escalier* had to be wide enough for two people to pass each other or to proceed together without disrupting their conversation.[22]

The remainder of the ground floor was arranged into three types of suites, called *appartements,* which composed the well-designed house. Two of these suites, belonging to the space of display, had to be located to either side of the *salon,* which they shared. To the left, Blondel situated the *appartement de société* (A) for receiving friends in the afternoon; to the right, the *appartement de parade* (B) for morning business visits. In the lower right corner, off the *enfilade* and removed from the more animated places, is the *appartement de commodité* (C) for the owners' personal use. Each of these suites is composed of several rooms selected from an extensive repertory of types that Blondel enumerated before explaining the choices and exclusions made for this house.

There is a loose hierarchy of rooms, which, in descending order of importance and size, would read: for the public rooms, *le salon, la salle, le cabinet;* for the service spaces, *l'antichambre, la garde-robe;* and finally, in its own category, for the bedroom, *chambre de parade en alcôve* (with columns), *chambre de parade, chambre en niche.* When combined as a unit with rooms ranging from large to small, from more public to more private, from formal to informal, and including the appropriate service spaces, the *appartement* was the pride of the mid-century architect and home owner.[23]

In this modest dwelling, each type of room was employed but certainly not each variation of the type. For instance, whereas Blondel listed the different purposes and thus aspects that a *salle* might assume—*salle d'assemblée, salle du dais, salle de conseil, salle de bal, salle de concert, salle de festin, salle à manger,* and *salle de compagnie*—he furnished his house only with the basic ones. The *salon* would serve the function of a party room, just as the antechamber (A-3) doubled as a dining room (*salle à manger*). Whereas the *appartement de société* was given a *salle de compagnie,* the *appartement de parade* in this relatively modest dwelling did not merit a comparable *salle d'assemblée.* Instead, a smaller *cabinet* (B-10) had to serve this function.

The designated activity for each room required not only a particular size and location but also an appropriate ambience. The *cabinet* (B-10), which functioned as a *salle d'assemblée,* was to be suited for business and hence required a more reserved decor. The *salle de compagnie* (A-4), which was the principal room of the *appartement de société,* was intended for the dinner guests who retire from the dining room (A-3). Since it had to provide an enjoyable atmosphere for conversation and table games, this room required a cheerful decoration. Next to the *salle de compagnie* was located a smaller room labeled *cabinet* (A-5), perhaps in-

tended to provide a more intimate place for conversation. Further retreat could be had in the even smaller *cabinets* situated still farther away.
The *cabinet* (A-6) called *méridienne* is for "rest and solitude," just as the
arrière-cabinet (B-12) is where the master "can be alone with his thoughts
far from the presence of the guests."[24]

The *appartement de commodité* was cozier, mentally and physically, than
the public rooms of the other two suites. Not only did you have lower
ceilings over your shoulders, but you also knew that somebody lived
close above tucked away in the *entresol*. The polarity between display and
retreat attains its fullest development in the *entresol* where a young man
is assured a quiet sanctum far away from the gay atmosphere of the *appartement de société*.[25]

The service spaces constituted a major aspect of the *commodité* that
each suite enjoyed. As *garde-robes,* they provided storage, toilet facilities,
and hidden passageways and staircases for servants and masters. In
the *appartement de société,* the room G is a closet and A-7 a flush toilet
with direct access from both the dining room (A-3) and the living room
(A-4). Blondel takes pleasure in explaining that the interior closet
(A-7) receives natural daylight, albeit diminished, through a mirror
placed behind the bed in the adjacent *cabinet* (A-6). Finally, the *antichambre servant de réchauffoir* is a service room that provides a place to keep
the food warm until it is served. The two other suites each have a bedroom that share one toilet (B-14). For economy Blondel suggests that a
simple *chaise percée* could be substituted for a flush toilet. Behind the
arrière-cabinet (B-12) the master has a small *garde-robe* (B-13) in which to
secure his valuables. The function of neither the *garde-robe* (A-8) nor the
antichamber (C-17) is explained.[26]

Whereas both B-11 and C-16 are bedrooms, their presence in radically different suites has obliged an equally dissimilar treatment. After the manner of the *chambre de parade* found in more sumptuous
homes, the *chambre à coucher* (B-11) is decorated with fabric in the zone
around the bed and *lambris* (wood paneling) to the far side, which can
be seen from elsewhere along the *enfilade*. As a vestige of the seventeenth-century practice of receiving distinguished visitors while in a *lit
de parade*, this bed is still placed within the *appartement de parade*, although
the concomitant social ritual had fallen out of use. In contrast to the
more formal *appartement de parade*, the bedroom in the *appartement de
commodité* was arranged as a *chambre en niche* (C-16). By placing the bed
within a cozy niche, the architect obtained residual side spaces for important service functions.[27]

The first floor above the ground (*premier étage*), as was customary,

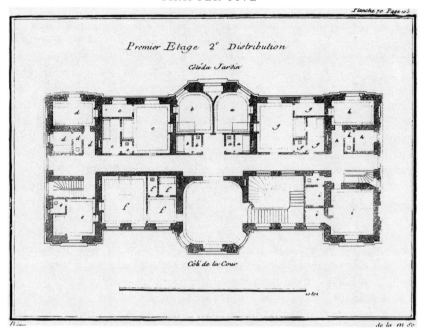

Figure 72. Charles-Etienne Briseux, country house, second-floor plan. From *L'Art de bâtir des maisons de campagne, où l'on traite de leur distribution, de leur construction, et de leur décoration . . .* (1743).

was consecrated primarily to private suites. Here Blondel has arranged two *appartements de maître* (A, D) and two smaller ones (B, G). By organizing his plan without true corridors, Blondel took sides in the contemporary debate about the merits of the traditional system of *antichambres* and hidden service passageways (*dégagements*) within the walls versus the relatively new system of corridors.

According to Blondel, the corridor had serious disadvantages that disqualified it for use in domestic architecture. Blondel objected to the way in which the corridor divided the floor plan into two separate parts. Furthermore, the corridor was noisy: domestics could not work there without troubling the repose of those in the adjoining rooms.[28] Briseux, who championed the use of the corridor (fig. 72), argued that the corridor did not, as its critics maintained, waste space. Rather, it used less room than the various extra staircases and antechambers required by the rival system. By locating the small service stairs at either end of the long corridor, these noisy passageways could be removed from the proximity of many of the bedrooms. As for disturbing the sleepers in bedrooms along the length of the hallway, these rooms could be acoustically buffered from this service zone.[29] An examination of his plan shows the repeated use of a *garde-robe* for this purpose.

In comparing the plan designs of this period, especially with respect to the ground floor, one finds an organic quality to the overall arrangement of rooms. The architect proceeded with a hierarchical distribution moving outward from the center much as a tree develops. Within the subgroups of rooms, spaces cluster around each other in familiar variations of generic patterns. If the house is viewed in this manner, one can understand Courtonne's insistence that a successful *distribution* does not consist primarily in giving each room a different contour but rather in realizing a certain "natural arrangement of all the rooms of the building."[30]

A Taxonomic Age

The organizational clarity of the Rococo *hôtel,* prompted by a need to classify functions separately and then in clusters and according to hierarchical arrangements, reflects a *mentalité* or frame of mind that is found throughout the eighteenth century.[31] This period, which gave the world the great classificatory systems in the natural sciences of Georges Buffon, Carolus Linnaeus, and Baron Georges Cuvier was truly a taxonomic age. Buffon was the author of a "monumental compendium on natural history," the forty-four volume *Histoire naturelle* (1749–1804). Linnaeus is "considered the founder of the binomial system of nomenclature and the originator of modern scientific classification of plants and animals." His classification system, published in *Systema naturae* (1735) and *Genera plantarum* (1737), "remains the basis for modern taxonomy." Cuvier, a "pioneer in comparative anatomy, . . . originated a system of zoological classification based on structural differences of the skeleton and organs."[32] He "began to develop this concept in his lessons on Comparative Anatomy at the Museum of Natural History in 1795; these lessons were published in 1800."[33]

Architectural historians have been fond of suggesting the influence of these men on the architectural thinking of the period. Whereas this is highly likely, it is also possible that these men profited from a widespread mental outlook to which they, as much as the architects, were indebted. If we consider the chronology of their respective works, we find that the taxonomic development of the French *hôtel* occurs before the pioneering work of these illustrious scientists. This would suggest the emergence or even crystallization of this classificatory outlook in the years immedi-

Figure 73. Claude-Nicolas Ledoux, prison (unbuilt), Aix-en-Provence, c. 1785. From *L'Architecture considérée sous le rapport de l'art, des moeurs et de la législation* (1847 ed.).

ately preceding the scientific work.

This taxonomic impulse served the development of both the new functional and symbolic building arrangements that characterize the age. This same period that saw the rise of strictly functional planning through a clearly articulated taxonomic arrangement of spaces also saw the flowering of symbolic systems of classification as well. The former was applied to hospitals and prisons; the latter dominated houses, churches, cemeteries, with all three availing themselves of functional taxonomic criteria as well.

The new hospital designs arose largely in response to the fire in 1772 that burned the Hôtel-Dieu. There ensued a dual debate as to whether the hospital should be rebuilt at its current location in the center of the city by the cathedral Notre-Dame or to the periphery and as to the proper form to give a hospital building. The reason for the separate wards in the functional hospital designs mentioned in Chapter 1 was not simply for cross-ventilation but also to group patients according to their problems and needs. Different types of illnesses were to be separated into different wards; patients for surgery as well as convalescing patients also were to be given their own respective wings.[34]

Prisons, as suggested above in Chapter 1, also were now to be designed according to a taxonomic classification combined with features that promoted hygiene. Whereas the forbidding outside of Ledoux's unrealized prison design (c. 1785) commissioned for the city of Aix-en-Provence (fig. 73) adheres to Blondel's precepts for *une architecture terri-*

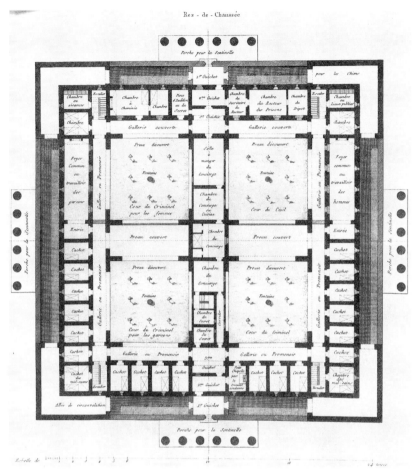

Figure 74. Ledoux, prison (unbuilt), Aix-en-Provence, plan. From *L'Architecture considérée sous le rapport de l'art, des moeurs et de la législation* (1847 ed.).

ble, achieved through both expressive and metaphorical *caractère,* with massive, oppressive, and somber forms, as well as a fortress-like and funerary appearance, the inside (fig. 74) reveals a fully functional plan conceived according to this taxonomic spirit.[35] The prisoners are separated according to whether they are female criminals, male criminals, civil inmates, or criminal male youths. Using a cruciform arrangement within a square, Ledoux segregated the inmates into four groups, each with its own cells, its own workshop, and its own exercise court. With the four exercise courts in the middle of the building and the rooms distributed in long rows one room deep, all rooms are provided with

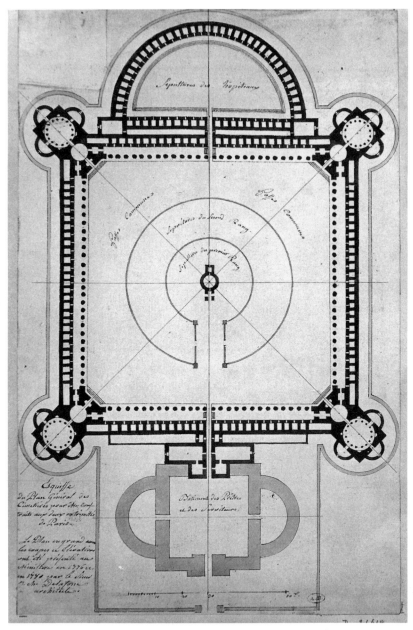

Figure 75. Jean-Charles Delafosse, cemetery (project), Paris, 1776.

natural ventilation and most with cross-ventilation as well, thereby satisfying contemporary requirements for hygiene.[36]

Whereas the new cemetery designs were dominated by a similar concern for hygiene, achieved primarily by forbidding all plantings and sometimes facilitated by openings in walls or floors to permit the passage of air, the major organizational features of the designs, as found in projects associated with private entrepreneurs, was a geometrical ordering to perpetuate the social distinctions of existing burial grounds. Thus, in the balance between public hygiene and social status, hence between function and symbolic code, it was the latter that dominated the ordering of space in this building type. In the existing cemeteries, various places had been consecrated by tradition and hence were more desirable—and more expensive—as places for interment. These places were located according to architectural or sculptural features, such as a chapel or a cross, which might be found anywhere in the cemetery. The new cemeteries, though, whose land was like a tabula rasa, could offer no places consecrated by tradition. Thus, the architects turned to a taxonomic division of space through geometry. The points of focus in any precinct will be the center and the periphery, both of which were used to establish the most desirable (and most expensive) places for burial. At the center was placed the chapel. Along the periphery were individual sepulchral vaults. Corners too offered ideal locations for chapels and costly private burials. As for the undifferentiated space enclosed within the cemetery's walls, it would be divided into concentric zones of decreasing distinction and price as one moved away from the center. All of these features can be found, for example, in Jean-Charles Delafosse's cemetery project of 1776 (fig. 75), which in addition placed the hospital's burial ground beyond the main precinct in its own semicircular zone. This last separation reflected both cultural and hygienic concerns, for the people who died in the hospital were most likely to have been diseased and were of a low social status.

The taxonomic organization of space in eighteenth-century monumental architecture did not reach the same degree of compulsive separation and hierarchy until the advent of ideal church design. Around 1766, Blondel offered his project for a new type of parish church (fig. 76), subsequently published in his *Cours d'architecture*, which was as elaborate as the *hôtel* designs that he had recently been popularizing. Once again, the building is organized according to a binary system of display and retreat. Even more significant is the impetus behind Blondel's classificatory system. The architect's explanation of his design reveals that he

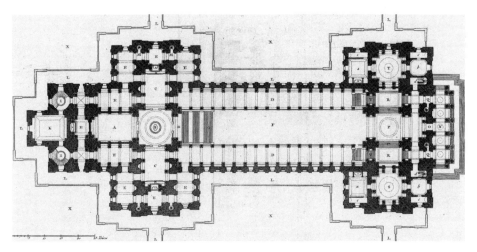

Figure 76. Jacques-François Blondel, ideal parish church (project), c. 1766.

was guided by a strong desire to avoid what he saw as confusion resulting from different activities taking place in the same or neighboring spaces and thereby disrupting each other. Furthermore, each activity required its own, designated place. The reasoning was both symbolic and functional. It was as if only by giving an activity its own space could it acquire its full identity. This attitude is very close to the impulse to create symbolic spaces dedicated to high ideals, discussed above in Chapter 1 in my discussion of character. As for the functional justification, by providing a room for each different activity the architect could invest it with appropriate character through size, lighting, and decoration, just as in the highly differentiated spaces of the *hôtel*. At the same time, each designated place would receive a cluster of related service rooms, also like the suites (*appartements*) in *hôtel* design.

The primary systems of triage in Blondel's ideal parish church separate the living from the dead and the main service from all secondary functions. Forbidding the customary burials within the main level of the church, Blondel banished them to a crypt below. To focus attention on the main service, to make it appear as resplendent as possible, and to eliminate distractions, Blondel elevated the altar (B) and choir (A) from nave (F) and side aisles. The extensive flights of steps and intermediary landings (G), used to this end, were also for distributing the officiating clergy in an impressive visual display. Side chapels for competing masses, with their "comings and goings" that disrupt the main service, are eliminated. The presence of women among men in the church, deemed another disruptive feature, was solved by creating for the female sex elevated tribunes over the side aisles. Religious paintings, also a source of distraction when scattered throughout the church proper, are relegated to sacristies and to cloisters. If possible, Blondel even would have used an architectural arrangement to keep the poor from circulating around the church where they disrupt the service. With no spatial solution coming to mind, he had to content himself with an expression of dismay about their behavior.

Having assured the tranquility of the main space of display, as well as its activities, Blondel turned to the more private functions, distributed around the periphery of the church. The list is too long to consider in its entirety. Let us note, with relative brevity, several of the main features. The parish church has a front porch (N) elevated by several steps off the ground of the public space outside to provide the appropriate dignity. From this porch issue three doors. The central portal (O) opens onto a vestibule for the nave. The front door to the left (Q) leads to a foyer (R) for the chapel with the baptismal font (S) located at the front left corner of the church. This chapel is surrounded by service rooms (a,b,c,d), which, like the *appartement de commodité* in the *hôtel,* have mezzanine spaces above reached by private stairs. The same arrangement applies to the right side of the church where the right door (Q) leads to the vestibule (R) to the wedding chapel (T), with its cluster of circumferential service rooms (a,b,c,d) and mezzanine floor above. The vestibules to these side chapels also lead to the steps placed just beyond them that give access to the women's galleries (D) flanking the nave to either side. The side aisles off the nave wrap around the transept at floor level and hence are lower than the altar (B), choir (A), and the arms of the transept itself (C). These aisles lead to private stairs (M) at the perimeter of the transept for the musicians to use as they climb out of the church's basement level. The stair to one side is for the vocalists who will occupy one side of the transept; the stair to the other side is for the musicians who will occupy the other side of the transept. Another pair of stairs (I) to the rear of the church lead down to the lower level for access to the sepulchers and for church functions such as penitence and catechism.[37]

Ledoux's church project for the town of Chaux exhibits a similar concern with the classification, articulation, and separation of discrete functional and symbolic realms (figs. 77, 78). As with Blondel, there is an upper and a lower church, the former for the celebration of life, the latter for death. Even the upper church is arranged with separate entrances at opposite sides for baptism and marriage. Funeral parties enter the crypt along the cross axis. In this way, people participating in functions with "conflicting purposes" would not run into each other.

Figure 77. Claude-Nicolas Ledoux, church (project), Chaux. From *L'Architecture considérée sous le rapport de l'art, des moeurs et de la législation* (1804).

Placing the Greek cross of the church building within a square precinct with low surrounding walls at the corners, Ledoux designated the four remaining square areas at the corners for burials, assigned, once again as in the prison, according to sex and age: young men, young women, adult males, and adult females. Contemporary sensibilities were offended by the practice of mass graves containing many corpses, when men and women, especially female virgins and experienced men, would be mixed together in a physical proximity that seemed revoltingly promiscuous.

Each level of Ledoux's church received the proper character. For the upper church, reached by ascending stairs, there was a tall nave, elegant Ionic columns, barrel vaults and central dome opened with skylights. In contrast, the crypt had a low ceiling, whose claustrophobic atmosphere was heightened by a baseless, Doric order with thick, stubby shafts, squatter even than the customary proportions of Tuscan columns, illustrative of what Blondel termed *une architecture terrible,* appropriate for an underground realm of death. Funereal dark cypresses rose from below out of each of the four corner cemetery quadrants.[38] In hospitals, prisons, cemeteries, and churches, then, as well as in the *hôtel,* we find the taxonomic spirit of the age of Enlightenment where functional and symbolic concerns directed, in varying degrees, the highly articulated and hierarchically organized arrangement of spaces.

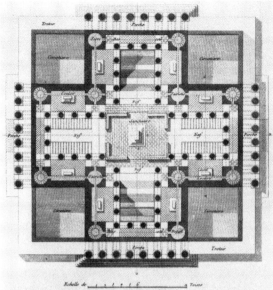

Echelle de _____ Toises

Plan Souterain de l'Église de chaux

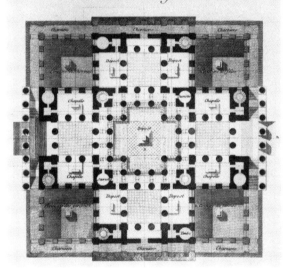

Figure 78. Ledoux, church (project), Chaux, plans of
the sanctuary and the crypt. From *L'Architecture considérée
sous le rapport de l'art, des moeurs et de la législation* (1804).

CHAPTER FIVE

The Polarity of "La Distribution" and "La Décoration"

Although Courtonne mocked the architect who would neglect *la distribu-tion* in favor of an elaborate exterior, the facades of a house at this time were, in the judgment of Blondel and Briseux, a subject of neglect. Blondel felt that the architects of the time of Colbert had been more successful in facade design. He, along with Briseux, hoped to reverse the current "décadence" in this area by counsel and exhortation. The problem arose largely from the modest program and budget for a house, in comparison with civic buildings, which often meant that the architec-tural orders were not used. In that case, the designer too often neglected to decorate the facade "simply and nobly."[39] Like the interior of the *hôtel,* the exterior also had its systems and rules. One was the overall concept of ordering, grounded in regularity and bilateral symmetry. The other was the need to invest all aspects of the facade with appropriate expres-sive character.

Just as the interior spaces had to be arranged in an organic manner, so too did all aspects of the exterior have to be coordinated according to one of five genres of expression: "rustique, solide, moyenne, délicate, ou composée [rustic, firm or solid, medium, delicate, or composite]."[40] These genres were obviously based on the five architectural orders—Tuscan, Doric, Ionic, Corinthian, Composite. Yet Blondel names them according to their expressive characteristics rather than by their order, because the orders were not necessarily going to be employed. Through proportions, solid-void relationships, and ornamental detailing, the spirit of the order, which characterized each genre, would have to be infused into the design.[41]

To demonstrate the importance of applying the proportions of the orders, as well as the characteristic degree of force or grace that they embodied, while not actually using them, Blondel furnished the court-yard facade (fig. 68) with Ionic columns for the ground level and Corin-thian pilasters above, while omitting them entirely from the garden fa-cade (fig. 69). Having provided the reader with the means for making the comparison, Blondel argued that each floor of the garden facade successfully applied the requisite proportions and captured the essence of the respective genres. Comparing the two elevations, Blondel decided in favor of the simplicity of the garden side. Were Blondel actually to construct this home, he might have redesigned the front facade without the orders, as he had in a comparable building published in *De la Distri-bution.*[42]

The compositional system based on regularity and bilateral symme-

144

try, usually with a central entrance, was fundamental to the design of classical architecture as it had been revived during the Renaissance. From Alberti to Boullée, the metaphysical underpinning for this design philosophy resided in the analogy to the human body considered as a reflection of divine order. Just as the body was considered disfigured and grotesque if one limb were missing or if corresponding body parts were not aligned but rather askew, so too a building's facade had to be regular and symmetrical.[43]

Although Palladio made the correspondence between interior and exterior regularity a principle in his domestic architecture, neither the architects of the earlier Renaissance nor those of the later Rococo *hôtel* adhered to this approach. Thus, in composing the dwelling, the French eighteenth-century architect had to coordinate two different systems of organization with their often opposing demands. While the decoration of the interior required an individuality for each type of room, as well as a hierarchy among the sizes of the rooms, the decoration of the exterior prescribed uniformity along the facade. The difficulty resided in combining a facade with regularly spaced windows all the same size with correctly proportioned rooms of different dimensions.

In the illustrative building of the "Abrégé," Blondel applied these precepts as strictly as possible to the main facades. In contrast, the side facades were organized with greater compositional freedom, which reflected the functional needs of the interior more than the requirement for exterior order. Yet even on the principal facades, Blondel encountered conflicting situations that had to be resolved through architectural sleights of hand.

In one instance, the difference in the treatment of the solid portions of the corners of the courtyard and garden facades created a difficulty for one of the corner rooms facing the rear of the house. With its projecting side bays, the courtyard facade has corners proportioned to the width of these secondary parts, whose overall size, in turn, relates to the other recessed sections of the facade as well as to the whole. The garden facade, on the other hand, has only the central projecting bay. Thus, Blondel has given a greater width to the solid end pieces of this facade, whose aesthetic function is visually to terminate the composition with a proportional scheme that relates to the projection of the central *salon,* to the uninterrupted range of windows to either side of this *salon,* and to the height and length of the two entablatures and cornices, as well as to the building's overall proportions. Yet, on the inside, this wider corner mass creates problems for the regularity of the important corner rooms located to the far left on both floors, the *cabinet* (A-5) and the *chambre en niche* (D-3). In both cases, Blondel has used a nonstructural wall to create convenient closets (labeled G on the ground floor). In saving, so to speak, the regularity of these rooms that are placed along the main *enfilade,* he has preserved the nobility that is required for the home's space of display.

In the other instance, the needs of a particular room would have broken the regularity and symmetry of the facade. The *arrière-cabinet* (B-12), a place of retreat which housed the personal papers of the master of the house, and the *cabinet de toilette* (A-5) on the floor above, each required a fireplace that could be located only along the wall of the garden facade opposite the bed. Since Blondel needed a window in virtually the same position as the fireplace in order to balance the window on the other side of the facade, as well as to provide a void next to the solid corner of the building, he solved the problem by providing a false aperture. Thus, from the outside it appears as if there is a window. In this manner the requirements of symmetry and appropriate solid-void relationships are maintained without sacrificing the commodity required in the interior.

The underlying system of compositional order, based on regularity and bilateral symmetry, would, as is well known, come under attack in the nineteenth century. Asymmetry in the arrangement of the parts and picturesque assemblage of forms in the profile of the building would now be seen as affording more functional planning and a livelier aspect. At first, in the early years of the nineteenth century, the differences between these two systems of architectural order would be considered a function of a building's status in the social hierarchy. Thus, we find Edmund Bartell, Jr., explaining in 1804 that the mansion and other large edifices required symmetry whereas the more modest cottage benefited from irregularity:

> In a mansion, or any building of considerable magnitude, particularly after the Grecian model, we expect to see a correspondence of parts. In such buildings, the eye is disgusted with anything wearing the appearance of irregularity: we survey it as a piece of architecture which is intended to command attention; while in the cottage, whether ornamented or not, we look only for comfort and general effect; which I think is altogether assisted, rather than injured, by studying to make the situations of particular parts of such buildings appear to be more the effects of convenience, than objects of solicitous attention.[44]

Within a few decades, though, asymmetrical and picturesque design became available for larger and more prestigious building types. As Kenneth Clark has observed, until the competition for rebuilding the Houses of Parliament was decided in 1836, "no one had ever suggested that a large secular public building should be designed" in the Gothic style.[45] After that time, there were then two rival systems of architectural ordering, which each could be justified through appeal to a greater natural order.

6

Landscapes of Eternity

The cemetery truly entered the architect's repertory of building types in the second half of the eighteenth century. Like the hospital and prison, it received a new attention as part of the radical rethinking of the city in France that was explored above in Chapter 1. The relationship of these tainted institutions to the city was reflected in a matter-of-fact way by J.-N.-L. Durand when he explained to his students in 1805 that a city would be suitably arranged if those buildings that ought not to be located within its boundaries, "such as hospitals, cemeteries, etc., were relegated to land outside the city walls."[1] The self-evident tone of Durand's lesson contrasts vividly with the idealized vision of a new "radiant" city that the abbé Porée had imagined in 1743:

> What a sight for the traveler! Let us imagine it now. . . . This apparently will be its only reality unless those in authority adopt our ideas. . . . From afar I spy the city; its towers, whose points disappear into the sky, inform me of its religion. Further along, I remark its ramparts, which show me its protective forces; then, approaching the city, I see its buildings, which tell me about its size, its commerce, its riches, its taste. There I am sure to find the living, for I know that the dead are all within the expansive confines of those funerary buildings that I noticed along the way.[2]

Porée was writing at the beginning of a reform movement that was centered in France, which not only questioned the traditional relationship of these institutions to the city but also rocked the foundations of customary notions about death. For about a thousand years, since the seventh or eighth century, Christians had been burying their dead inside parish churches and in adjacent or neighboring cemeteries. The dead played an important role in the spiritual life of the community. Their presence served as *memento mori*, reminders of human mortality. This became especially vivid through the evidence of their skulls and bones visible in the charnel houses, created beginning in the late fourteenth and early fifteenth centuries, that enclosed the burial grounds. In a reciprocal manner, the presence of the dead both in and by the church also reminded the living to pray for their souls as a regular aspect of worship.[3]

As one of the pioneering crusaders in the cemetery reform movement, which sought to end burials inside churches and their neighboring cemeteries in favor of opening new burial grounds just outside the city, the abbé Porée could not know that it would take sixty years to realize their goals. It would require the dislocation caused by the French Revolution to disrupt profoundly the status quo, and then the creation of a unified and strong government, in the form of the Napoleonic prefectorial system, to replace the fractured authority shared under the Ancien Régime by the king, the *Parlement,* and the city. Porée also could not anticipate the major changes in the image of the cemetery that would accompany the reform movement over the ensuing six decades. Perhaps the fear and revulsion experienced by the initial reformers at the presence of the dead within their midst had to become intensified to the point that made even the customary mode of burial no longer suitable as further impetus to reform. In any event, when the Cemetery of Père Lachaise was opened as the first municipal cemetery for Paris in 1804, its image as a landscape garden would have astounded Porée and his contemporaries.

The long-term consequences of this new image of the cemetery as a landscape garden were several and enduring. On the one hand, Père Lachaise served as the prototype for the garden cemeteries founded in the United States and Great Britain beginning in the 1820s and 1830s, when these countries underwent their own reform movements to end churchyard interment. By 1849, Andrew Jackson Downing could write that there was scarcely an American city of note "that did not have its rural cemetery," as the new American burial grounds were called.[4] With people flocking to these rural cemeteries on weekends for family picnics, it was observed that this inappropriate use revealed a need for public parks. The two major figures in the field of landscape development in nineteenth-century America, Downing and Olmsted, both felt, as David Schuyler explains, "that the success of rural cemeteries reinforced the public recognition of the importance of naturalistic parks as part of the new urban landscape." "Eight years before the commencement of construction of New York's Central Park," continues Schuyler, "Downing wrote, 'In the absence of great public parks, such as we must surely have one day in America, our rural cemeteries are doing a great deal to enlarge and educate the popular taste in rural embellishment.' . . .

Olmsted concurred, pointing out that the use of cemeteries for recreational purposes 'indicates, as much as any thing else, the need that exists in every town and village for a proper pleasure ground.' "[5] The subsequent history of public parks is well known and extends beyond the bounds of this chapter. As for the cemetery, we have only to look around us to ascertain the persistence of the verdant burial ground as an integral part of nineteenth- and twentieth-century Western culture. This chapter then will consider briefly the main stages of the sixty-year period of the cemetery reform movement to chart its course and to note its interface with the radically new type of garden design, known as the picturesque or landscape garden.[6]

Architectural Solutions

The cemeteries proposed by architects and others during the first forty years of the reform movement were architectural precincts, bounded by walls and often containing a central chapel or religious marker (fig. 75). The imagery was traditionally Christian with the cross and the customary *memento mori* placed in prominent positions, such as at the entrance and over the chapel (fig. 79). The macabre force of the *memento mori* usually was held in check by the discreet use of a single death's-head rather than the Baroque exuberance of the pell-mell piling of skulls and bones in the eaves of contemporary ossuaries. Sometimes classical funerary urns and sarcophagi also were used to decorate and characterize the architecture. Variations of the pyramid and obelisk, each usually a crowning feature raised above a rectangular or square base, further characterized the monuments, as did the generally austere and somber aspect of the walls, often marked with pronounced rustication, albeit with regular, smooth-faced ashlar.

The architectural prototype for these designs was the walled precinct of the thirteenth-century Campo Santo of Pisa. The eighteenth-century counterparts, though, often differed by presenting more elaborate geometries in the subdivision of the central space into zones and in the articulation of the peripheral galleries with additional chapels and special sepulchral chambers. Inspiration for these more elaborate geometries seems to have come from engravings of ancient Roman baths and gardens as well as of Italian Renaissance and Baroque gardens.[7]

As mentioned above in Chapter 1, two concepts of the cemetery developed in this period. The architects working for entrepreneurs who hoped to be awarded the commission to construct and operate the new

NASCITUR AD MORTEM,
MORITUR AD VITAM.

Figure 79. Capron, cemetery (project), Paris, 1782. Detail of the entrance.

cemeteries used these spatial divisions to create social distinctions that would perpetuate the hierarchies in burials actually found in contemporary churches and their burial grounds (fig. 75). Without the benefit of places consecrated by tradition, these designers used the geometrical subdivision of the open space into concentric rings to achieve this end. Their cemeteries offered the most expensive and prestigious places around the central chapel and in the private sepulchral chambers along the perimeter. In contrast, the Académie Royale d'Architecture offered an alternative vision of funerary distinctions based on public recognition of meritorious contributions to society.[8] In accordance with ecclesiastical tradition and in adherence with current notions of public hygiene, there were generally no plantings in these proposed cemeteries. Trees, it was feared, would block the cleansing action of the air, which had to sweep away what were deemed as the dangerous miasmata that arose from the mass graves, containing dozens and even hundreds of corpses.

The *Grand Prix* competition of 1785 focused attention on a new image of the cemetery in which a pantheistic celebration of Nature replaced the earlier version of the new Christian burial ground. Pierre Fontaine's competition design presented a vast Egyptian wasteland (fig. 80) with a gigantic central pyramid at the center, the entire scene shown at the time of a violent storm with lightning momentarily illuminating

the scene. The dramatic depiction of the sublime in these drawings earned the young architect a reprimand from the academicians who demoted Fontaine's project from the first to the second prize. Nevertheless, it was Fontaine rather than the first prizewinner, Jean-Charles Moreau, who provided the example to be followed in a 1788 *prix d'émulation* competition for a cenotaph to honor the explorers who perished in the voyage of La Pérouse (fig. 81). The mid-1780s is also the time generally assigned to Boullée's pantheistic cemetery projects, in which Nature rises in triumph through the form of the central pyramid (figs. 9, 55). As Jean Starobinski has observed, Nature is depicted here as a *puissance,* a vital force.[9] Boullée's central pyramid presents the image of Nature incarnate, timeless, chthonic, primitive, fertile, and crystalline.

The central pyramid in Boullée's cemeteries is the final destination in the sequencing of spaces and forms that begins in a highly directed manner at the entrance (fig. 54). As we saw in Chapter 4, Jacques-François Blondel had counseled architects to lower the level of the ground a few steps from the surrounding terrain. That way the kinesthesis of walking down into the earth would affect the visitors in a powerful way, engaging the senses along with the imagination, to give an intimation about one's own mortality. Boullée adhered to this advice by dropping the ground of the cemetery abruptly at the entrance with a long descent down into the central precinct. This same strategy can be found in Fontaine's second *Grand Prix* of 1785 (fig. 80) and can be traced back to Louis-Jean Desprez's 1766 *prix d'émulation* for a parish cemetery, whose entrance sequence had earned Blondel's praise.

Figure 80. Pierre Fontaine, cemetery, Paris, second *Grand Prix* of 1785.

The experiential basis of neoclassical architecture explored in Chapter 4 with respect to walking through a "forest of columns" (figs. 52, 53) or running the eye over the immensity of the spherical cavity inside Boullée's Cenotaph to Newton (fig. 13) also pertained to Boullée's cemetery design. We have seen in Chapter 4 that Boullée created a claustrophobic sense in his funerary architecture through vastly elongated horizontal bands that compressed relatively diminutive versions of columns and through low-lying peripheral buildings that seem to hug the ground. Repeating an observation by Jean-Jacques Rousseau, whose reflections on "le sentiment de l'existence," the feeling of life, of sentience, were instrumental in forming contemporary sensibilities, the architect Nicolas Le Camus de Mézières, in *Le Génie de l'architecture, ou l'analogie de cet art avec nos sensations* (The genius of architecture, or the analogy of this art with our sensations) (1780), explained, "In effect, we are made such that, when we are happy our heart expands and loses itself in immensity." Sadness, on the other hand, prompts the contrary feeling, a tightening up inside. Architecture, Le Camus de Mézières argued, could foster such feelings by the qualities of its forms.[10]

Boullée attempted to impart the latter type of feeling with his claustrophobic images, as well as with simple, unadorned, monotonous surfaces and with the extensive use of darkness. All of these features, advocated by Le Camus de Mézières, became the constituent elements to Boullée's funerary architecture which had three components. One was a naked architecture, consisting of unadorned walls constructed of unpolished stone that absorbs light. Another was a "buried architecture."

Figure 81. Vien, "Cenotaph in honor of the explorers who perished in the voyage of M. de La Pérouse," first prize, *prix d'émulation*, 1788.

This was achieved in part by suggesting the presence of columns buried and hence hidden from view under pediments or domes placed on or close to the ground (fig. 55). The sloping forms of the triangular roofs

154

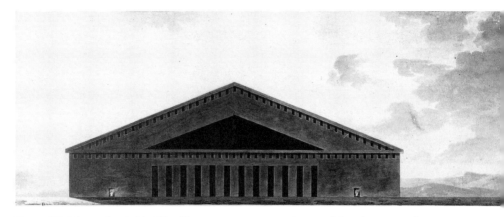

Figure 82. Etienne-Louis Boullée, "Funerary monument characterizing the genre of an architecture of shadows," Paris, c. 1785.

of the cemetery entrance (fig. 54) and the peripheral mortuary chapels contributed further to the effect of a buried architecture by also appearing to be sliding down into the ground. The third element of Boullée's funerary architecture was an "architecture of shadows," in which negative shapes filled with dark shadows would form ghostly images of columns and pediments, the entire scene viewed under a somber moonlight (fig. 82). Together these three principles constituted what Boullée termed a "new genre of architecture."[11]

The experiential program that Le Camus de Mézières and Boullée postulated for architecture, grounded in a desire to inspire appropriate emotions, ranging from gaiety to sadness, by using simple geometric shapes viewed under varying conditions of light and shade, was largely inspired by the contemporary interest in landscape gardens where the characteristics of different scenes, visited at different times of day and across the seasons, were to serve similar ends. Unlike Boullée's contemporaries, who considered the seasons as moving in a gradually changing cycle that progressed from birth (spring), developed to fruition (summer), entered a decline (autumn), and passed into death (winter) before the cycle recommenced, Boullée understood nature in a simple bipolar opposition. For Boullée, there were three seasons of life and one of death. Perhaps this bipolar vision, which saw the seasons as analogous to human existence, an alteration between life and death, was instrumental in prompting the architect to develop complementary worlds of the living and the dead, with a coordinated and complementary visual vocabulary, discussed above in Chapter 4. In any event, it is winter that is reflected in Boullée's funerary architecture, an architecture that renders in simple stereometric forms viewed under moonlight the essence

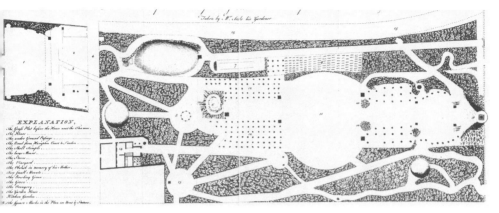

Figure 83. Alexander Pope, garden at Twickenham. From J. Serle, *A Plan of Mr. Pope's Garden* (London, 1745).

of the "black" season:

> What sad days! The celestial torch has disappeared! Darkness envelops us! Frightful winter comes to chill our hearts! It is brought by time! Night follows as it spreads its somber veils over the earth, which it covers in shadows. The brilliant glimmer of the waves is already tarnished by the cruel blowing of the cold winds. The delightful shelter of the woods offers us nothing more than its skeleton. A funerary crepe covers nature. The ravishing image of life has vanished: that of death has taken its place! Objects have lost their brilliance and their color; forms are no longer vibrant, their contours are angular and hard; and the denuded earth offers to our eyes nothing but the vast expanse of a universal sepulcher![12]

The Elegiac Landscape Garden

The landscape garden was influential not only for the pantheistic cemetery designs of the mid-1780s. By the same time, it was actually being invoked as the ideal model for the new cemeteries themselves. Whereas at first glance it might seem astounding that a pleasure garden should serve as a burial ground, it must be remembered that commemoration, often associated with death considered through elegiac feeling, was as integral to the development of the landscape garden as the ha-ha and the serpentine path. In addition, a new sensibility about death and burial, which rejected as abhorrent the mass grave and the macabre *memento mori,* encouraged people to turn to the setting of the garden as the

Figure 84. Stowe. View of the Elysian Fields showing the Temple of British Worthies. From J. Seeley, *Stowe, A Description of the House and Garden* (Buckingham, 1797).

appropriate ambience for death.

Beginning with the earliest English gardens designed in the new picturesque or landscape mode we find commemorative monuments for the dead. The result was to offer an image of a peaceful rest in a pastoral landscape. In the fields of Castle Howard, whose productivity was idealized as recreating the Golden Age and whose tranquility was deemed to promise the peace of mind of the Elysian Fields, rose in the 1720s the new family mausoleum as well as the pyramid honoring the ancestral founder of the Howard estate.[13] Alexander Pope in his garden at Twickenham, started in 1719 and developed until the writer's death in 1744, created an irregular plan in a limited terrain, which, nonetheless, presented a carefully orchestrated sequence of open and closed spaces that culminated at an obelisk in memory of his mother set against a screen of evergreens (fig. 83).[14] This personal elegiac focus was also to be found at the writer William Shenstone's "Arcadian farm," the Leasowes. Here the emotional highlight of the Lover's Walk was a gilt urn nestled among the shrubs and inscribed to the memory of Maria Dolman, whose tragic

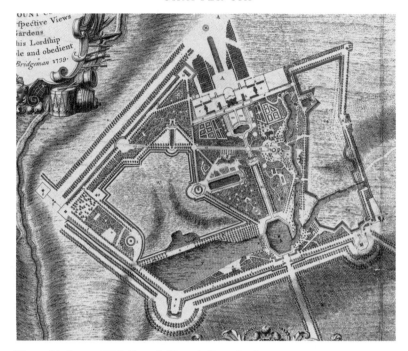

Figure 85. Stowe, 1739. From J. Rigaud, *Stowe Gardens in Buckinghamshire* (London, 1746).

death at twenty-one had left the poet in mourning. Inscribed with the epigram, *Et in Arcadia ego,* taken from Nicolas Poussin's famous painting of this title that had become so popular at this time, to suggest not only the nostalgia for a lost Arcadian bliss but even the sense that in death a loved one's presence remained in the garden, this urn presented the type of image that would have such a powerful hold on the imagination of continental observers who would soon propose the landscape garden as a model for the new cemetery.[15]

Two gardens, in particular, Stowe in Buckinghamshire and Jaegerspris in Denmark, provided the model for what could be achieved.[16] Although conceived in the 1730s as a political allegory, the Elysian Fields at Stowe (fig. 84), with the Temple of Ancient Virtue and the Temple of British Worthies set in a more "natural" landscape than the rest of the garden, were widely admired for their commemorative aspect. With the addition of the rostral column to Captain Thomas Grenville, which was moved from the Grecian Valley to the Elysian Fields after Richard Grenville, later Lord Temple, took charge of the gardens in 1749, the character of the Elysian Fields changed from a closed political allegory to an

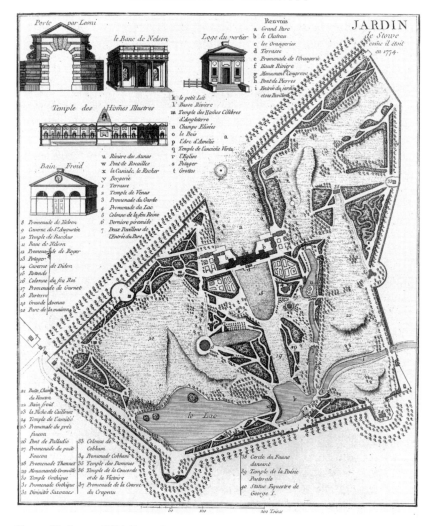

Figure 86. Stowe, 1774. From G.-L. Le Rouge, *Détail des nouveaux jardins à la mode* (Paris, 1776–1788).

open-ended memorial setting.[17] As the contours of the remainder of the garden softened (figs. 85, 86), other monuments at Stowe, such as the pyramid for William Congreve, the observatory column dedicated to the memory of Lord Cobham, and the obelisk to General Wolfe, seemed to make the entire garden into a memorial park.[18] On the continent, Prince Frederick of Denmark and Norway, between 1773–1784, created

an actual memorial park to Danish worthies at Jaegerspris near Copen-
hagen. Fifty-four monuments, including several tombs erected in honor
of national heroes and meritorious citizens, were scattered throughout
a landscape garden.[19]

In France, the death and burial of the "friend of nature," Jean-
Jacques Rousseau in 1778 at Ermenonville, focused attention on the con-
soling aspects of the tomb in the garden. Rousseau's classical sarcophagus on the poplar island became a place of pilgrimage. Even after the
marquis de Girardin forbade visits to the island itself, which was being
ruined by tourists, there was still the unnamed Englishman who, over-
come by emotion, swam across the lake to weep upon the tomb. The
visitor to Ermenonville found a series of pastoral scenes, many of them
with tombs or memorials placed in an intimate setting. It was a fitting
development for a landscape garden called by its owner "the Leasowes
of France."[20]

Girardin had included in his 1777 treatise on landscape design a
stinging condemnation of the "lugubrious" contemporary urban burial
grounds, "depots of cadavers and of putrefaction." The grave, he admon-
ished his readers, belonged in the beautiful countryside. Rousseau's subsequent burial at Ermenonville gave compelling witness to that ideal.[21]

Literature also helped prepare the public spirit for the tomb in the
garden. The Swiss author Salomon Gessner published immensely popular and highly regarded pastorals in the third quarter of the century that
circulated throughout Europe in German and in translation. Gessner's
"idylls" greatly stimulated the cult of making a sentimental visit to the
tomb of a loved one in an Arcadian setting. Gessner's tombs became a
type of family altar to which the living often returned to pay homage,
shed tears, and commune with the dead.[22]

Gessner's idylls were joined in the 1780s by three important works
on gardening that advocated the creation of cemeteries in the form of
the landscape garden where mourners could visit their dead loved ones
whose graves would be marked by individual tombs. Christian Cay L.
Hirschfeld published a five-volume in-quarto treatise on garden design
with German and French editions appearing between 1779 and 1785. If
Hirschfeld's readers had not been able to visit the memorials and tombs
in contemporary gardens, this author provided them with a literary tour
ranging from the isolated chapel for meditation dedicated to Shenstone
in the garden of Envil to Rousseau's tomb at Ermenonville, described as
covered with roses and set upon a green lawn on the *Ile des Peupliers*
where the tall poplars were reflected in the peaceful waters of the lake.
Hirschfeld praised the Elysian Fields of Stowe for having provided the

first instance of an entire area in a garden consecrated to honoring the worthy dead, but judged that this British example could hardly compare with the memorial park of Jaegerspris.

Perhaps the highlight of Hirschfeld's study can be found in volume 2 with the moonlit pilgrimage to a park outside Berlin to visit the tomb of Johann Georg Sulzer, author of *Tableau des beautés de la nature* (1755) and *Allgemeine Theorie der schönen Künste* (1771–1774). Hirschfeld dedicated his first volume to the ailing Sulzer, whom he praised as the first true champion of the landscape garden in Germany. In subsequently depicting the scene at Sulzer's tomb, Hirschfeld encouraged the reader to imagine himself or herself leaning against a venerable tree with the moon reflected in the placid waters of the pond and a small rill murmuring at the foot of Sulzer's grave. There was nothing macabre about this "touching" scene, where the "idea of death loses all of its frightfulness." Hirschfeld contrasted such scenes with the "barbaric custom" of burying within cities and inside churches. He suggested that people with sufficient property use a park or woods for a family cemetery.[23]

Like Hirschfeld, the abbé Delille, in his poem, *Les Jardins, ou l'art d'embellir les paysages* (Gardens, or the art of embellishing the countryside) of 1782, took cue from the "sweet sadness" of Poussin's *Et in Arcadia ego*. "Imitate Poussin," counseled the popular French poet. Delille suggested creating a tomb in a pastoral setting and dedicating it to a loved one or some other cherished person, with an inscription that proclaimed the virtues of the deceased: "Here lies the good son, the good father, the good husband." As in an idyll by Gessner, a visitor to the tomb would hang as an offering a garland among the "pious" trees, somber yews, pines, and cypresses, and scatter flowers upon the grave. Like Gessner and Hirschfeld, Delille understood the emotive power of invoking "the woods, the water, and the flowers" as companions to the tomb. Like Claude-Henri Watelet, author of *Essai sur les jardins* (1774), Delille proposed the creation of a garden Elysium with statues of the benefactors of humanity.[24]

Just as it is uncertain as to whether Delille was suggesting actual tombs in a garden rather than false ones, which were popular at the time, albeit with sincere dedications, and as to whether his Elysium was to be an actual cemetery rather than a commemorative garden, the decisive step was taken in 1784 by Bernardin de Saint-Pierre in his *Etudes de la nature* (Studies of nature). Bernardin not only advocated an Elysium for the worthy dead in the form of a landscape garden, he also proposed creating public cemeteries in the environs of a city according to the same model. Paris, he argued, should have public burial grounds in which bosquets of cypresses and pines mixed with flowering and fruit-bearing trees. The combination of this landscape and its memorials would inspire a "profound and sweet melancholy" through the "moral feelings" that they would sustain. In such a setting the tombs would appear as "monuments placed on the frontiers of two worlds."

In describing his proposed national Elysium for the worthy dead, Bernardin was even more explicit in stipulating its features. The landscape was to be in the new picturesque manner, with none of the formal elements of the previous era: "There will be ... no alignments ... no bowling greens, no pruned and shaped trees, nothing that resembles our [formal gardens]." The tombs and mausoleums "would not be crowded together as in a warehouse but spread about with taste."[25] Bernardin's vision of a public cemetery and a garden of fame within a picturesque landscape setting was to become a standard point of reference throughout the remainder of the century.

In the last book of his garden treatise, which appeared in 1785, Hirschfeld also described a new type of public cemetery, which had been briefly announced in 1783 in his outline for the remaining volumes. Like Bernardin, Hirschfeld employed the aesthetics of the landscape garden. This cemetery was to be surrounded with a "peaceful, solitary, and serious" countryside, which would prepare the visitor psychologically for the visit by removing distracting influences. The cemetery itself would be united visually with its surroundings yet protected with either a very low wall, a hedge, or a ha-ha. Trees, now welcomed by scientists for "purifying" the air, would adorn the burial ground as would aromatic plants that would add an enchanting balm.[26]

The first volume of Quatremère de Quincy's encyclopedia on architecture, published as part of the *Encylopédie méthodique* in 1788, contained a long entry on cemeteries that proposed combining the *campo santo* and the picturesque garden. As a model for the former, Quatremère turned to the famed Campo Santo of Pisa; for the latter, he lifted verbatim long passages from Hirschfeld's text of 1785 on the garden cemetery without reference to its author. Quatremère's article not only further popularized the idea of the garden cemetery, it registered a desire to alter the very vocabulary of death. The text began by observing that there was a close analogy between words and things. No word, explained Quatremère, could better convey the "infectious dumping grounds," the "hideous depots of cadavers and skeletons" that constituted the cemeteries of Paris than the term *charnier,* or charnel house. The word "cemetery," on the other hand, came from the Greek *coimeterion.* Wishing to reestablish a correspondence between "les mots" and "les choses," Quatremère proceeded to outline his ideal cemetery that would be worthy of the meaning of the word. For this new landscape garden cemetery would offer a message that death was a "rest" for all "eternity."[27]

The Field of Rest

The French Revolution brought to a head the crisis that had prompted the cemetery reform movement decades before. With the expropriation of church property, the dissolution of the traditional clergy, and the closing of former parish burial grounds, the customary rituals of the funeral were gravely disrupted. The privileged lost their prerogative of a grave inside the church; the traditional funeral procession was gone. Everybody was now buried in mass graves that contained several hundred and sometimes even more than one thousand corpses. All of these drastic changes occurred in the midst of revolutionary violence and bloodshed whose traumatizing effects produced, under the Directory and the Consulate, an outpouring of sentiment about dignified funerals and decent cemeteries.

The desire to establish a correspondence between words and things, articulated by Quatremère de Quincy just before the Revolution, became even stronger after 1789, with the word "cemetery" itself now being associated with the hated mass graves and charnel houses. Throughout the Revolution, people preferred to refer to the burial ground as a "field of rest" (*champ de repos*), a "place of rest" (*lieu de repos*), or an Elysium (*Elysée*). Important citizens were honored with monuments or graves in garden settings: the monument to Carolus Linnaeus erected in the Jardin des Plantes in Paris in 1790 and the burial of the naturalist Louis Daubenton in 1800 in this same garden, the temporary tomb erected for Jean-Paul Marat in the garden of the former Cordeliers' monastery in 1793 and for Rousseau in the Tuileries in 1794, the latter two on their way to the French Panthéon. It was seen in Chapter 2 that the transformation of the former Church of Sainte-Geneviève into the French Panthéon in 1791 to honor France's worthy dead prompted a controversy in which critics shuddered at the thought of entombing these people within the cold stone walls of a building when a tranquil verdant setting seemed more appropriate. Even Quatremère de Quincy, as was noted, had hoped to surround the Panthéon with "sacred woods."

Paris was given its landscape Elysium when in 1794 Alexandre Lenoir opened an Elysium Garden in the garden of the former convent of the Petits-Augustins as part of the new Musée des Monuments Français

Figure 87. Alexandre Lenoir, Elysium Garden, Musée des Monuments Français, Paris. Painting by Hubert Robert, c. 1800.

(fig. 87). Although merely charged to rescue from destruction France's artistic patrimony, Lenoir took this opportunity to create the Elysium of French worthies that had been so ardently desired. As he explained:

> An Elysium seemed to suit the character that I gave to my establishment, and the garden offered me all the necessary means to execute my project. In this calm and peaceful garden, you will find more than forty statues. Tombs, placed here and there on a grass lawn, rise with dignity in the midst of silence and tranquility. Pine trees, cypresses, and poplars accompany them. *Larvae* and cinerary urns positioned upon the walls help establish within this place of happiness a sweet melancholy that speaks to the sensitive soul.[28]

Within this garden, Lenoir gathered the mausoleums of renowned Frenchmen, such as Boileau, Descartes, Molière, and Turenne. Yet the monument most conducive to sweet melancholy was the Gothic tomb of Abélard and Héloïse. According to René Schneider, "all of elegiac Paris flocked" there to weep at the tomb of the unfortunate lovers.[29]

Among the various projects for landscape garden cemeteries proposed during the Revolution, one of the most striking was submitted by Jacques Cambry, former administrator of the Department of the Seine, in collaboration with Jacques Molinos, architect and inspector of civil buildings for the same department (fig. 88). This project was actually approved by the Department of the Seine on 14 Floréal, year VII (May 3, 1799), which half a year later ordered the printing and distribution of a sumptuous book complete with a learned and sentimental text on burials by Cambry and beautiful engravings of Molinos's design. Although published under the aegis of the government, this proposal was

Figure 88. Jacques Molinos, "Field of Rest" (unexecuted project for transforming the quarries of Montmartre into a cemetery), Paris, 1799.

being sponsored by private entrepreneurs who hoped to build and manage the cemetery for the city.

Molinos's *Champ de repos* was to be a picturesque garden with meandering paths and funerary monuments of all types scattered among the variegated plantings. Since the cemetery was to be built over former quarries at Montmartre, the architect envisaged the provision of underground catacombs, thereby offering an alternative place of burial for the wealthy. People of modest means would be buried in trenches two bodies deep or cremated in the furnaces of the central pyramid. Cremation, it should be noted, was totally alien to the traditions and sensibilities of the times. Borrowing the concept of freestanding neoclassical pavilions of different shapes placed at the perimeter of the city that Ledoux had used for the *barrières,* or tax gates, of Paris, Molinos proposed erecting mortuary depots around the city where the funeral party would terminate its procession (figs. 89, 90). At the end of the day chariots would make the rounds to collect all the corpses, which would then be taken to the cemetery. Like Ledoux, Molinos conceived these pavilions after the manner of garden *folies,* serving here as intermediaries between the city and the garden cemetery. The scale of the buildings and the simple geometries used, along with their cosmological symbolism and traditional imagery of immortality, such as the butterfly hovering over the entrance, all would combine to reassure the citizens of Paris that the cemetery was the realm of tender feelings and sentimental memories.[30]

With the project submitted by Cambry and Molinos, the ideal of equality in death, which had dominated the Terror when the cemetery became a "Garden of Equality" and which had remained a concern under the Directory, was abandoned in favor of the prerevolutionary system of demonstrating socioeconomic differences. In Cambry's text, the egalitarianism of the immediate past was jettisoned in favor of celebrating the contrasts between the humble memorials for the people of modest means and the magnificent mausoleums for the rich. This was the sentiment that guided the creation of the first municipal cemetery, the now famous Cemetery of Père Lachaise.

Before the land was even purchased for Père Lachaise, the first prefect of the Seine, N.-T.-B. Frochot, proposed to the minister of the interior that the Parc Monceau, one of the first picturesque gardens in France, which had been created for the duc de Chartres in 1779 at the outskirts of Paris and hence, as confiscated property, now belonged to the nation, be given to the city for burials:

This solitary place, located at one of the extremities of Paris, presents a surface of ninety-nine *arpents,* ornamented with the

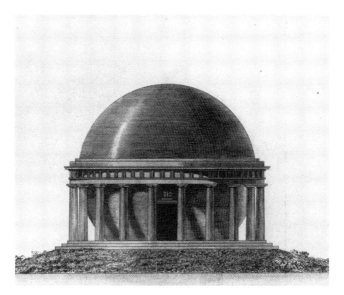

Figure 89. Molinos, mortuary depot (unexecuted), Paris, 1799.

Figure 90. Molinos, mortuary depot (unexecuted), Paris, 1799.

most beautiful plantings. Through the picturesque way in which it is designed and by the irregularity of its forms and the surprise of its movements, it offers a delectable Elysium where death would hold sway only through the memories of those who live on, through the monument that would cover the cherished remains, through the simple epitaph hung from the foliage of funerary trees.[31]

Among the reasons enumerated for rejecting Frochot's request two stand out. First, because the city was required to reduce its outstanding debts as much as possible, neither the purchase of this luxurious property nor even its gift achieved through private donations would be permissible. Second, because the garden could not accommodate the burials for the entire city, it would become "the privileged cemetery of the wealthy," since the other new cemeteries would not be equal to its splendor.[32]

Undaunted by this setback, Frochot acquired for the city the magnificent hilltop estate known as Mont-Louis, which had once belonged to the Jesuits and which had housed among its extensive formal gardens the confessor to Louis XIV, Père Lachaise. In December 1802 and March 1803, the Conseil Général of the Seine recognized the use of the two burial grounds to the north and south of the city at Montmartre and Montparnasse, respectively, as municipal cemeteries and designated the Mont-Louis property to the east of the city as a third place of burial. In March 1804, the Mont-Louis estate was purchased. By an arrêté of 22 Floréal, year XII (May 12, 1804), Frochot designated this property as the Cemetery of the East, or, as it was popularly called, the Cemetery of Père Lachaise. The burial ground was inaugurated on May 21. Thus, the cemeteries that would serve nineteenth-century Paris were now in place.

Less than one month after the opening of the Cemetery of Père Lachaise, Napoleon issued the Imperial Decree on Burials of 23 Prairial, year XII (June 12, 1804). This document reiterated the terms of the entire sixty-year reform movement and would become the fundamental law on burials for the succeeding century. Burials in closed places and within the city were henceforth forbidden. For reasons of decency and salubrity, the communal grave was proscribed in favor of individual graves separated by a minimum of thirty to forty centimeters to the sides and by thirty to fifty centimeters at the head and foot. Ordinary graves would be reused after five years, but in the interim tombstones or other markers would be permitted. Only if the cemeteries had adequate space could land be sold for permanent graves marked by tombstones or mausoleums or fashioned as sepulchral vaults for individuals or families.

In designing the Cemetery of Père Lachaise according to the stipulated goals of both Prefect Frochot and the Municipal Council, dominated by the energetic Quatremère de Quincy, the city's architect,
Alexandre-Théodore Brongniart, created a vast landscape garden for
private burials (fig. 91), while reserving a restricted area on the plain to
the lower left corner of the site for the communal graves where the poor
would be buried without charge. According to a special commission on
cemeteries reporting in 1874, the provision of Napoleon's Imperial Decree of 1804 stipulating separate graves for everybody had never been
applied in Paris. At first, coffins of the poor had been superimposed and
then later aligned side by side in long rows without the required space
between them.[33] By reserving most of the land for the temporary concessions, regularized in 1825 as five-year renewable plots, and for the more
prestigious and expensive *concessions à perpétuité,* the Cemetery of Père
Lachaise effectively reversed the terms of the Imperial Decree, which
would have permitted the more opulent sepulchers only to the degree
that space remained.

In arranging the terrain for burials, Brongniart created a carriage
path that looped around the perimeter of the site. He further designed
serpentine footpaths to cross the entire garden. The entrance was
shifted to the foot of the hill, where the architect created an esplanade
that led up to the house upon the crest. The architect hoped to replace
this house with a mortuary chapel in the form of a pyramid (figs. 92,
93), a popular image in contemporary projects for garden cemeteries
and one that actually graced the Protestant Cemetery in Rome, where
the ancient Roman tomb of Caius Cestius was the focal point of the
burial ground which had by then become a garden cemetery. After
Brongniart's death his successor, Hippolyte Godde, constructed instead
a classical chapel of more modest size. He also erected a variant of
Brongniart's first project (fig. 92) for the cemetery entrance using cippi
rather than the more dramatic second project (fig. 93) based upon the
classical sarcophagus. Among the architectural features envisaged by the
architect that were not built was the peripheral gallery of sepulchral
vaults, which Quatremère de Quincy and Frochot had favored.

By the early 1820s the Cemetery of Père Lachaise had become a
magnificent garden cemetery with different landscape features that gave
identity and character to its parts. To the lower right was the zone known
as the valley. The tomb of Abélard and Héloïse, along with the lovers'
remains, transferred here in 1817 from the recently closed Museum of
French Monuments, served as a sentimental focal point here. Above the
valley rose the hillside that culminated in an escarpment, this crest being

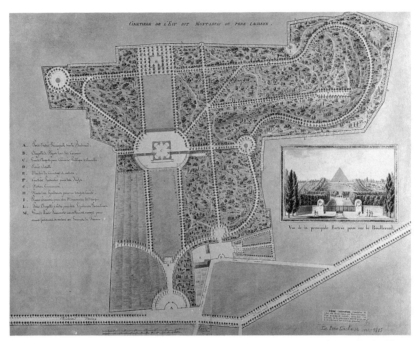

Figure 91. Alexandre-Théodore Brongniart, Cemetery of Père Lachaise, Paris. First project, c. 1812.

Figure 92. Brongniart, Cemetery of Père Lachaise, view of the entrance and main chapel (unexecuted), Paris. First project, c. 1812. Enlargement, showing the inset in figure 91.

Figure 93. Brongniart, Cemetery of Père Lachaise, view of the entrance and main chapel (unexecuted), Paris. Second project, c. 1812.

favored by Napoleon's generals whose burials there gave the sobriquet of the "Rendez-vous des Braves," the heroes' rendez-vous. Their funerary monuments appeared dramatically against the sky when viewed from below. Within the garden there were other special places. On the escarpment could also be found a dense bosquet where "everything is romantic," named the "Bosquet du Dragon." This bosquet had been developed out of a formal bosquet from the earlier garden that still remained on the site. Further back was another bosquet, called "La Charmette," which was favored by Protestants, who clustered their tombs there. To the left of the "Bosquet du Dragon" were two sunken bosquets, which once had been formal basins of rectangular outline, long since fallen into ruin.[34] A formal bosquet to the right of the chapel became the "Bosquet Delille," named after the famous poet who had championed the tomb in the garden and who was buried there in 1813. The following lines, found that year written in French on a terrace wall in Père Lachaise, convey the feelings of comfort and solace that this garden cemetery had conveyed and that still can be experienced there today:

> At this peaceful site, amid trees and flowers,
> Sorrows and laments come to cry their tears:
> Here they can find a sympathetic shade:
> Death hides from their eyes its hideous scythe.
> As it spreads its subjects throughout a vast garden;
> For the home of the dead has become a new Eden.[35]

7

The Space of Absence

My theme in this final chapter is the type of place whose distinguishing characteristic is a mysterious solemnity that takes us out of this world into a type of limbo. It is a place of paradoxes, neither of this world nor of the next, neither the space of the living nor the place of death. It is a void whose overwhelming message is the absence of the dead person, no longer with us in life and yet somehow present within the aura of the monument. The projects that I group under the rubric of the space of absence are all characterized by a search for the basic and primal. They define a place set off from the world of the living either by making a temple-like enclosure, by opening a cavity in the ground, or by gathering a dense mass of stone around a constricted area. They often employ a descent into the earth or an ascent toward the sky; they sometimes use a special light, luminous and crystalline or somber and ghostly.

The space of absence is a space associated with commemoration. It derives its character from the mental and spiritual outlook of the Enlightenment when architects were fond of setting aside empty places fashioned as temple-like enclosures dedicated to some abstract concept. To enter that space was to commune, so to speak, with a high ideal, to make the abstract present through the aura associated with a specially designated precinct. It is no accident that the great neoclassical architect Etienne-Louis Boullée was the master in his age both of temple-like spaces for the architecture of the world of the living and of the funerary architecture of shadows that evoked a negative self, incorporeal and yet seeming very real.

The symbolic aspect of this space is grounded in the same intuition about abstract presence as is symbolic character. It is also a species within the broader genus of numinous space. It differs from both of these, though, in that its subject is extremely personal. It is about the encounter of two or more spirits or souls in a way that defies reason.

Beginning with the Enlightenment and extending to the present day, the theme of the space of absence has sponsored some of the most deeply spiritual architecture in the West. Although recurring as a motivating force in commemorative design, it is not certain that the space of absence has been subject to a clear chronological development. Rather, as is often the case in matters that touch the spirit so intimately, it seems to have arisen in different forms largely in relationship to the artist's particular creative persona. This does not mean to say, though, that individual projects did not spur an entire series of related developments. At times, this occurred as well. My approach in this chapter, however, will be thematic rather than chronological. I will survey the subject according to type.

Temple-Like Enclosures

Perhaps it comes as no surprise that one of the finest temple-like spaces envisaged for a mausoleum is a project of about 1799 by Friedrich Gilly (fig. 94), the German architect who learned well the spirit and principles of French neoclassicism through a visit to Paris. In their study of German neoclassical architecture, David Watkin and Tilman Mellinghoff note that this "square-piered mausoleum, in which the conventional trappings of the orders have been pared away, is well known as one of the most advanced statements of the reductionist style which appeared in various European centres around 1800." "Associated with the Greek Revival at its most imaginatively austere," these authors continue, "this is represented by the outline engraving style of Carstens, Flaxman, Percier and Fontaine, and Hope; by the sans-serif lettering adopted, for example, by Soane; and by the linear disembodied architecture of the younger Dance and his pupil Soane."[1] Whereas this is certainly true, there is another explanation of the primitive aspect to this composition, which is detailed as a trabeated construction of monolithic piers and beams, devoid of ornamentation and stout in their proportions. This is a quest for a primitive aspect, like an *Ur-Architektur,* deemed most appropriate for the building type. One is reminded here of Boullée's drawing for a funerary chapel in the form of a stark, unadorned pyramid, viewed in the midst of a thunderstorm.[2] In both cases, the architect is seeking to give presence to a cosmic realm of Nature through the primitive quality of the architecture.

We have seen in Chapter 3 the degree to which the Beaux-Arts architect Paul Philippe Cret imbued his institutional architecture with the spirit of late eighteenth-century symbolic character. Once again, it should not be surprising to learn that he also conveyed a sense of the

173

Figure 94. Friedrich Gilly, mausoleum (project), c. 1799.

space of absence in his war memorials. The Pennsylvania State War Memorial (fig. 95) at Varennes, France (1924), for example, designed in conjunction with Thomas Atherton, Jr., uses the temple-like precinct of neoclassical architecture to create a realm of symbolic space. This monument at the edge of a cliff features a plateau that is defined by two peripheral rows of classical piers each carrying an entablature.

Cret's move from such spaces dominated by symbolic character into the more primitive and chthonic space of absence comes in the Bushy Run Battlefield Memorial projects of 1927 (fig. 96). Here Cret plunged

Figure 95. Paul Philippe Cret and Thomas H. Atherton, Jr., Pennsylvania State War Memorial, Varennes, France, 1924. Scheme "A."

Figure 96. Paul Philippe Cret, Bushy Run Battlefield Memorial (project), 1927.

Figure 97. Frank Lloyd Wright, Unity Temple and Cenotaph (project), Taliesin Valley (Spring Green), Wisconsin, July 1958.

into a world of primitivism with rough stone piers, either in a straight row or in a circle, reminiscent of the monoliths at Stonehenge on the Salisbury plain.[3]

At the end of Chapter 3, I pointed out that Frank Lloyd Wright invested his institutional buildings, centered upon what he called the "noble Room," with the same quality of symbolic character that could be found in the architecture of Boullée and Cret. When we turn to his commemorative buildings, we find that they are rich in the sense of a space of absence. His work will figure prominently in this chapter. Under the heading of the temple-like enclosure, we have Wright's unexecuted funerary chapel, the Unity Temple and Cenotaph project (figs. 97, 98) designed in the last years of the architect's life when he was about ninety years old. The project is doubly remarkable, not only as a fine example of the temple-like space of absence but also because it uses a trabeated stone architecture. Wright had spent a professional lifetime inveighing against Greek post-and-lintel construction and inventing alternative systems of construction and form. "If form really followed function," he had mused in *An Autobiography,* "why not throw away the implications of post or upright and beam or horizontal entirely? Have no beams or columns piling up as 'joinery.' Nor any cornices."[4] At a later point in Wright's life, though, to the architect's mind the most appropriate form for a funerary chapel was a temple-like space based on post-and-lintel construction, a space following in the tradition of Gilly's and Cret's un-

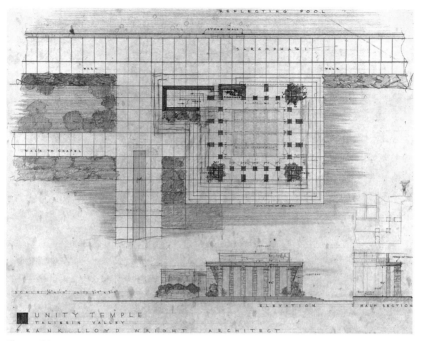

Figure 98. Wright, Unity Temple and Cenotaph (project), July 1958, plan and elevation.

executed projects and, more specifically, from the vantage of a possible precedent known to Wright, of Gunnar Asplund's crematorium of 1935–1940 at Woodland Cemetery in Stockholm.[5]

After experimenting with a sequence of three chapels with deep porches carried by a primitive trabeated architecture, Asplund replaced the multiple porches with a single giant loggia, open in the center to the sky like an ancient Roman impluvium. Viewed at the top of the slope with a low wall to the left and a giant stone cross to the right, this temple-like space has a powerful effect issuing in part from the primitive simplicity of the forms and in part from their ability to engage into the composition a landscape scene of cosmic character.

Wright's initial scheme follows the example of Asplund's design by combining a square temple-like space, similarly defined by rows of piers along the periphery, with a vertical monument, which here is a cenotaph inscribed with names and featuring a towering bronze lantern. In this first scheme for Unity Temple, Wright arranged these two elements in an axial fashion.[6]

This Unity Temple was to be located close to the Lloyd-Jones family

177

burial ground and chapel. It was a site pregnant with meaning for Wright, who cherished the memory of his Welsh ancestors and who loved the valley in which he had been raised and to which he returned in 1911 to create his headquarters, Taliesin, the Welsh word for "shining brow." Wright's projected new building was to be named Unity Temple, ostensibly after the "Unitarianism of the Lloyd-Joneses . . . [which] was an attempt to amplify in the confusion of the creeds of their day, the idea of life as a gift from a Divine Source, one God omnipotent, all things at one with Him."[7]

Between the old chapel and the projected Unity Temple rose the grove of fir trees that Wright's Uncle Thomas had planted, as Wright explains in his autobiography, "beside the chapel so future Sunday picnics might have shade." "On the east side of the shingle-sided chapel," Wright continued, "with its quaint belfry opposite the fir grove, was the churchyard where the simple white marble obelisk did reverence to the memory of 'EinTad' and 'EinMam' [that is, the pioneering immigrant Welsh grandparents who had founded the Lloyd-Jones clan in 'the Valley']. Grouped around the tall slender obelisk were the family graves. Every Sunday, spring and summer of these youthful years, up to September fifth, the boy would put on his city clothes and go to these chapel gatherings. . . . This family chapel was the simple wooden temple in which the valley-clan worshipped the images it had lovingly created and which in turn reacted upon the family in their own image."[8] Wright's new Unity Temple was for his second family, the Taliesin Fellowship, whose members would be buried in a row of graves by the funerary chapel.

As Wright developed the project, he worked with three issues: the form of the funerary chapel, the nature of the sarcophagus, and the link with the preexisting family chapel and burial ground. The project dated September 1, 1957, shows the obelisk-like cenotaph shifted to the left of Unity Temple. In later schemes this vertical form disappears altogether. As for the site plan, as shown in this drawing dated July 1958 (fig. 98), Wright rotated the row of Taliesin Fellowship graves ninety degrees so that it and the adjacent walk aligned with the grandparents' obelisk to the other side of the grove of fir trees. A second and parallel walk leads from the old family chapel to the entrance of the new Unity Temple.

In the project of July 1958, Wright's major change in plan was to create a double range of piers, with square stone piers forming the inner ring that defines the temple-like space of the chapel and rectangular piers to the periphery. At three of the corners are exterior plantings over which rise crystalline "lanterns," as Wright calls them, upside down, stepped glass pyramids of light. The sixteen central squares in the center of the funerary chapel are lit from above, after the manner of the building's namesake, the Unity Temple that Wright had built at the turn of the century in Oak Park. The floor of the funerary chapel was to be black marble. A staircase would lead to a crypt below the sanctuary where Wright and his wife would be buried.[9]

Wright's July 1958 funerary chapel was like a meeting between the Greek temple and Stonehenge, filtered through the creative persona of this inimitable organic architect. The trabeated stone forms rose upon a stepped platform reminiscent of a Greek temple's stylobate; the central space defined by the double square ring of stone piers, devoid of any ornamentation or further articulation, called forth the image of Stonehenge; the open outside corners and cantilevered roof, as well as the ceiling of skylights, were hallmarks of Wright's architecture.

The architect, though, was not satisfied with this scheme. To one side of the perspective view he sketched a new detail to articulate the juncture between the pier and the beam. In the subsequent set of drawings, Wright gave the piers this modern version of a classical capital. It is a pinched form, slighter than the pier and faced in wood with a decorative geometric pattern. The directness of the stone beams carried by the stone piers in the earlier scheme is gone now as a lapped wooden fascia forms a sort of entablature.[10] The simplicity of the Stonehenge detailing has been replaced by a sophisticated, abstract rendition of the Greek orders. All these details pale, though, before the power of the silent empty space contained within this grove of columns, with the black marble floor and the central top lighting.

The Descent into the Earth

There is a reassuring quality to the temple-like enclosures dedicated to the space of absence that is not present in those funerary projects that take the visitor down into the earth. We have seen above in Chapters 4 and 6 that it was the great teacher Jacques-François Blondel who, toward the middle of the eighteenth century, instructed his students to lower the level of the cemetery a few steps from the surrounding terrain in order to convey an intimation of the "terrible but inescapable realm which we must inhabit when we die."[11] We also saw that this advice was applied by Louis-Jean Desprez in his prize-winning design of 1766 for a parish cemetery, by Pierre Fontaine in his second *Grand Prix* for a cemetery in 1785 (fig. 80), and by Boullée, who not only used the principle

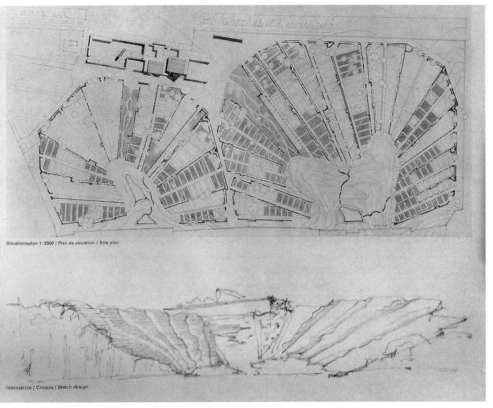

Figure 99. Alvar Aalto, cemetery project, Lyngby, Denmark, 1952. Unbuilt competition design, site plan and sketch.

in his cemetery projects but also focused on this theme in his drawings which show the land dropping suddenly and precipitously at the cemetery's entrance or inner precinct (figs. 9, 54).

It is not simply the difference in level but rather the kinesthetic feeling of walking down into the earth that stirs powerful emotions. Looking at the section through one of Boullée's proposed cemeteries or through Alvar Aalto's unbuilt competition design of 1952 for the cemetery at Lyngby, Denmark (fig. 99), we find an entire world removed from the space of everyday life, where the descent into the earth, while open to the sky, would have placed one in a perfect space of absence. As much as in any temple-like space above the ground, the air around the visitor would seem as filled with the premonition of death and of the dead. Of course, in Aalto's scheme the greenery and the watercourse that would accompany each descending path would lighten the mood.

One of the prime reasons for the effectiveness of Maya Lin's Vietnam Veterans Memorial (Washington, D.C., 1982) is the gentle descent into the V-shaped wedge of space. To this powerful effect of kinesthesia Lin added the even more moving sense of touch, such that with a single finger you can sense the absent life contained within a name, one of the tens of thousands of names, inscribed in the polished black marble wall. It is the reverse of Michelangelo's *The Creation of Adam* on the ceiling of the Sistine Chapel, for this is not a life-giving touch but its opposite, an evocation of a life lost, cut off in its prime, an existence felt through the tip of the finger but impossible to retrieve across the stone barrier. The experience is even more eerie if the reflection of the blue sky with moving clouds passes over the wall at that moment.

The Gaping Tomb

The analog to moving down into the earth is looking down into a cavity that evokes the realm of the dead, of the absent person. This is the subterranean equivalent to the Stonehenge-like funerary temple above the earth. I am not referring to the totally underground crypt but rather to an opening in the floor that reveals a zone of space directly below. In the *Grand Prix* competition of 1755 for a sepulchral chapel, the first and third prizes were awarded to designs that opened the floor to the crypt below and ringed it with a circular columnar temple above. The whole scene was placed under a hemispherical dome. For anybody interested in the space of absence, though, it was Jacques Rousseau's sepulchral chapel that deserved not the third but rather the first prize. Charles Maréchaux's first-prize design made the sarcophagus rise within the central cavity to the height of the viewer.[12] In contrast, Rousseau kept the sarcophagus below the level of the main floor (fig. 100). Nearly a century later in 1841, Ludovico Visconti used the idea of opening the floor to a crypt below with a sarcophagus on display to win the competition for Napoleon's tomb under the dome of Les Invalides.[13] I wonder, though, whether the considerable breadth of the opening in the floor as well as the large size of the sarcophagus detract from the overall effect, which might have been more powerful on a more modest and intimate scale.

Henri Labrouste's entry in this competition (fig. 101) presents a variant on the theme of a realm of death evoked by a cavity in the ground. He envisaged a giant metal shield suspended above the opening where Napoleon's ebony sarcophagus would be glimpsed, as César Daly explained, in "partial darkness." "The underlying idea behind this com-

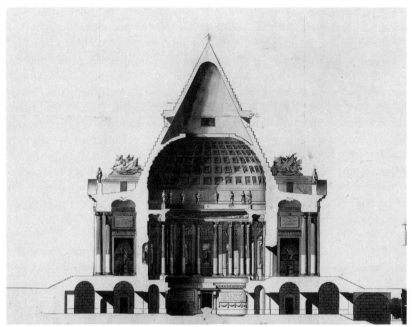

Figure 100. Jacques Rousseau, sepulchral chapel, section. Third Prize, *Grand Prix* of 1755.

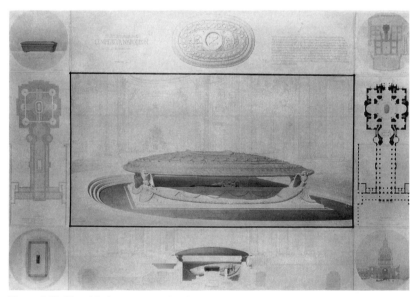

Figure 101. Henri Labrouste, tomb of Napoleon Bonaparte (project), competition entry, 1841.

position," affirmed Daly, "is absolutely new: there is nothing like it in antiquity nor in any other age."[14] Perhaps Daly was correct about the originality of the tomb, but he certainly missed the parallel to the Campidoglio, not only in the gigantic curved surface of the shield but also in the ring of three steps that set off the space of the raised shield from the surrounding floor. If you have ever lingered for a while on the Capitoline Hill and pondered the genius of Michelangelo's composition, as we can imagine that Labrouste might have done during his five-year sojourn at the French Academy in Rome, perhaps you were struck by the way the two rings that step downward toward the oval isolate the central convex surface in a manner that keeps you away, making it seem like a transgression to cross the threshold and trespass on a sacred space contained within. Once this feeling takes hold, then you are prepared to experience the power of the raised oval floor that appears as the omphalos of the world. You are faced with a total world of architecture, and yet the gently curved oval seems to rise from below the surrounding surface you occupy. All the power of the center of that special hill, as a force of nature, is present before your eyes.

Labrouste certainly understood the design of the Capitoline Hill and translated its lessons into his project for Napoleon's tomb. There the curved surface of the immense elevated shield reads as both the raised cover of the tomb and as the earth's surface. As at the Campidoglio, you do not want to cross the line created by the triple ring of steps that descend toward the central point of focus. In the Preface to this book, I recounted that Louis Kahn used to say that the Pantheon was a perfect building except that it had a door. What he meant was that the moment you pass the threshold you immediately occupy the interior space as if you were at the center under the oculus, from which point you fill the surrounding volume with your spatial sense of self. The purported fault in the design was the need to traverse the distance between the door and the center, where you already are in your mind. Labrouste's proposed tomb for Napoleon operates in a similar way. You fill the space from the center of the shield to the outer edge of the triple ring of steps. Yet, unlike at the Pantheon, you cannot physically occupy the center nor should you violate the central zone by attempting to enter it. Here the space of absence requires you to join it only through the eye and the mind. That is why it would have been so effective.[15]

Labrouste's design shows how simple it would be to create a space of absence, for the mere suggestion of the lid of a sarcophagus lifted off the ground changes the qualitative aspect of the space below it and removes it from the realm of the living. Certainly the eminent Italian Ra-

Figure 102. Giuseppe Terragni, monument to Roberto Sarfatti, Col d'Echele, 1935.

tionalist architect Giuseppe Terragni understood this when he tested various schemes for the monument of 1935 to Roberto Sarfatti, killed in World War I. In one variant, an asymmetrical composition of horizontal and vertical planes, a short run of steps carries the visitor to an upper level where two raised horizontal surfaces capture space below, which evokes a realm of death. In another scheme, dating from 1934, Terragni combined an ascent up a centrally placed stair to a platform with a facing inscription, followed by a descent to either side under an enormous, thick, and hovering horizontal roof that weighs down upon the visitor with a force that far exceeds its actual mass and makes the space which it embraces and which it encloses below it a powerful place of communion with the dead soldier.[16] Terragni's executed design (fig. 102), however, used another design typology, in which spirit is sensed to have been captured within an impenetrable mass.

The Impenetrable Mass

In the executed design for the monument to Roberto Sarfatti, Terragni found a powerful sense of containment in the density of a cruciform massing of large stone blocks with a roughly stippled finish. The center of this composition is punctuated with a flight of steps leading to a

Figure 103. Franz Metzner, "Entwurf für einen monumentalen Brunnen" (sketch for a monumental fountain). From *Der Architekt*, 1904.

crowning cubical stone that carries an inscription on its vertical surface. It is as if the spirit of the deceased has been concentrated into the impenetrable stone and most especially into this central block.

Here we encounter the paradoxical opposite of the temple-like space of death with its Stonehenge-like ring that encloses and consecrates the volume of air that it encircles. We have no interior space here but just dense stone, the earth in which the dead are buried, sublimated into the image of noble immutability, the stone cube. Yet there is also a temple here, defined by the arms of the stone walls and treated with reverence by the staircase that controls the approach.

It is uncanny that at the turn of the century the sculptor Franz Metzner conceived a similar project (fig. 103) that was published in 1904 in *Der Architekt*, the avant-garde architectural journal of the Viennese Secession. This design appeared in an article written by Josef Lux entitled "Schöne Brunnen" (Beautiful Fountains). Although labeled "Entwurf für einen monumentalen Brunnen" (Sketch for a monumental fountain), this project was accompanied by analogous fountain designs by Metzner clearly designated as funerary architecture, such as the "Brunnendenkmal für Herrn v. L." and "Entwurf für eine Gruft," which suggest that the "monumental fountain" too was intended as a funerary monument.[17] Decades before Terragni, Metzner discovered the power

185

that thick walls have for creating a space of absence by partially enclosing a zone next to the grave. He also appreciated the force of the ponderous mass of regular ashlar stone arranged in a cross with the center cut out in the form of a stair. In both Terragni's Sarfatti memorial and Metzner's monumental fountain there is a strong sense of enclosure established through the most economical compositional means. At the same time, the concentrated forms of the simple prismatic blocks of stone mark a place as suggestive as any temple-like space. Both monuments, considered in their broader landscape setting of cosmic dimensions, give the impression of a timeless presence firmly anchored in the boundless universe. All of these points can be found in Frank Lloyd Wright's unexecuted project of 1928 for a "blue sky sarcophagus" or "burial terrace" (fig. 104) for one of his favorite clients, Darwin D. Martin. Yet the dominance of the staircase here suggests that it belongs to another typology, what might be called the staircase to heaven.

Staircase to Heaven

In Frank Lloyd Wright's "blue sky sarcophagus" project, a central marble stair rises between two sides of a stepped terrace, each level covered with a giant marble slab with inscription serving as lid to the sepulchral chamber below. On axis and at the head of the stair is a giant rectangular block, which Wright called a "head stone or cenotaph." In a variant to this scheme, to either side of the headstone are low, enclosing walls with shrubs and trees.[18] In the version shown here, instead of these low walls, Wright has placed a horizontal stone slab to either side of the central headstone. These slabs cantilever beyond their recessed supports so that they appear to hover in the air. Wright explained his project to Mr. Martin as follows:

> This is burial facing the open sky—
> a dignified great head-stone common to all.
> There is a nice symbolism in the stepping terraces, it seems—
> This scheme is a compromise between the grave and the mausoleum.
> It may have the better points of both.
> Executed in good material, the inscriptions either well carved
> or inlaid in bronze—the whole could not fail of noble effect.[19]

This unexecuted "burial terrace" is a hybrid between the staircase-within-the-mass-of-the-monument type typified by Terragni's Sarfatti memorial and the staircase-to-the-monument type, which can be found in

THE SKY SARCOPHAGUS FOR D.D. MARTIN FAMILY FRANK LLOYD WRIGHT ARCHITECT

Figure 104. Frank Lloyd Wright, "blue sky sarcophagus" or "burial terrace" for Darwin D. Martin (project), 1928.

Terragni's World War I memorial of 1928–1932 for the small town of Erba Incino (figs. 105, 106), located near the architect's hometown of Como. Of course, the differences here are a matter of degree, since the staircase in all three cases is an integral part of the composition.

At Erba Incino the temple-like space at the top of the steep and lengthy slope consists of two parts: a concave screen wall with arches and square openings, which embraces the lower sacrarium that projects outward with a contrapuntal convex curve. This sacrarium is created by two opposing arcs of a circle that make a shallow interior space with a low, flat ceiling and roof; inside it features a crucifix rising from a broken fragment of a cannon shell placed within a central niche. To either side are thick engaged columns without base or capital. The stone in both temple-like spaces is rusticated and laid up in uneven courses. The cross, with its crown of barbed wire, is similarly plain, unfinished wood. Whereas the concave screen wall captures fragments of the sky, the enclosed sacrarium has an oppressive quality that is reinforced by the low ceiling, the tight framing around the cross, and the articulation of the walls such that the columns seem engaged within their thickness. We

187

Figure 105. Giuseppe Terragni, World War I Memorial, Erba Incino (Como), 1928–1932.

Figure 106. Terragni, World War I Memorial, Erba Incino (Como), detail of the sacrarium.

should not be surprised that Terragni conceived of this space of absence, into which the visitor peers but does not enter, as a bunker.[20] Everything about the architecture contributes to the desired effect.

Terragni also envisaged the long and steep stone staircase as "una scala santa," a holy stair. The "sacrifice" of the arduous ascent was to be a form of homage to those who had made the ultimate sacrifice on their behalf. The inscription on the entablature of the bunker-like sacrarium dedicates the place to the dead, to the living, and to future generations: "per quelli che furono, per quelli che sono, per quelli che saranno." The staircase itself consists of three parts, a semicircular convex spread of steps below a lower retaining wall; a long central flight with landings to reach the terrace with the sacrarium, and finally a flight that curves around both sides of the sacrarium to reach the upper terrace with the open screen wall.

Terragni's war memorial at Erba Incino follows directly the precedent set by the important national competition after World War I for a memorial to the Italian infantryman in which the long flight of steps up a hillside to a sacrarium was a favored theme.[21] In all of these schemes there is an integration of architecture with landscape whose prototypes are the monuments designed in honor of the explorers who perished in the voyage of La Pérouse, projects that date from the 1788 *prix d'émulation*, sponsored by the French Académie Royale d'Architecture, and then from 1830, when part of the debris from the shipwreck was found. In the prizewinning projects by Vien (fig. 81) and Dumannet, as well as in the later design by Labrouste (fig. 107), the space of absence is created both by the amphitheater of rocks or steps as well as by the interior of the cenotaph, which, in the last design, contains the few remnants of the ship, like relics of the explorers' sacrifice. In all three cases, the architecture is fashioned out of the earth in varying degrees of finish, ranging from an amphitheater of living rock to one of smooth ashlar that seems to emerge from the natural setting.

Matter into Spirit

The use of glass to suggest the transubstantiation of matter into spirit presents another approach to the space of absence. In Chapter 1 we encountered the project for a "Field of Rest" dating from the last decade of the eighteenth century by the architect Pierre Giraud, where the covered arcade that defines the perimeter of the crematorium was to be constructed of clear glass columns fashioned somehow out of mortal

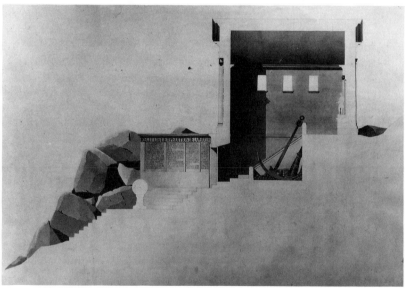

Figure 107. Henri Labrouste, Cenotaph to La Pérouse (project), 1830.

remains in the furnaces hidden within the central pyramid. Giraud's scheme had been inspired by the German chemist Johann Joachim Becker's treatise *Physica subterranea* (1669, 1734, 1768), which popularized the idea of saving the dead from the horror of putrefaction by transformation into a beautiful, imperishable, luminous glass. No less a personage than Jean-Jacques Rousseau had been similarly fascinated by Becker's proposition.[22] Frank Lloyd Wright designed a funerary chapel in which the theme of the faceted crystal, as an image of transubstantiated matter, dominated. This was the unexecuted Rhododendron Chapel with its copper and glass pyramidal roof (figs. 108, 109). This project, dating from 1953, was to be a memorial to Edgar Kaufmann's wife, Liliane, who had died recently. The site was the Kaufmann property near Fallingwater.[23]

Wright's Rhododendron chapel project followed his Chapel of the Soil project of 1937 (figs. 110–112), which also used prismatic mass to suggest the transubstantiation of matter into spirit. The architect conceived this building as a "memorial to the tiller of the ground making the earth a feature of the monument or vice versa."[24] Bruce Brooks Pfeiffer, director of archives at the Frank Lloyd Wright Memorial Foundation, whose long association with Wright dates back to his first year as an apprentice at Taliesin in 1949, reminds us of the importance of this theme to the architect:

> The design for this chapel, intended for southern Wisconsin, was entitled by Mr. Wright "Memorial to the Soil." The particular area for which it was intended was the section of the state in which Mr. Wright was born, where he grew up, and where he built his home, Taliesin. It is a pastoral landscape rich in produce and noted for large dairy farms. . . . Mr. Wright's boyhood was spent on the farm of his uncle James. . . . Mr. Wright's mother, Anna Lloyd Wright, . . . firmly believed that the rigor, the hard work, the training, and the demands that life on a farm would impose upon him would be a necessary counterpart to those other creative and artistic tendencies that were evident so early in his life.[25]

As any reader of Wright's autobiography will vividly remember, and as the often repeated phrase of "adding tired to tired and adding it all over again" conveys, Wright intimately knew the hard work and determination required of the "tillers of the ground."[26] This project is, in many respects, a memorial to Wright's mother, to his uncles and their families on the farm, to his ancestral Lloyd-Jones clan, and to all farmers everywhere, as well as a reaffirmation of the need to marry architecture to

Figure 108. Frank Lloyd Wright, Rhododendron Chapel (project for a memorial to Liliane Kaufmann), Bear Run, Pennsylvania, 1953.

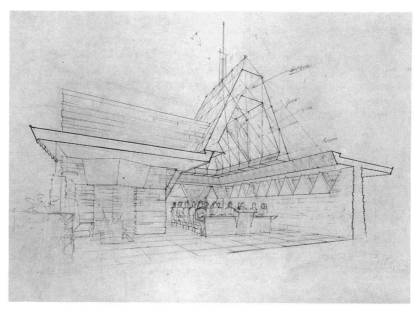

Figure 109. Wright, Rhododendron Chapel (project).

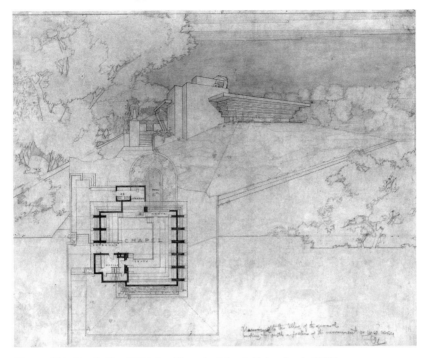

Figure 110. Frank Lloyd Wright, Chapel of the Soil (project), 1937.

the ground both literally and metaphorically and to make it seem as if it has grown out of the earth, a constant theme of Wright's entire career, from the prairie houses onward.

"The plan," explains Pfeiffer,

> is basically a square, chosen as a symbol of integrity and solidarity, oneness and unity. The entrance to the chapel is from the side, passing a large cast concrete sculptural abstraction. Inside, the walls of the chapel are ledges of packed earth, or berms, set into the ground, since the essence of the design was conceived as a memorial to the soil. . . . Part of the berm wall ends in a perimeter garden of flowers at the window level. At the opposite side the wall extends down to floor level with a half-circle curve outside to hold a pool and fountain. Thus, from inside the chapel, a view at eye level on two sides reveals flowers and foliage planted on the berm. The third wall of glass looks into the sunken fountain pool. Everything in the design, its forms, shapes, and human scale, emphasizes the ground, the soil.[27]

Figure 111. Wright, Chapel of the Soil.

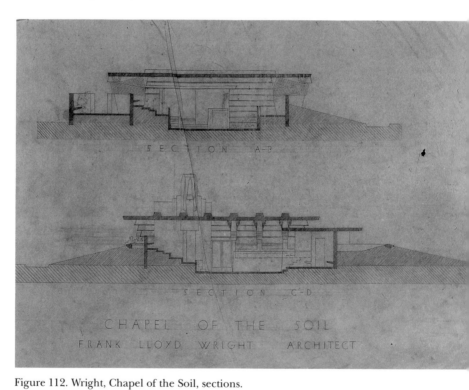

Figure 112. Wright, Chapel of the Soil, sections.

There are several ways to consider this building that is partially buried in the ground. We can read it as a pair of inverted pyramids: a pyramid of earth reaching upward toward a point and an inverted stepped pyramid of glass, a crystalline space of transubstantiated matter rising outward, with the two forms meeting at the level of the worshipers. Body and soul, life and death, life and afterlife, raw matter and finished creation, tilled earth and the fruit of the harvest—all of these paired concepts come to mind in looking at these paired pyramidal images.

Then again, we can see the building as a giant grave, its tombstone lid lifted off the ground and hovering over the interior space like the suspended shield that Labrouste had proposed for Napoleon's tomb. Wright accentuates this roof plan by extending the concrete slab with a dramatically cantilevered overhang. Certainly the feeling inside the half-buried chapel under the hovering roof would be conducive to the impression of an underground cave or grave. As in the giant pyramidal funerary chapels that Boullée imagined a century and a half earlier, the partially buried quality of the forms and the underground location of the chapel are conceived to make one feel in contact with the larger world of nature. This is made particularly forceful in Wright's design of the massive piers, whose decorative patterns bring to mind great upheavals of rock formations over vast periods of time as well as suggesting a crystalline presence of Nature incarnate.

The Hovering Roof

Wright's Chapel of the Soil also uses another typology, what might be called the hovering roof. We know the powerful effect of spirituality, the sense of a special realm removed from merely ordinary space that this can create, thanks to Le Corbusier's pilgrimage chapel of Notre-Dame-du-Haut (1950–1955) at Ronchamp. We must transfer that experience to the earlier project for a sacrarium to the so-called martyrs of the Italian Fascist revolution proposed by the Rationalist architect Giuseppe Samonà in his competition entry of 1934 for the Palazzo del Littorio (fig. 113), the new Fascist party headquarters with Museum of the Revolution. Samonà's entire edifice is conceived as a temple within a temple. The front facade curves outward and the building's mass pulls back to make a temple-like space around the semicircular sacrarium buried below the ground.[28]

This "martyr's sacrarium and votive chapel," as Samonà called it, was to present an austere volume whose mystical sense was highlighted by the narrow slice of light that separated the tall walls from the flat ceiling, which seems to hover above. This, of course, is a modern-day rendition of the ring of sacred light at the base of the dome of Hagia Sophia in Istanbul. Within the semicircular enclosure of Samonà's project, a platinum-covered ring of steel, carried on four cylindrical "columns" of the whitest marble, defined an inner ring of sacrality in which rose the black granite monolith, square in section, with each side carrying a giant inlaid platinum cross. The elevated platinum ring would be like an inner circle of sacred light, whose luminosity would be enhanced by the contrast with the red granite floor, the dark granite of the lower perimeter walls, and by the blackness of the monolith itself.

This sacrarium combined form, space, material, light, shade, and the associative value of color to attain its desired effect. It is an austere variation on the actual sacrarium erected according to the design of the Rationalists Adalberto Libera and Antonio Valente in 1932 for the Exhibition of the Fascist Revolution that celebrated the tenth anniversary of the Fascist March on Rome (fig. 18).

The Architecture of Shadows

Libera and Valente's sacrarium for what were then termed Fascist "martyrs," briefly introduced in Chapter 2, was a circular room in which the magic of luminosity and shadow were the primary compositional elements. In the reigning darkness, a wall of light, elevated on polished metal piers, shone through the repeated visual iteration of PRESENTE! lit from the rear, so as to appear as a luminous irradiation of the so-called martyrs' souls as they answered the roll call. After World War I the Italian army instituted a ritual of calling aloud the names of each dead soldier, after which somebody would call out "*presente*" as if the dead man were still there. Under the elevated, luminous ring in this sacrarium Libera and Valente arranged the pennons of the early *Fasci di Combattimento*, each flag sporting the name of a fallen Fascist. In the center of the room a giant metal cross rose from a circular base bathed in what was described at the time as a "blood red" light. On the top section of the cross another set of luminous letters proclaimed that the dead Fascists honored here had attained immortality by giving their lives for their country. A recording of the Fascist anthem, *Giovinezza,* wafted faintly through the silence of this space.[29]

This Fascist sacrarium used light the way Boullée used darkness, or rather a negative light, in his funerary architecture. One of the most

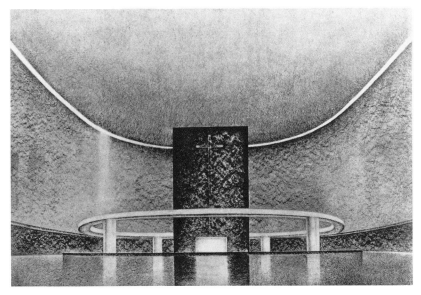

Figure 113. Giuseppe Samonà, Palazzo del Littorio, Rome, 1934. Competition entry. Interior of the buried central "martyr's sacrarium and votive chapel."

moving accounts of an architect's motivation behind creating not merely a funerary architecture but specifically a space of absence can be found in Boullée's manuscript, *Architecture, essai sur l'art:*

> Finding myself in the countryside, I skirted the edge of a woods in the moonlight. My shadow caused by the light excited my attention (certainly, this was not a novelty for me). Because I was in a special mood, the effect of this image of myself prompted a feeling of extreme sadness. The shadows on the ground of the trees made the most profound impression on me. This scene intensified in my imagination. I became aware of all that is most somber in nature. What did I see? The mass of objects detached as black silhouettes against a background of extremely pale light. Nature seemed to offer itself in mourning to my view. Moved by the feelings that I was experiencing, I applied myself, from that moment onward, to translate them in a precise manner into architecture.[30]

That night by the forest Boullée had an uncanny sense about himself, about the silent partner that every mortal carries within, and about the unending nothingness that each person will become. It appeared to him in the form of his shadow and then in the shadows of the entire forest. It was a vision of what the French today are fond of calling "l'Autre," the

197

Other; it was the presence of the self in death, a black silhouette without substance, a being of purely negative space and shadow. To render that experience in architectural form, Boullée developed his three principles of a naked architecture, a buried architecture, and an architecture of shadows, discussed above in Chapter 6. In one design in particular (fig. 82), he presented the image of a ghostly pediment that hovers above its equally ghostly colonnade. This is not merely the absence of light but rather the presence of a dark light, existing in its own right.

Boullée in many ways was the spiritual godfather of all of the designs discussed here, for his account of what he termed "this new genre of architecture" brings us the closest to the meaning of the space of absence. In his funerary designs, we can experience the presence of the departed who simultaneously remain on the other side of the void. We are there ourselves in an eternal space of nothingness, but still part of a larger order. Curiously, because we can occupy that space and feel that condition as an alternative mode of our own condition, not dispersed but rather confined within a negative image of our positive form, it offers a possibility of hope or consolation, or, at the very least, understanding.

NOTES

PREFACE

1. Edward T. Hall, *The Hidden Dimension* (Garden City, N.Y.: Doubleday, 1966), 107–122; and *The Silent Language* (New York: Fawcett, 1966 [1959]), 158–164.
2. Richard A. Etlin, "At the Still Point of the Turning World," *Connections* ([Cambridge, Mass.: Harvard Graduate School of Design], 1971), [21–31].
3. Mircea Eliade, *The Sacred and the Profane: The Nature of Religion,* tr. Willard R. Trask (New York: Harper & Row, 1959), esp. 20–65; Joseph Rykwert, *The Idea of a Town: The Anthropology of Urban Form in Rome, Italy and the Ancient World* (Princeton: Princeton University Press, 1976).
4. Claude Lévi-Strauss, *Structural Anthropology,* tr. Claire Jacobson and Brooke Grundfest Schoepf (New York: Anchor Books, 1967 [1963]), 128–160.

CHAPTER ONE

1. On this theme, see Raymond Trousson, "Introduction," in Louis-Sébastien Mercier, *L'An deux mille quatre cent quarante: Rêve s'il en fut jamais,* ed. R. Trousson (Bordeaux: Editions Ducros, 1971), 57–59. I take the word "uchronia" from Trousson: "de l'utopie à l'uchronie."
2. Guillaume Poncet de la Grave, *Projet des embellissements de la ville et faubourgs de Paris,* 2 vols. (Paris, 1756). Mercier's book was reprinted numerous times, sometimes with additions, between 1771 and 1799.
3. Kevin Lynch, *The Image of the City* (Cambridge, Mass.: MIT Press, 1960).
4. Donald J. Olsen, *The City as a Work of Art: London, Paris, Vienna* (New Haven: Yale University Press, 1986), 3–5.
5. Louis Combes, "Dissertation sur l'architecture, comparée aux productions de la nature, à la poésie et aux beaux-arts." Bibliothèque Municipale de Bordeaux, MS. 48, no. 4, fol. 3.
6. François-Joseph Belanger, *Monument d'utilité publique, décrété par sa Majesté Napoléon 1er, . . . construction d'une halle aux vins, aux eaux-de-vie et autres liquides à Paris* (Paris, [1808]), 1–2.
7. Abbé Marc-Antoine Laugier, *Essai sur l'architecture,* rev. ed. (Paris, 1755), 214.
8. Poncet de la Grave, *Projet,* 1:77–79.
9. Voltaire, "Babouc ou le monde comme il va," in *Recueil des pièces en vers et en prose, par l'auteur de la tragédie de Sémiramis* (Amsterdam, 1750), 98.

10. Poncet de la Grave, *Projet*, 1:75.

11. On Blondel, see Wolfgang Herrmann, "François Blondel," *Macmillan Encyclopedia of Architects* (New York, 1982), 1:219; Christian Dupavillon and Francis Lacloche, *Le Triomphe des Arcs* (Paris: Gallimard, 1989), 51.

12. Jacques-Guillaume Legrand and Charles-Paul Landon, *Description de Paris et de ses édifices, avec un précis historique et des observations sur le caractère de leur architecture . . .* (Paris, 1809), 2:55–56.

13. Claude-Nicolas Ledoux, *L'Architecture considérée sous le rapport des moeurs, de la législation et de l'art* (Paris, 1804), 1:16, 163, 176, 187.

14. Other "propylaea" included the paired "propilei neoclassici" of Porta Nuova (1837) in Bergamo and Leo von Klenze's Propyläen (1846–1860) in Munich. The characterization of the Bergamo entrance pavilions is by Walter Barbero, *Bergamo* (Milan: Electa, 1985), 175–176.

15. James Dao, "Amtrak's Envious Look at Post Office," *New York Times*, May 13, 1992, B1.

16. L.-P. Bachaumont, *Essai sur la peinture, la sculpture et l'architecture* (n.p., 1752), 55; Laugier, *Essai*, 211–212; Jean-Nicolas-Louis Durand, *Précis des leçons d'architecture données à l'Ecole Polytechnique* (Paris, year XIII, 1805), 2:21–22.

17. Laugier, *Essai*, 212, 219. For partial illustrations of the winning entries of the 1738 competition, see Jean-Marie Pérouse de Montclos, *"Les Prix de Rome" concours de l'Académie Royale d'Architecture au XVIIIᵉ siècle* (Paris: Berger-Levrault and Ecole Nationale Supérieure des Beaux-Arts, 1984), 43–44.

18. On the successive development of the *grande croisée* through the First Empire, the Second Republic, and, finally, the Second Empire, see David H. Pinkney, *Napoleon III and the Rebuilding of Paris* (Princeton: Princeton University Press, 1972 [1958]), 56–58; Olsen, *The City*, 46–47.

19. See Yvan Christ, *Paris des utopies*, rev. ed. (Paris: Balland, 1977), 120–121; Dupavillon and Lacloche, *Le Triomphe*, 1.

20. Pierre Chaussard, *Monuments de l'héroisme français; nécessité de ramener à un plan unique, et de coordiner à ceux déjà existents, les monuments qu'on propose d'élever à Paris sur l'étendue comprise entre les Tuileries et l'Etoile . . .* ([Paris, year X]).

21. Charles de Wailly, "Projet général relatif aux Louvre, aux palais et jardins des Thuilleries, place Louis XV, et Champs Elisées." Bibliothèque Nationale, MS. NAF 2479, fol. 441.

22. For a survey of the *grand projets*, see Yves Dauge, ed., *Paris 1979–1989*, tr. Bert McClure (New York: Rizzoli, 1988).

23. Laugier, *Essai*, 213.

24. Charles Villette, *Lettres choisies de Charles Villette, sur les principaux évènements de la Révolution* (Paris, 1792), 149–150.

25. S. Granet, *La Place de la Concorde* (Paris, 1963), 10.

26. Jean-Louis Viel de Saint-Maux, *Lettres sur l'architecture des anciens et celles des modernes dans lesquelles se trouve développé le génie symbolique qui présida aux monuments de l'antiquité* (Paris, 1787), letter vii.

27. See Gaston Bardet, *Paris: Naissance et méconnaissance de l'urbanisme* (Paris: Editions S.A.B.R.I., 1951), 284.

28. For an illustration of Bailleul's urban square, see Pérouse de Montclos, "*Les Prix de Rome*," 40.

29. Jean-François Sobry, *De l'Architecture* (Amsterdam and Paris, 1776), 160.

30. For an illustration of Combes's square, see Pérouse de Montclos, "*Les Prix de Rome*," 173.

31. Jacques-François Blondel, *Cours d'architecture . . . contenant les leçons données en 1750 et les années suivantes . . .* , 9 vols. (Paris, 1771–1777), 1:423–424, 2:309.

32. Etienne-Louis Boullée, *Architecture, essai sur l'art*, ed. Jean-Marie Pérouse de Montclos (Paris: Hermann, 1968), 85 (fol. 90v).

33. Alain-Charles Gruber, *Les grandes Fêtes et leurs décors à l'époque de Louis XVI* (Geneva: Librairie Droz, 1972), xii.

34. This discussion of the space of hygiene has been adapted from Richard A. Etlin, "L'Air dans l'urbanisme des Lumières," *Dix-Huitième Siècle* no. 9 (1977), 123–134.

35. Jacques Dehorne, *Mémoire sur quelques objets qui intéressent plus particulièrement la salubrité de la ville de Paris* (Paris, 1788), 1.

36. Abbé Marc-Antoine Laugier, *Observations sur l'architecture* (The Hague and Paris, 1765), 168.

37. On domestic sanitation, see Pierre Saddy, "Le Cycle des immondices," *Dix-Huitième Siècle* no. 9 (1977), 206–208; on mechanical ventilation, see Richard A. Etlin, *The Architecture of Death: The Transformation of the Cemetery in Eighteenth-Century Paris* (Cambridge, Mass.: MIT Press, 1984), 27.

38. Laugier, *Observations,* 168.

39. Olivier, *Sépultures des anciens où l'on démontre qu'elles étaient hors des villes . . .* (Marseille, 1771), xi.

40. Laugier, *Observations,* 169–171.

41. Mathieu Géraud, *Essai sur la suppression des fosses d'aisances, et de toutes espèces de voiries . . .* (Amsterdam and Paris, 1786), 94–95, 160–161.

42. Nicolas Goulet, *Observations sur les embellissements de Paris et sur les monuments qui s'y construisent* (Paris, 1808), 25–27.

43. In the nineteenth century, public parks were seen as serving two main purposes—to prompt better dress, manners, and morality in the working classes, and to promote public health. Commenting on these matters, Pinkney, in *Napoleon III,* 94, observes: "The Emperor instructed Haussmann to use every opportunity that the transformation of Paris might present to create small parks . . . , for he maintained that they would benefit the public health and . . . gradually effect a revolution in working class morality. Haussmann did not share the latter hope, but he was convinced of the value of parks to public health."

44. Th. Weyl and M. M. Weinberg, *Histoire de l'hygiène sociale,* tr. Robert André (Paris, 1910), 64.

45. See Pinkney, *Napoleon III,* chap. 6.

46. See, for example, Marie-Joseph Peyre, *Oeuvres d'architecture* (Paris, 1765), 25; P.-J. Le Moine, *Le Parallèle du Paris de la république, avec le Paris des rois* ([Paris], year II), 20. For illustrations of street drainage and of shooting fountains, see Etlin, *The Architecture of Death,* 28–29.

47. Jean-Jacques Menuret de Chambaud, *Essais sur l'histoire médico-topographique de Paris . . .* (Paris, 1786), 28.

48. Pierre Patte, *Mémoires sur les objets les plus importants de l'architecture* (Paris, 1769), 8.

49. Menuret de Chambaud, *Essais,* 84.

50. See Mouillefarine le fils, "Mémoire présenté à l'Assemblée Nationale le 9 avril 1790," Archives Nationales, N IV Seine 87; Jean-Charles Désessartz, "Une analyse de la topographie médicale du canton de Paris," *Moniteur Universel* (July 4, 1807); Jacques-Antoine Dulaure, *Réclamation d'un citoyen, contre la nouvelle enceinte de Paris, élévée par les Fermiers-Généraux* (n.p., 1787), 13.

51. Dulaure, *Réclamation,* 24.

52. On this theme, see Helen Rosenau, *Social Purpose in Architecture: Paris and London Compared, 1760–1800* (London: Studio Vista, 1970), 51–96; Bruno Fortier, "La Politique de l'espace parisien à la fin de l'ancien régime," in Fortier et al., *La Politique de l'espace parisien (à la fin de l'ancien régime)* (Paris: CORDA, 1975), 73–111; Etlin, "L'Air," 128–133, and *The Architecture of Death,* esp. chaps. 1–2; Anthony Vidler, "Confinement and Cure: Reforming the Hospital, 1770–1789," in *The Writing of the Walls: Architectural Theory in the Late Enlightenment* (Princeton: Princeton Architectural Press, 1987), 51–69.

53. On associationism, see George L. Hersey, *High Victorian Gothic: A Study in Associationism* (Baltimore: Johns Hopkins University Press, 1972).

54. Olsen, *The City,* 283.

55. Vitruvius, *The Ten Books of Architecture,* tr. Morris Hicky Morgan (New York: Dover, 1960 [1914]), 14–15 (I.2.v). Quatremère de Quincy relates Vitruvius's discussion of "propriety" in three articles of his *Encyclopédie méthodique: Architecture* (1788, 1801) and *Dictionnaire historique d'architecture* (1832): "Bienséance," "Caractère," and "Convenance."

56. Blondel, *Cours d'architecture,* 1:410.

57. For Blondel's application of this principle in his own designs, see Chap. 5 below, "The System of the Home."

58. Emil Kaufmann, *Von Ledoux bis Le Corbusier, Ursprung und Entwicklung der autonomen Architektur* (Vienna and Leipzig: Dr. R. Passer, 1934). One need not accept all of the philosophical and social implications of the concept of "autonomy" as argued by Kaufmann to recognize the usefulness of this word for describing Ledoux's architecture. Moreover, my own characterization of the Renaissance and Baroque periods, as well as of Ledoux's compositional strategies, differs in part from Kaufmann's.

59. Boullée, *Architecture,* 73 (fol. 84).

60. Ibid., 35 (fols. 54–54v).

61. *Procès-verbal de la première séance du Jury des Arts, nommé par la Convention Nationale, et assemblé dans une des salles du muséum, en vertu des décrets des 9 et 25 jours de Brumaire, an II, . . . pour juger les ouvrages de peinture, sculpture et architecture mis au concours pour obtenir le prix* (Paris, year II), 56. Archives Nationales, AD VIII, 13.

62. Boullée, *Architecture,* 113 (fol. 107v).

63. For illustrations of Boullée's city hall project, see Jean-Marie Pérouse de Montclos, *Etienne-Louis Boullée, 1728–1799: De l'Architecture classique à l'architecture révolutionnaire* (Paris: Arts et Métiers Graphiques, 1969), plates 110–112.

64. [Léon Vaudoyer], "Etudes d'architecture en France, ou notions relatives à l'âge et au style des monuments élevés à différentes époques de notre histoire. Suite. Règne de Louis XVI," *Le Magasin Pittoresque* 20 (1852), 388. Although scholars have not found an earlier source for this term, it should be noted that in using it Vaudoyer wrote, "Ledoux was a partisan of what has since been called *l'architecture parlante*." I am following Vidler in assigning this article to the architect Léon Vaudoyer. See Anthony Vidler, *Claude-Nicolas Ledoux: Architecture and Social Reform at the End of the Ancien Régime* (Cambridge, Mass.: MIT Press, 1990), ix.

65. Boullée, *Architecture*, 127 (fol. 119v): "Le monument . . . qui renferme toutes les connaissances acquises."

66. Ibid., 137–139 (fols. 127–128).

67. Werner Szambien has commented on the sacred quality of the central space in Durand's museum design in *Jean-Nicolas-Louis Durand, 1760–1834: De l'Imitation à la norme* (Paris: Picard, 1984), 223.

68. Voltaire, *Lettres philosophiques*, ed. René Pomeau (Paris: Garnier-Flammarion, 1964 [1734]), 149.

69. June Hargrove, "Shaping the National Image: The Cult of Statues to Great Men in the Third Republic," in Richard A. Etlin, ed., *Nationalism in the Visual Arts*, Studies in the History of Art, vol. 29 (Washington, D.C.: National Gallery of Art, 1991), 49.

70. A.-R. Mopinot de la Chapotte, *Proposition d'un monument à élever dans la capitale de la France, pour transmettre aux races futures l'époque de l'heureuse révolution qui l'a revivifiée sous le règne de Louis XVI* (Paris, 1790), 14–15.

71. Pierre Patte, *Monumens érigés en France à la gloire de Louis XV . . .* (Paris, 1765), 212.

72. D.-V. Ramel, *Discours par forme de motion d'ordre, prononcé au Conseil des Cinq-Cents, . . . sur la construction d'une galerie pour le muséum, parallèle à celle du Louvre . . .* , Corps législatif, séance du 8 pluviôse, an 4 (Paris, year IV), 10.

73. Laugier, *Observations*, 233.

74. Maille Dussausoy, *Le Citoyen désintéressé, ou diverses idées patriotiques, concernant quelques établissements et embellissements utiles à la ville de Paris . . .* (Paris, 1767), 1:145–146.

75. Francis H. Dowley, "D'Angiviller's *Grands Hommes* and the Significant Moment," *Art Bulletin* 39 (December, 1957), 259–277. D'Angiviller was also the directeur général des Bâtiments.

76. For a further discussion of this building, see Chaps. 2, 4, 6 below.

77. Abbé Charles-Gabriel Porée, *Observations sur les sépultures dans les églises, et réflexions sur les Lettres écrites à ce sujet* (Caen, 1749), 26.

78. [Guillaume-François-Roger Molé], *Lettre de M. M*** à M. J***, sur les moyens de transférer les cimetières hors l'enceinte des villes* (n.p., [1776]), 22.

79. *Procès-verbaux de l'Académie Royale d'Architecture,* ed. Henri Lemonnier, 10 vols. (Paris, 1911–1929), 7:228.

80. Louis-Jean Desprez, *Oeuvres,* Bibliothèque Nationale, Estampes Ha 52. For illustrations, see Etlin, *The Architecture of Death,* 44–45.

81. For a further discussion of this theme, see Etlin, *The Architecture of Death,* Chap. 2.

82. *Programme pour les Grands prix d'architecture de l'an 7, donné par l'Institut.* Archives de l'Institut de France, Réserve 6B10.

83. For illustrations, see Etlin, *The Architecture of Death,* 289.

84. A.-R. Mopinot de la Chapotte, *Eloge historique de Pigalle, . . . suivie d'un mémoire sur la sculpture in France . . .* (London and Paris, 1765), 21.

85. Pierre-Louis Roederer, *Des Institutions funéraires convenables à une république qui permet tous les cultes, et n'en adopte aucun; mémoire lu . . . dans la séance publique de l'Institut national . . . le 15 messidor, l'an 4* (Paris, year IV), 9–11.

86. Pierre Giraud, *Essai sur les sépultures . . . composé en l'an 4, et déposé, au Département de la Seine, le 11 Nivôse, an 7 . . .* (Paris, [year VII]), 5–8, 11–12, and *Les Tombeaux, ou essai sur les sépultures . . .* (Paris, year IX, 1801), 18, 21–22. For an illustration, see Etlin, *The Architecture of Death,* 257.

87. See Etlin, *The Architecture of Death,* 256, 258.

88. Wilbur Fisk, *Travels in Europe,* 4th ed. (New York, 1838), 40.

CHAPTER TWO

1. In *The Idea of the Holy,* tr. John W. Harvey (Oxford and London: Oxford University Press, 1923 [1917]), 6–7, Rudolf Otto explains the word "numinous" " . . . I adopt a word coined from the Latin *numen. Omen* has given us 'ominous,' and there is no reason why from *numen* we should not similarly form a word 'numinous.' "

2. Readers interested in pursuing further the subject of architecture for the French Revolution should consult James A. Leith's magisterial *Space and Revolution: Projects for Monuments, Squares, and Public Buildings in France, 1789–1799* (Montreal and Kingston: McGill-Queen's University Press, 1991), as well as Mona Ozouf, "Le Cortège et la ville: Les itinéraires parisiens des fêtes révolutionnaires," *Annales Économies Sociétés Civilisations* (September–October 1971), 889–916, and *La Fête Révolutionnaire 1789–1799* (Paris: Gallimard, 1976), 149–187; Jean-Marie Pérouse de Montclos, "L'Architecture à l'antique et la Révolution," *Art de France* (1964), 325–327; Daniel Rabreau, "Architecture et fêtes dans la nouvelle Rome: Notes sur l'esthétique urbain de la fin de l'ancien régime et de la Révolution. Le Colisée. Le Cirque. L'Amphithéâtre," in Jean Ehrard and Paul Viallaneix, eds., *Les Fêtes de la Révolution: Colloque de Clermont-Ferrand (juin 1974),* Bibliothèque d'Histoire Révolutionnaire, 3ᵉ série, no. 17 (Paris: Société des Etudes Robespierristes, 1977), 355–375; James A. Leith, "Projects for a Revolutionary Center: Verly's Plans for Lille," *Daidalos,* no. 7, March 15, 1983, 56–63; Werner Szambien, "Le Style républican," *Monuments Historiques,* no. 144 (April–May 1986), 39–43; Annie Jacques and Jean-Pierre Mouilleseaux, *Les Architectes de la liberté*

(Paris: Gallimard, 1988); Annie Jacques and Jean-Pierre Mouilleseaux, eds., *Les Architectes de la liberté, 1789–1799,* exhibition catalog, Ecole Nationale Supérieure des Beaux-Arts, Paris, October 4, 1989–January 7, 1990 (Paris, 1989); Anthony Vidler, "Researching Revolutionary Architecture," *Journal of Architectural Education* 44 (August 1991), 206–210.

3. This was one of two plans by Perrault. While reporting that Perrault was less pleased with the design of the individual elements in this project than in a later design, Jacques-François Blondel nonetheless praised the earlier plan for its skillful resolution of the skewed axis: " . . . et si la forme générale des cours n'y est pas plus heureuse, du moins l'obliquité de l'axe des deux Palais du Louvre et des Tuileries y est masquée très ingénieusement." The round form here is an oval amphitheater. Jacques-François Blondel, *Architecture françoise, ou recueil des plans, élévations, coupes et profils des . . . édifices les plus considérables de Paris . . .* (Paris, 1756), 4:14. For the other plan, see 4:9–13, and plate 1. See Christ, *Paris des utopies,* 8; and Szambien, *Jean-Nicolas-Louis Durand, 1760–1834,* 110 and fig. 167 for a historical summary of projects to complete the Louvre depicted on an engraving of 1811. See also Wolfgang Herrmann, *The Theory of Claude Perrault* (London: A. Zwemmer Ltd., 1973), 25.

4. Bernard Poyet, "Plan général des terreins et bâtimens situés entre la Rivière et la Rue St. Honoré, depuis le Pont Neuf jusqu'aux Champs-Elisées, avec un projet . . . pour réunir dans la même enceinte le Palais de nos Rois, celui de l'Assemblée Nationale, le Louvre dont on feroit l'Hôtel-de-Ville et la place de Louis XVI, afin de réunir les pouvoirs civile et militaire . . . présenté et dédié à la Commune de Paris le 21 mars 1790."

5. H. Grégoire, *Système de dénominations topographiques pour les places, rues, quais, etc. de toutes les communes de la République* (Paris, [year II, 1794]), 13–14. See also P. Grunebaum-Ballin, "Le 'Système de dénominations topographiques pour les rues, places et quais des communes de la République du citoyen Grégoire' et l'application de ce système aux XIX^c et XX^c siècles," *La Vie Urbaine* (1959), 251–256.

6. B. Barère, *Rapport fait au nom du Comité de Salut Public, sur la suite des événements du siège d'Ypres, et sur les monuments nationaux environnans Paris. Convention Nationale, séance du 13 messidor l'an 2* (Paris [1794]), 3.

7. "Extrait des registres des délibérations de l'Administration centrale du Département de la Seine, du 22 vendémiaire, an 7." Archives de la Seine, DL^1.2.

8. Mouillefarine le fils, "Carte générale des environs de la Bastille . . . afin d'en former des allignements à une place royale nationale de la Liberté sur les ruines de la Bastille et à un pont dit de la Réunion," along with accompanying "Mémoire." Archives Nationales, N IV Seine 87. For an illustration of the obelisk, see Richard A. Etlin, "Architecture and the Festival of Federation, Paris, 1790," *Architectural History* 18 (1975), fig. 18b. For other illustrations of this project, see Leith, *Space and Revolution,* 88–90.

9. Robert Darnton, "What Was Revolutionary about the French Revolution?" *New York Review of Books* 35, January 19, 1989, 4.

10. *Rapport de l'Administration des Travaux Publics, sur les cimetières; lu au Conseil-Général par le Citoyen Avril* ([Paris, 21 Nivôse, year II, January 10, 1794]), 12, 18.

11. For illustrations of the cemetery projects by Grandjean de Montigny and Détournelle, see Etlin, *The Architecture of Death,* 289, 296–298.

12. Yvan Christ, "Ledoux et son temps," in *L'Oeuvre et les rêves de Claude-Nicolas Ledoux* (n.p.: Editions du Chêne, 1971 [1961]), 23–24. See also Allan Braham, *The Architecture of the French Enlightenment* (Berkeley and Los Angeles: University of California Press, 1980), 196; and Anthony Vidler, *Claude-Nicolas Ledoux,* 209–235.

13. For contemporary illustrations, see Jacques and Mouilleseaux, *Les Architectes de la liberté,* 24–25.

14. Charles Villette, letter of May 1, 1791, in *Lettres choisies de Charles Villette, sur les principaux événements de la Révolution* (Paris, 1792), 122–124.

15. B. G. E. Lacépède, "Lettre relative aux établissemens publics destinés à renfermer des animaux vivants, et connus sous le nom de ménageries," *La Décade philosophique, littéraire, et politique,* 20 Frimaire, year IV [December 11, 1795], 451–462.

16. Arrêté du Départment de la Seine, 28 Germinal, year VII, Archives de la Seine, DZ^6 carton 3.

17. Maurice Dommanget, "La Déchristianisation à Beauvais: Les Sacrements civiques," *Annales révolutionnaires* 11 (1919), 187: "'jardin de l'Egalité.'"

18. See Etlin, *The Architecture of Death,* 236, 238.

19. *Rapport de l'Administration des Travaux Publics, sur les cimetières,* (21 Nivôse, year II, January 10, 1794), 5–6, 8.

20. C. P. Le Sueur, "Idées pour la propreté de Paris" (year II). Archives Nationales, F^{14} 187^B. For the hygienic reform movement, see Richard A. Etlin, "L'Air dans l'urbanisme des Lumières," 123–134, and *The Architecture of Death,* 12–39.

21. Giraud, *Place patriotique avec un palais pour la permanence de l'auguste Assemblée Nationale, et la description d'une fête annuelle pour le renouvellement du serment civique . . .* (Paris, 1790), 2–3.

22. F. Lanthenas, *De l'Influence de la liberté sur la santé, la morale, et le bonheur* (Paris, 1792), 7–8.

23. Félix-Marie Faulcon, *Anniversaire, ou journal de ce qui s'est passé pendant la semaine de la Confédération* (Paris, 1790), 15–16. See also Alexandre-Théodore Brongniart's project for a square at the site of the Bastille where "un monument simple" would be erected. Bibliothèque Nationale, MS. NAF 3456. A poster printed under the signature of Pierre Benezech, the minister of the interior, in Floréal, year IV (Spring 1796), addressed to artists ("Appel aux artistes"), called for "monuments to genius and liberty" that should be "simples et majestueux." Bibliothèque Nationale, Fol. Lb^{42}.2732.

24. Sobre le jeune, *Projet d'un monument à élever dans le Champ de la Fédération* (n.p., n.d.); N.-M. Gatteaux, *Projet d'un monument pour consacrer la Révolution.*

Archives Nationales, C 120, or Bibliothèque Nationale, Estampes Ha 66b for the printed booklet.

25. *Songe patriotique, ou le monument et la fête* (Paris, 1790), 7, 14, 19.

26. Louis Combes, "Projet d'un palais de la nation dédié à l'Assemblée Nationale," which accompanies Combes's "Plan général d'une place et d'un palais de la nation pour la tenue de l'Assemblée Nationale, projettés sur l'emplacement de la Bastille: A Bordeaux le 6 novembre 1789." Archives Nationales, N IV Seine 87.

27. Faulcon, *Anniversaire,* 35.

28. F. L. Aubrey, *Projet d'un monument à la gloire des défenseurs de la patrie* (Douai, 12 Floréal, year V, [1797]). Archives Nationales, AD XIII, 13.

29. See Etlin, "Architecture and the Festival of Federation, Paris, 1790," *Architectural History* 18 (1975), 30–31.

30. Bernard Poyet, *Idées générales par le sieur Poyet, architecte du roi et la ville, sur le projet de la fête du 14 juillet . . .* (Paris, June 16, 1790), 5–6.

31. For a description and illustrations, see *Les Fêtes de la Révolution,* exhibition catalog, Musée Bargoin, Clermont-Ferrand, June 15–September 15, 1974 (Clermont-Ferrand, [1974]), 28–29, figs. 39–40.

32. Ferdinand Boyer, "Projets de salles pour les assemblées révolutionnaires à Paris (1789–1792)," *Bulletin de la Société de l'Histoire de l'Art français* (1933), 170–183; Armand-Guy Kersaint, *Discours sur les monuments publics, prononcé le 15 décembre 1791* (Paris, 1792), 64 (for the project by Molinos and Legrand). For illustrations, see also Leith, *Space and Revolution,* chap. 4.

33. Combes, "Projet d'un palais de la nation." For an illustration, see Jacques and Mouilleseaux, *Les Architectes de la liberté,* 49.

34. As reported in Jean-Marie Pérouse de Montclos, *Etienne-Louis Boullée, 1728–1799,* 182. For Boullée's own account, see Etienne-Louis Boullée, *Architecture, essai sur l'art,* 115.

35. Robert Rosenblum, *Transformations in Late Eighteenth Century Art* (Princeton: Princeton University Press, 1969), 127.

36. See Le Corbusier and Pierre Jeanneret, *Oeuvre complète 1910–1929,* 9th ed. (Zurich: Les Editions d'Architecture, 1967), 89–90.

37. Antoine-Chrysostôme Quatremère de Quincy, *Rapport sur l'édifice dit de Sainte-Geneviève, fait au directoire du Département de Paris* (Paris, 1791), 28, and *Rapport fait au directoire du Département de Paris, le 13 novembre 1792, . . . sur l'état actuel du Panthéon français . . .* (Paris, n.d.), 11–13.

38. Quatremère de Quincy, *Rapport sur Sainte-Geneviève,* 33. See also his *Rapport sur l'état actuel du Panthéon français,* 18–19.

39. Jean-Charles Laveaux, "Sur les Sépultures des grands hommes, et celles des autres citoyens," *Journal de la Montagne,* July 19, 1793.

40. Louis-Marie de La Revellière-Lépeaux, *Du Panthéon et d'un théâtre national* (Paris, frimaire, year VI), 7.

41. Richard A. Etlin, *Modernism in Italian Architecture, 1890–1940* (Cambridge, Mass.: MIT Press, 1991), 439–447.

42. Thomas L. Schumacher, *Surface and Symbol: Giuseppe Terragni and the Architecture of Italian Rationalism* (New York: Princeton Architectural Press, 1991), 116.

43. For a description of this monument, see Samir al-Khalil [Kanan Makiya], *The Monument: Art, Vulgarity and Responsibility in Iraq* (Berkeley: University of California Press, 1991), 2, 4.

44. Ibid., 3–4. Makiya points out that the Arc de Triomphe rises sixteen meters whereas the Victory Arch reaches forty. The monument is actually double, that is, a pair of arches "marking the two entrances of a vast new parade-ground in central Baghdad."

45. On Nazi Germany, see Alex Scobie, *Hitler's State Architecture: The Impact of Classical Antiquity,* College Art Association Monograph 45 (University Park: Pennsylvania State University Press, 1990), 75–87.

46. Etlin, *Modernism,* 399, 481–492, 501–504.

47. For the comparison between these Roman sites, see Riccardo Mariani, *E 42: Un progetto per l'"Ordine Nuovo"* (Milan: Edizione di Comunità, 1987), 51 (with illus.).

48. Scobie, *Hitler's State Architecture,* 56–59, 64.

49. As quoted in ibid., 69.

50. Ibid.

51. Ibid., 72–73.

CHAPTER THREE

1. Blondel, *Cours d'architecture . . . ,* 1:423, 2:309.

2. "L'Examen de tous les projets de construction et de réparations qui sont adressés au Ministre de l'Intérieur relativement aux bâtiments civils . . . " Archives Nationales, Paris, F¹³.201. This report is concerned with buildings from all of France.

3. David Van Zanten, "Architectural Composition at the Ecole des Beaux-Arts from Charles Percier to Charles Garnier," in Arthur Drexler, ed., *The Architecture of the Ecole des Beaux-Arts* (New York: Museum of Modern Art, 1977), 160.

4. The characterization is from Donald Drew Egbert, *The Beaux-Arts Tradition in French Architecture Illustrated by the Grands Prix de Rome,* ed. David Van Zanten (Princeton: Princeton University Press, 1980), 48.

5. René Descartes, *Discours de la méthode,* ed. Maurice Dorolle (Paris: Librairie Larousse, 1935 [1637]), 27.

6. Jean-Nicolas-Louis Durand, *Partie graphique des cours d'architecture faits à l'Ecole Royale Polytechnique depuis sa réorganization: Précédée d'un sommaire des leçons relatives à ce nouveau travail* (Paris, 1821), 1–2.

7. In *Jean-Nicolas-Louis Durand,* 67, Werner Szambien explains that before 1811 Durand's students rarely used graph paper. By the end of the 1820s the procedure of designing buildings on graph paper had become standard at the Ecole Polytechnique.

8. These last two matters are discussed below in Chap. 4.

9. J.-N.-L. Durand, *Précis des leçons d'architecture données à l'Ecole Polytechnique* (Paris, 1802–1805), 1:4–24, 2:4–7. I have translated *la convenance* and *convenable* as "function" and "functional."

10. Werner Szambien, "Durand and the Continuity of Tradition," in Robin Middleton, ed., *The Beaux-Arts and Nineteenth-Century French Architecture* (Cambridge, Mass.: MIT Press, 1982), 18–33; Szambien, *Durand*, 94–95, fig. 106. Durand proceeded in the same way in his historical studies. In an announcement for his *Recueil et parallèle des édifices de tout genre* (1799–1801), Durand explained that he had taken the liberty to "simplify" several of the historical buildings depicted there, not to correct them but rather to clarify the main idea (Durand, *Précis,* 2:101).

11. Next to the section of Gay's design Cret wrote: "Cénotaphe à Newton—etoiles découpées dans la voûte." Paul Philippe Cret Archives, conserved in the Architectural Archives of the University of Pennsylvania (AAUP).

12. Paul Cret, "The Ecole des Beaux Arts: What Its Architectural Teaching Means," *Architectural Record* 23 (May 1908), 369.

13. For an illustration of the former, see Carol McMichael, *Paul Cret at Texas: Architectural Drawing and the Image of the University in the 1930s,* exhibition catalog, Archer M. Huntington Art Gallery, University of Texas at Austin, March 31–May 22, 1983 (Austin, 1983), 165 (fig. 90); for the latter, see AAUP, Paul Philippe Cret, 3.44 (left sheet).

14. See AAUP, Paul Philippe Cret, 17.2 (left sheet).

15. Elizabeth Grossman, "Paul Cret and the Pan American Union Competition," *Modulus/The University of Virginia School of Architecture Review* (1982), 31. Paul Cret's role as the designer of this building is clearly established in the letter of April 15, 1907, from Albert Kelsey to Cret, in which Kelsey confirms the subject matter of their talk that morning during which they agreed to associate together for this competition. Kelsey wrote, "It is agreed that you will make all studies up to the Watman paper stage, and that this office shall make the finished drawings with such occasional assistance as you may deem wise and necessary on your part." The continuing nature of Cret's role as the principal architect continued after the competition had been won and as the design was refined. This is made clear in Kelsey's letter of July 18, 1907, in which he assured Cret that all changes being made during his absence in France are consistent with his original prize-winning design and that furthermore, when Cret returns, there would be opportunity for him to amend and further polish the scheme: "Do not allow the building to worry you. The work is progressing nicely, and under the continued criticisms of [the jurors, Charles Follen] McKim and [Henry] Hornbostel, I am evolving a good thing. The design adheres closely to your original scheme though certain changes have been made. . . . I shall arrange to push the work as rapidly as possible, but will leave certain loop-holes open, so that you can make any corrections you desire after your return. . . . While it will be natural for you to be uneasy in entrusting the preparation of these drawings so largely to me, I can assure you on the other hand that I shall do

nothing that is startling, and I will in every way endeavor to make opportunities for you to give the finishing touches to the design upon your return." Paul Philippe Cret Papers, Box 13a, Special Collections, Van Pelt Library, University of Pennsylvania.

16. Paul Philippe Cret, "The Pan American Union Building," in Edward Warren Hoak and Willis Humphrey Church, *Masterpieces of Architecture in the United States . . . Selected by a Jury of Architects: Measured and Drawn by Edward Warren Hoak and Willis Humphrey Church with an Introduction by Paul Cret* (New York: Scribner's, 1930), 127.

17. Grossman, "Paul Cret and the Pan American Union Competition," 33, 35–37.

18. Albert Kelsey, letter to Paul Cret, June 22, 1907. Cret Papers, Box 13a, Special Collections, Van Pelt Library, University of Pennsylvania. This passage is reproduced in Grossman, "Paul Cret and the Pan American Union Competition," 36–37.

19. Cret, "The Pan American Union Building," in Hoak and Church, *Masterpieces,* 127.

20. Ibid.

21. Since the *galerie* played a major role in Cret's architecture, the reader may wish to familiarize himself or herself with the history of this type of room, conveniently presented in Julien Guadet, *Eléments et théorie de l'architecture: Cours professé à l'Ecole Nationale et Spéciale des Beaux-Arts,* 5th ed. (Paris: Librairie de la Construction Moderne, n.d.). 2:87–93, 4:282, 314–317.

22. Elizabeth Grossman, "Paul Philippe Cret: Rationalism and Imagery in American Architecture" (Ph.D. diss., Brown University, 1980), 51–52, 55.

23. Grossman, "Paul Cret and the Pan American Union Competition," 35.

24. W. R. E. and R. R. B., "Indianapolis, Indiana: Indianapolis Public Library, Completed 1917," *Library Journal* 42 (November 1917), [Notes to the frontispiece].

25. Boullée, *Architecture, essai sur l'art,* 131 (fol. 122).

26. For an illustration, see Etlin, *The Architecture of Death,* 140.

27. Jean-Marie Pérouse de Montclos has suggested this dating in "*Les Prix de Rome,*" 205.

28. Charles-Paul Landon, *Annales du Musée et de l'Ecole Moderne des Beaux-Arts* (Paris, year IX, 1801), 1:137–138.

29. Frederick D. Nichols, "Section of the Rotunda, University of Virginia," in William Howard Adams, ed., *The Eye of Thomas Jefferson* (Washington, D.C.: National Gallery of Art, 1976), 296. Nichols questions whether Jefferson's project was ever fully realized: "But no bills for blue paint could be found in the university archives."

30. Neil Levine, "The Romantic Idea of Legibility: Henri Labrouste and the Neo-Grec," in Drexler, ed., *The Architecture of the Ecole des Beaux-Arts,* 351.

31. Ibid., 348.

32. Milton B. Medary, "The Public Library Building, Indianapolis," in Hoak and Church, *Masterpieces,* 69.

33. For an illustration, see McMichael, *Paul Cret at Texas,* 135 (fig. 49).

34. Medary, "The Public Library Building," in Hoak and Church, *Masterpieces,* 69.

35. McMichael, *Paul Cret at Texas,* 76, 78.

36. Ibid., 66.

37. Ibid., 64.

38. Ibid., 50.

39. Clyde H. Burroughs, letter of December 2, 1919, to Paul Cret. Museum Archives of the Detroit Institute of Arts, BCR 1/1.

40. Paul Philippe Cret, "Preliminary Report," January 10, 1920, pp. 2–3. Museum Archives of the Detroit Institute of Arts, BCR 5/3.

41. Ibid., 6, 9, 3.

42. Ibid., 9, 5–6.

43. Cret's drawing of the entrance hall is conserved in the Museum Archives of the Detroit Institute of Arts.

44. Paul P. Cret, "Report on Plans for the New Museum of the Detroit Institute of Arts," December 27, 1920, p. 3. Museum Archives of the Detroit Institute of Arts, BCR 5/5.

45. For plans, see *The Detroit Institute of Arts: The Architecture* (Detroit: Detroit Institute of Arts, 1928), figs. 1 and 2.

46. S[usan] W[atkins], "The Detroit Institute of Arts," in ibid., 4–5.

47. For a view of the entrance foyer, see "Federal Reserve Building. Paul P. Cret, Architect," *American Architect and Architecture* (December 1937), 33.

48. For a chronology of these institutions, see Annie Jacques and Anthony Vidler, "Chronology: The Ecole des Beaux-Arts, 1671–1900," *Oppositions,* no. 8 (Spring 1977), 153–154.

49. Frank Lloyd Wright, *An Autobiography* (London, New York; and Toronto: Longmans, Green and Co., 1932), 154, 156.

50. See Patrick Pinell, "Academic Tradition and the Individual Talent: Similarity and Difference in the Formation of Frank Lloyd Wright," in Robert McCarter, ed., *Frank Lloyd Wright: A Primer on Architectural Principles* (New York: Princeton Architectural Press, 1991), 18–58; Richard A. Etlin, *Frank Lloyd Wright and Le Corbusier: The Romantic Legacy* (Manchester: Manchester University Press, 1994), 158–160.

51. John Lobell, *Between Silence and Light: Spirit in the Architecture of Louis I. Kahn* (Boulder: Shambhala, 1979), 106.

52. Louis Kahn, "Twelve Lines," in *Visionary Architects: Boullée, Ledoux, Lequeu,* exhibition catalog, University of St. Thomas, Houston, October 19, 1967–October 29, 1968 (Houston: University of St. Thomas, 1968), 9.

CHAPTER FOUR

1. Emil Kaufmann, *Von Ledoux bis Le Corbusier: Ursprung und Entwicklung der autonomen Architektur* (Vienna and Leipzig: Dr. R. Passer, 1933). In utilizing Kaufmann's term "autonomous architecture" to distinguish the work of Boullée and Ledoux from that of the Renaissance and Baroque eras, I do not adhere completely to Kaufmann's explanations. See Chap. 1, n. 58.

2. Etienne-Louis Boullée, *Architettura: Saggio sull'arte*, tr. A. Rossi (Padua: Marsilio, [1967]).

3. Meyer Schapiro, "The New Viennese School," *Art Bulletin* 18 (June 1936), 266.

4. The term "visionary architect" was used for the exhibition sponsored by the University of St. Thomas, Houston, which opened on October 19, 1967: "Visionary Architects: Boullée, Ledoux, Lequeu." This term was a felicitous variation on "revolutionary architect," which had been popularized by Emil Kaufmann, notably in *Three Revolutionary Architects—Boullée, Ledoux and Lequeu*, Transactions of the American Philosophical Society 42 (1952). A bibliography of Kaufmann's earlier work on this era is published in the preface to his *Von Ledoux bis Le Corbusier*. He subsequently wrote *Architecture in the Age of Reason: Baroque and Post-Baroque in England, Italy, France* (New York: Dover, 1968 [1955]). Kaufmann repeatedly confused the "revolutionary" aesthetic aspect of these architects' work with the "architecture of the French Revolution" with which, as he was well aware, it does not always coincide, either chronologically or ideologically. For a recent discussion of the problems that this confusion has caused, see Anthony Vidler, "Researching Revolutionary Architecture," *Journal of Architectural Education* 44 (August 1991), 206–210.

5. Amaury Duval, *Paris et ses monuments* (Paris, 1803), 23.

6. Abbé Jean-Louis de Cordemoy, *Nouveau Traité de toute l'architecture ou l'art de bastir* (Farnsborough: Gregg Press, 1966 [1706; 1714 rev. ed.]), 92–94, 112, 157–159, 161–162; Abbé Marc-Antoine Laugier, *Essai sur l'architecture*, 29, 35, 39–42, 44–45; and *Observations sur l'architecture* (Paris, 1765), 181. Laugier argues that a complete entablature signals the base for the roof of a building. Thus, only an architrave or an architrave with a few of the parts of a cornice was to be used to demarcate an intermediary floor.

7. Jacques Gondoin, *Descriptions des Ecoles de Chirurgie . . .* (Paris, 1780), 6.

8. Cordemoy, *Nouveau Traité*, 61–63, 129, 141–143; Laugier, *Essai*, 13–20; Etienne-Louis Boullée, *Architecture, essai sur l'art*, 81 (fols. 88v–89). See also Wolfgang Herrmann, *Laugier and Eighteenth Century French Theory* (London: A. Zwemmer Ltd., 1962), 110–112, 247–248 (appendix 11: "Pilaster versus Column"). Whereas Cordemoy accepted engaged piers, he rejected the pilaster "with only one face extending out from the wall . . . by one sixth part only," as "poorly conceived and . . . not beautiful" and indicative of the "architect's sterility and lack of taste." Engaged columns were simply "unbearable." For Laugier, the engaged column "sees its grace infinitely diminished"; the pilaster is both "maussade" (disagreeable, dull) and a "colifichet" (a trinket). Boullée contemptuously dismissed the pilaster as "un plaquis de quelques pouces d'épaisseur," a mere relief several inches thick.

9. Cordemoy, *Nouveau Traité*, 118.

10. Alan Colquhoun, *Modernity and the Classical Tradition: Architectural Essays 1980–1987* (Cambridge, Mass.: MIT Press, 1989), 29–30.

11. Neil Levine, "Frank Lloyd Wright's Own Houses and His Changing Concept

of Representation," in Carol R. Bolon et al., eds., *The Nature of Frank Lloyd Wright* (Chicago: University of Chicago Press, 1988), 26.

12. Herrmann, *Laugier,* 47–50.

13. Anthony Vidler, "The Idea of Type: The Transformation of the Academic Ideal, 1750–1830," *Oppositions,* no. 8 (Spring 1977), 95.

14. Laugier, *Essai,* 49. I have used here the translation in Marc-Antoine Laugier, *An Essay on Architecture,* tr. Wolfgang and Anni Herrmann (Los Angeles: Hennessey and Ingalls, 1977), 32.

15. Laugier, *Essai,* 56.

16. Boullée, *Architecture,* 83 (fol. 90), 133 (fol. 124), 131 (fol. 122).

17. The phrase "forest of columns" comes from Sidonius, "silva per columnas," which is repeatedly quoted by Cordemoy in his *Nouveau Traité,* 138, 195, 198–199, 202.

18. For illustrations, see Jean-Marie Pérouse de Montclos, *"Les Prix de Rome,"* 172–173.

19. Boullée, *Architecture,* 133–135 (fols. 124–125v). For an illustration of such a dome inside a pyramidal mortuary chapel, see Richard A. Etlin, *The Architecture of Death,* 120.

20. Jacques-François Blondel, *Cours d'architecture,* 2:341–342.

21. Allan Braham, *The Architecture of the French Enlightenment* (Berkeley: University of California Press, 1980), 48–49.

22. Laugier, *Essai,* 46–47, 178, 198.

23. Boullée, *Architecture,* 91–95 (fols. 94v–97).

24. For illustrations of these last three buildings, see Pérouse de Montclos, *Boullée,* plates 108, 109, 111, 113. Illustrations of other projects by Boullée discussed below also can be found in this book.

25. For illustrations, see Jean-Marie Pérouse de Montclos, *Boullée,* plates 102, 99, 101. My labeling of these variants does not necessarily follow the chronological order of their creation.

26. Anthony Vidler, *Claude-Nicolas Ledoux,* 114.

27. Claude-Nicolas Ledoux, *L'Architecture,* 1:179.

28. Ibid., 1:115–116, 235–239.

29. Anthony Vidler, *The Writing of the Walls,* 19.

30. For illustrations, see, for example, Demetri Porphyrios, ed., *Classicism Is Not a Style* (London: Architectural Design and Academy Editions, 1982), 59–69.

31. Laugier, *Essai,* 174, as quoted in Herrmann, *Laugier,* 69. I have used Herrmann's translation here with a minor change.

32. Jacques-Germain Soufflot, "Mémoire sur l'architecture gothique" (April 12, 1741), in Michael Petzet, *Soufflots Sainte-Geneviève und der französische Kirchenbau des 18. Jahrhunderts* (Berlin: Walter de Gruyter and Co., 1961), 131–142 (appendix III).

33. Maximilien Brébion, "Mémoire à Monsieur le Comte de la Billarderie d'Angiviller, directeur et ordonnateur général des Bâtimens" (1780), in Petzet, *Soufflots Sainte-Geneviève,* 147 (appendix IV).

34. Cordemoy, *Nouveau Traité,* 110–111: "On ne peut douter que je ne sois pour les colonnes; et c'est peut-être un foible que j'ai de commun avec les anciens, dont je ne me sçaurois défaire." See also p. 117.

35. Ibid., 50, 52, 57, 88, 93, 109–111, 120, 138–139, 144, 147, 195–199, 202.

36. Julien-David Leroy, *Histoire de la disposition et des formes différentes que les Chrétiens ont données à leurs temples, depuis le règne de Constantin le Grand, jusqu'à nous* (Paris, 1764), 47.

37. Ibid., 2–3, 48–49, 86–89.

38. For illustrations, see Joseph Rykwert, *The First Moderns: The Architects of the Eighteenth Century* (Cambridge, Mass.: MIT Press, 1980), 418–419.

39. Laugier, though, had limited his expression of aesthetic appreciation of the freestanding column to mentioning that when one used a pilaster or an engaged column, one "lost the grace" inherent to the individual column. Leroy emphasized the effects derived from large numbers of columns viewed in the same scene.

40. Leroy, *Histoire,* 50–63, 71 ("cette partie Metaphysique, et très-intéressante de l'Architecture"), 83–84.

41. On the sublime, see Edmund Burke, *A Philosophical Enquiry into the Origins of Our Ideas of the Sublime and the Beautiful* (London, 1757); and Marjorie Hope Nicholson, *Mountain Gloom and Mountain Glory* (New York, 1973).

42. Boullée, *Architecture,* 82–83 (fols. 89v–90), my emphasis.

43. Ibid., 83–84 (fols. 90–90v).

44. Leroy, *Histoire,* 1. This is the opening phrase of the book.

45. Dr. Eugène Minkowski, *Vers une Cosmologie: Fragments philosophiques* (Paris: Aubier- Montaigne, 1967 [1936]), esp. 69–78; Gaston Bachelard, *La Poétique de l'espace* (Paris: Presses Universitaires de France, 1970 [1957]), esp. 17.

46. Boullée, *Architecture,* 85 (fol. 91).

47. Ibid., 137–139 (fols. 127–127v).

48. As quoted by George Poulet in *Les Métamorphoses du cercle* (Paris: Plon, 1961), iii. Poulet explains that this phrase appeared the first time in a pseudohermetic manuscript of the twelfth century. In this book, Poulet traces the concept backward in time to Greek philosophers who defined eternity in a comparable way before he chronicles the persistent recurrence of the image into the twentieth century. For the varied use of the image during Boullée's time, see 72–132.

49. On this subject, see Etlin, *Frank Lloyd Wright and Le Corbusier: The Romantic Legacy,* 15–23.

CHAPTER FIVE

1. Julien Guadet, *Eléments et théorie de l'architecture: Cours professé à l'Ecole Nationale et Spéciale des Beaux-Arts,* 5th ed. (Paris: Librairie de la Construction Moderne, n.d.), 2:37. The chapter on "The Room in the Modern Dwelling" opens as follows: "It can be said that the modern dwelling was born in the eighteenth century, and Blondel, in his treatise on architecture, says, not without pride, that recently a veritable revolution had occurred in the architecture of *hôtels* and houses, especially with respect to *la distribution.*"

2. Brian Brace Taylor, "Sauvage et l'habitat hygiénique ou la révolution de la propreté à Paris," in Maurice Culot and Lise Grenier, eds., *Henri Sauvage, 1873–1932,* exhibition catalog, Société des Architectes Diplômés par le Gouvernement (Paris) and Ecole Nationale Supérieure d'Architecture et des Art Visuels (Brussels), November 1976–February 1977 (Brussels: Archives d'Architecture Moderne, 1976), 74, 76.

3. Pierre Saddy, "Perret et les idées reçues," *Architecture Mouvement Continuité,* no. 37 (November 1975), 22.

4. Peter Collins, *Concrete: The Vision of a New Architecture: A Study of Auguste Perret and His Precursors* (New York: Horizon Press, 1959), 166–168, 171, 218.

5. See Richard A. Etlin, "A Paradoxical Avant-Garde: Le Corbusier's Villas of the 1920s," *Architectural Review* 181 (January 1987), 24–25, and *Frank Lloyd Wright and Le Corbusier: The Romantic Legacy,* 118–125.

6. For Le Corbusier's repudiation of the picturesque design strategy typified by his own earlier La Roche-Jeanneret Houses (Paris, 1923–1924) and by Mallet-Stevens's work in favor of an exterior "mask," see Le Corbusier, "L'Exposition de l'Ecole Spéciale d'Architecture" (1924), *L'Esprit Nouveau,* no. 23, and reprinted with an English translation in *Rob Mallet-Stevens architecte* (Brussels: Archives d'Architecture Moderne, 1980), 379–384, where it is mistakenly identified as an unpublished manuscript. On the theme of the reasoned picturesque, see Etlin, *Frank Lloyd Wright and Le Corbusier,* 77–80, 120–121, 143–149.

7. Le Corbusier's debt to the eighteenth-century *hôtel* has been widely studied. See, for example, Colin Rowe, "The Mathematics of the Ideal Villa," in *The Mathematics of the Ideal Villa and Other Essays* (Cambridge, Mass.: MIT Press, 1982), 1–22; Kurt Forster, "Antiquity and Modernity in the La Roche-Jeanneret Houses of 1923," *Oppositions,* nos. 15/16 (Winter/Spring 1979), 131–153; Alan Colquhoun, "Displacement of Concepts in Le Corbusier," in *Essays in Architectural Criticism: Modern Architecture and Historical Change* (New York: Institute for Architecture and Urban Studies, 1981), 51; Michael Dennis, *Court & Garden: From the French Hôtel to the City of Modern Architecture,* Graham Foundation Architecture Series (Cambridge, Mass.: MIT Press, 1986), 190–219; Etlin, "A Paradoxical Avant-Garde," *Architectural Review* (January 1987), 24–26, 31; and *Frank Lloyd Wright and Le Corbusier,* 124–125.

8. This manuscript, whose title page features the coat of arms of the House of Grimaldi, is conserved in the Bibliothèque Mazarine in Paris as MS. 3691. It measures 22.4 cm × 18.2 cm and has eighty-eight pages and four pen-and-wash drawings. Whereas the author is given as "Blondel fils architecte," several references in the text confirm that this designation refers to Jacques-François Blondel. In five different places Blondel sends the reader to three of his principal works.

9. For other scholarly studies of the French hôtel, see Louis Hautecoeur, *Histoire de l'architecture classique en France* (Paris, 1950), 2:195–204; Michel Gallet, *Stately Mansions: Eighteenth Century Paris Architecture,* tr. James C. Palmes (New York: Praeger, 1972); Wend Graf Kalnein and Michael Levey, *Art and Architecture of the Eighteenth Century in France,* tr. of part II, "Architecture," by J. R.

Foster (Harmondsworth and Baltimore: Penguin Books, 1972), 218–250; Dennis, *Court & Garden*, passim.

10. Charles-Augustin d'Aviler, *Cours d'architecture qui comprend les ordres de Vignole* (Paris, 1691).

11. Charles-Etienne Briseux, *L'Art de bâtir des maisons de campagne, où l'on traite de leur distribution, de leur construction, et de leur décoration . . .* , 2 vols. (Paris, 1743).

12. Talbot Hamlin, *Architecture through the Ages* (New York: G. P. Putnam's Sons, 1940), 464–465. This passage, with minor modifications, is quoted in Dennis, *Court & Garden*, 91.

13. C. Oulmont, *La Maison* (Paris, 1929), 30.

14. Jean Courtonne, *Traité de perspective . . . , avec les remarques sur l'architecture . . .* (Paris, 1725), 92.

15. Jacques-François Blondel, *Architecture françoise . . .* (Paris, 1752), 1:21. See also Blondel, *De la Distribution des maisons de plaisance, et de la décoration des édifices en général* (Paris, 1737) 1:130, and *Discours sur la nécessité de l'étude de l'architecture . . .* (Paris, 1754), 43.

16. Courtonne, *Traité*, 92. See also Briseux, *L'Art de bâtir*, 1:27.

17. After introducing this terminology in "'Les dedans,' Jacques-François Blondel and the System of the Home," *Gazette des Beaux-Arts* 91 (April 1978), 139–145, I was gratified that Michael Dennis subsequently used the concept for the title of chap. 4, "Display and Retreat: The Rococo Hotel," in *Court & Garden,* to which the reader is referred for a further consideration of this theme. In Kalnein and Levey, *Art and Architecture of the Eighteenth Century in France,* 219, Kalnein, using earlier historical studies, explained that the separation of the "public sphere" from the "private" was one of the "decisive innovations" introduced by the eighteenth-century *hôtel.*

18. Blondel, "Abrégé," fol. 5.

19. D'Aviler, *Cours* (1710 ed.), 180.

20. Blondel, "Abrégé," fols. 5–6, 11–12.

21. Ibid., fols. 10–11, 26.

22. Ibid., fols. 27–29.

23. See Oulmont, *La Maison,* 30.

24. Blondel, "Abrégé" fols. 15–18.

25. Blondel, *De la Distribution,* 1:159. Unfortunately, neither the plan of the *entresol* nor the section is attached to Blondel's "Abrégé." The text, though, relates that the principal rooms measured eighteen-and-a-half feet high; the lower rooms ten feet; and the *entresol* seven-and-a-half feet, thereby leaving one foot for the thickness of the floor. See fol. 40.

26. Blondel, "Abrégé," fols. 18, 23, 41.

27. Ibid., fols. 19–20, 41.

28. Ibid., fol. 45.

29. Briseux, *L'Art de bâtir,* 1:26.

30. Courtonne, *Traité,* 96.

31. In "Le Cycle des immondices," *Dix-Huitième Siècle* 9 (1977), 214, Pierre Saddy concludes his article by referring to this period as "un siècle classificateur."

32. Judith S. Levey and Agnes Greenhall, eds., *The Concise Columbia Encyclopedia* (New York: Avon, 1983), 117, 212, 483.

33. Anthony Vidler, "The Idea of Type: The Transformation of the Academic Ideal, 1750–1830," *Oppositions*, no. 8 (Spring 1977), 106.

34. For sources for further reading, see Chap. 1 above, n. 52.

35. For *une architecture terrible*, see Blondel, *Cours*, 1:426–427.

36. For a discussion of the apparent influence on Ledoux of the ideal prison postulated by Jacques-Pierre Brissot de Warville in his *Théorie des lois criminelles*, published in 1781, see Anthony Vidler, *Claude-Nicolas Ledoux*, 203–206.

37. Blondel, *Cours*, 2:310–316; 3:383–391.

38. Claude-Nicolas Ledoux, *L'Architecture considérée*, 1:155–156; Blondel, *Cours*, 1:426–427.

39. Blondel, "Abrégé," fol. 50, and *Discours*, 21; Briseux, *L'Art de bâtir*, 2:116.

40. Blondel, "Abrégé," fol. 51.

41. Ibid., fols. 51–52, 55; See also, Briseux, *L'Art de bâtir*, 1:116–117, 120.

42. See Blondel, *De la Distribution*, I, pl. 34.

43. See, for example, Etienne-Louis Boullée, *Architecture, essai sur l'art*, 68–69 (fols. 81–81v).

44. Edmund Bartell, Jr., *Hints for Picturesque Improvements in Ornamented Cottages, and Their Scenery* . . . (London, 1804), 122. The text continues: " . . . principles should be in some measure laid aside . . . for a cottage or a shed; there all affectation should be avoided; blank windows in a cottage, for the sake of uniformity, would be as absurd, as the neglect of this principle would be in a palace" (123).

45. Kenneth Clark, *The Gothic Revival: An Essay in the History of Taste* (New York: Harper & Row, 1962), 114.

CHAPTER SIX

1. J.-N.-L. Durand, *Précis des leçons d'architecture*, 2:21.

2. Abbé Charles-Gabriel Porée, *Lettres sur la sépulture dans les églises* . . . (Caen, 1749), 41–42.

3. My work on this theme is greatly indebted to Philippe Ariès, author of *Essais sur l'histoire de la mort en Occident, du moyen âge à nos jours* (Paris, 1975), and *L'Homme devant la mort* (Paris, 1977).

4. Andrew Jackson Downing, "Public Cemeteries and Public Gardens," *The Horticulturalist* 4 (July 1849), 9. See also Richard A. Etlin, *The Architecture of Death*, 358–359; David Schuyler, *The New Urban Landscape: The Redefinition of City Form in Nineteenth-Century America* (Baltimore: Johns Hopkins University Press, 1986), 38–42.

5. Schuyler, *The New Urban Landscape*, 54–55.

6. For further reading, see Etlin, *The Architecture of Death*, chaps. 4–7.

7. For illustrations, see ibid., figs. 24, 31, 36, 45–46, 67–69.

8. On this theme, see "The Space of Emulation" above in Chap. 1; and Etlin, *The Architecture of Death*, 41–63, 119–130, 282–290.

9. Jean Starobinski, *L'Invention de la liberté, 1700–1789* (Geneva, 1964), 202.

10. Nicolas Le Camus de Mézières, *Le Génie de l'architecture, ou l'anaolgie de cet art avec nos sensations* (Paris, 1780), 1–78, 275–276.

11. Etienne-Louis Boullée, *Architecture, essai sur l'art,* 78–79, 133–137 (fols. 87, 123v–126v).

12. Ibid., 75 (fols. 85–85v).

13. Christopher Hussey, *English Gardens and Landscapes, 1700–1750* (New York, 1967), 114–115, 122–128.

14. "An Epistolary Description of the Late Mr. Pope's House and Garden at Twickenham" (1747), in John Dixon Hunt and Peter Willis, eds., *The Genius of the Place* (Cambridge, Mass.: MIT Press, 1988 [1975]), 247–253; Horace Walpole, *Essay on Modern Gardening* (Strawberry Hill, 1785), 63; Maynard Mack, *The Garden and the City: Retirement and Politics in the Late Poetry of Pope, 1731–1743* (Toronto: University of Toronto Press, 1969), 28–31; John Dixon Hunt, *The Figure in the Landscape: Poetry, Painting and Gardening during the Eighteenth Century* (Baltimore: Johns Hopkins University Press, 1976), 79–88; Morris R. Brownell, *Alexander Pope and the Arts in Georgian England* (Oxford, 1978), 133.

15. William Shenstone, *The Works in Verse and Prose of William Shenstone, Esq.,* ed. R. Dodsley, 3 vols. (London, 1764–1769), 1:3–6; 2:125–144, 333–392; 3:329–336; Thomas Whately, *Observations on Modern Gardening* (London, 1770), 170; Joseph Heeley, *Letter on the Beauties of Hagley, Envil, and the Leasowes, with Critical Remarks and Observations on the Modern Taste in Gardening,* 2 vols. (London, 1777), 1:192–193; 2:114–115; Beverly Sprague Allen, *Tides in English Taste (1619–1800): A Background for the Study of Literature,* 2 vols. (New York, 1958), 2:176–177; H. F. Clark, "Eighteenth-Century Elysiums: The Role of 'Association' in the Landscape Movement," *Journal of the Warburg Institute* 6 (1943), 175–177.

16. On the appreciation of the commemorative nature of Stowe with its Virgilian landscape and of Jaegerspris, see Etlin, *The Architecture of Death,* 193–197, 212.

17. For illustrations of monuments mentioned in this chapter, see ibid.

18. George B. Clark, "The History of Stowe," *The Stoic* (parts IV, VII, VIII, X, XIII, XIX) (March 1968–December 1973); "Grecian Taste and Gothic Virtue; Lord Cobham's Gardening Program and Its Iconography," in *The Splendors of Stowe,* offprint from *Apollo* (June 1973), 26–31; and "William Kent: Heresy in Stowe's Elysium" in *Furor Hortensis: Essays on the History of the English Landscape Garden in Memory of H. F. Clark,* ed. Peter Willis (Edinburgh, 1974), 48–56; Michael J. Gibbon, "The History of Stowe," *The Stoic* (parts IX, XI, XII, XXI) (March 1970–December 1974); Hussey, *English Gardens,* 93–103; Peter Willis, *Charles Bridgeman and the English Landscape Garden* (London, 1977), 107–112, 121–122; Michael McCarthy, "Eighteenth Century Amateur Architects and Their Gardens," in Nikolaus Pevsner, ed., *The Picturesque Garden and Its Influence outside the British Isles* (Washington, D.C.: Dumbarton Oaks, 1974), 31–55; Allen, *Tides,* 2:175–176; Ronald Paulson, *Emblem and Expression: Meaning in English Art of the Eighteenth Century* (Cambridge, 1975),

22–28; John Dixon Hunt, "Emblem and Expressionism in the Eighteenth-Century Landscape Garden," *Eighteenth-Century Studies* 4 (1971), 292–301.

19. Christian Cay L. Hirschfeld, *Théorie de l'art des jardins, traduit de l'allemand,* 5 vols. (Leipzig, 1779–1785), 3:226–237; Pierre-Maxime Schuhl, "Le mémorial de Jaegerspris," *Gazette des Beaux-Arts* 85 (February 1975), 49–60.

20. Hirschfeld, *Théorie,* 2:71–74, 5:302–305; [Stanislas-Xavier, comte de Girardin], *Promenade ou itinéraire des jardins d'Ermenonville . . .* (Paris, 1788), 17, 21–26; [Villeneuve], *Vues pittoresques . . . des principaux jardins anglois qui sont en France: Ermenonville* (Paris, c. 1788); Christopher Thacker, "Voltaire and Rousseau: Eighteenth-Century Gardeners," *Studies on Voltaire and the Eighteenth Century* 90 (1972), 1609–1610; Leslie G. Crocker, *Jean-Jacques Rousseau,* 2 vols. (New York, 1968–1973), 2:351–352; Eva Maria Neumeyer, "The Landscape Garden as a Symbol in Rousseau, Goethe and Flaubert," *Journal of the History of Ideas* 8 (1947), 196; Willis, *Bridgeman,* 145–146.

21. René-Louis de Girardin, *De la Composition des paysages, ou des moyens d'embellir la nature autour des habitations champêtres* (Geneva and Paris, 1777), 109–110.

22. Paul Van Tieghem, "Les *Idylles* de Gessner et le rêve pastoral," in *Le Préromantisme: Etudes d'histoire littéraire européenne,* 3 vols. (Paris: Librairie Félix Alcan, 1924–1930), 2:228–292; John Hibberd, *Salomon Gessner: His Creative Achievement and Influence* (Cambridge: Cambridge University Press, 1976). For summary accounts of several of Gessner's idylls, see Etlin, *The Architecture of Death,* 202.

23. Hirschfeld, *Théorie,* 1:64–74; 2:47–49, 71–74, 105, 123–124, 194, 201–206; 3:89–90, 153–171, 226–237, 263–274; 4:94–97, 271, 276; 5:131–133, 231, 247, 251–252, 262, 269, 302–305, 410–403.

24. Claude-Henri Watelet, *Essai sur les jardins* (Paris, 1774), 111–115; Abbé Jacques Delille, *Les Jardins, ou l'art d'embellir les paysages,* 4th ed. (Paris, 1782), 85, 100–101; Robert Mauzi, "Delille, peintre, poète et philosophe dans les *Jardins,*" in *Delille est-il mort?* (Clermont-Ferrand: G. de Bussac, 1967), 176.

25. Jacques-Henri Bernardin de Saint-Pierre, *Etudes de la nature* (Paris, 1784), 3:123, 357–376.

26. Hirschfeld, *Théorie,* 5:133–135.

27. Antoine-Chrysostôme Quatremère de Quincy, "Cimetière," *Architecture: Encyclopédie méthodique* (Paris, 1788), 1:677–683.

28. Alexandre Lenoir, *Description historique et chronologique des monuments de sculpture, réunis au Musée des Monuments Français,* 5th ed. (Paris, year VIII), 17, 363–367, and *Musée des monuments français . . .* (Paris, year IX, 1800), 18–20; Charles-Paul Landon, *Annales du Musée et de l'Ecole Moderne des Beaux-Arts . . . ,* 20 vols. (Paris, 1800–1809), 1:12; *Jardins en France 1760–1820: Pays d'illusion, terre d'expériences,* exhibition catalog, Caisse des Monuments Historiques et des Sites, Hôtel de Sully, Paris, May 18–September 11, 1977 (Paris, 1977), 149.

29. René Schneider, *Quatremère de Quincy et son intervention dans les arts* (Paris, 1910), 186.

30. Jacques Cambry, *Rapport sur les sépultures, présenté à l'Administration Centrale du Département de la Seine, par le citoyen Cambry* . . . (Paris, year VII).

31. Frochot, Préfet du Départment de la Seine, letter of 8 Prairial, year IX (May 28, 1801), to the minister of the interior, Archives Nationales, F³ ¹¹ Seine 20: "Ce lieu solitaire, placé à l'une des extrémités de Paris, présente une surface de 99 arpents, orné des plus belles plantations. Il offre par la manière pittoresque dont il est dessiné, par l'irrégularité de ses formes, la surprise de ses mouvements, un Elysée délicieux où la mort n'aurait d'empire que par les souvenirs de ceux qui survivent, par le monument qui couvrirait la cendre chérie, par la simple épitaphe suspendue au feuillage de l'arbre funéraire."

32. Minister of the interior, letter of 9 Prairial, year IX (May 29, 1801), to Frochot, préfet du Départment de la Seine, Archives Nationales, F³ ¹¹ Seine 20: "Enfin si ce champ de repos n'était pas unique, tous ceux qui existent déjà ou que l'on doit établir postérieurement ne pouvant réunir les avantages du Jardin de Monceau, il deviendrait en quelque sorte le cimetière privilégié des hommes riches." I have used the standard spelling of "Monceau" in transcribing this text.

33. *Rapport présenté par M. Hérold, au nom de la deuxième commission sur le projet de création d'un cimetière parisien à Méry-sur-Oise, Conseil Municipal de Paris, annexe au procès-verbal de la séance du 11 avril 1874* ([Paris, 1874]).

34. For plans of this terrain that illustrate these changes, see Etlin, *The Architecture of Death,* 341–342.

35. C.-P. Arnaud and Laurens l'aîné, *Recueil de tombeaux des quatre cimetières de Paris* (Paris, 1813), 16.

CHAPTER SEVEN

1. David Watkin and Tilman Mellinghoff, *German Architecture and the Classical Ideal* (Cambridge, Mass.: MIT Press, 1987), 72.

2. For an illustration, see *Visionary Architects: Boullée, Ledoux, Lequeu,* 23.

3. For illustrations of the two other variants of this project, see AAUP, Paul P. Cret, no. 160.

4. Frank Lloyd Wright, *An Autobiography* (London and New York: Longmans, Green and Co., 1932), 146.

5. For illustrations, see Stuart Wrede, *The Architecture of Erik Gunnar Asplund* (Cambridge, Mass.: MIT Press, 1980), figs. 173–180.

6. For illustrations, see Frank Lloyd Wright Archives, Taliesin West, nos. 5811.001, 5811.002.

7. Wright, *An Autobiography,* 14.

8. Ibid., 26.

9. I am grateful to Bruce Brooks Pfeiffer who, during my visit to the Frank Lloyd Wright Archives at Taliesin West in April 1991, explained this point as well as the alignment with the grandparent's obelisk and the project to bury the Taliesin Fellows in the long line of graves.

10. For illustrations, see Frank Lloyd Wright Archives, nos. 5811.011A, 5811.012.

11. See Richard A. Etlin, *The Architecture of Death,* 47.

12. For an illustration, see Jean-Marie Pérouse de Montclos, "*Les Prix de Rome,*" 60.

13. On this competition, see Michael Paul Driskel, "By Competition or Administrative Decree? The Contest for the Tomb of Napoleon in 1841," *Art Journal* 48 (Spring 1989), 46–52.

14. César Daly, "Exposition des projets de Tombeau pour Napoléon," *Revue Générale de l'Architecture* 2 (1841), 614.

15. For a discussion about human spatial projection from the place that one is occupying to a different place that one imagines, see the essay "L'Espace primitif" by the psychiatrist and philosopher Dr. Eugène Minkowski in *Vers une Cosmologie: Fragments philosophiques* (Paris: Aubier-Montaigne, 1967 [1936]), 69–78.

16. For illustrations, see Bruno Zevi, *Giuseppe Terragni* (Bologna: Zanichelli, 1980), 138; Ada Francesca Marcianò, *Giuseppe Terragni, opera completa 1925–1943* (Rome, 1987), 137; Thomas L. Schumacher, *Surface and Symbol: Giuseppe Terragni and the Architecture of Italian Rationalism* (New York: Princeton Architectural Press, 1991), 127–131.

17. For illustrations, see Josef Lux, "Schöne Brunnen," *Der Architekt* 10 (1904), 33 and pl. 9.

18. For an illustration, see Bruce Brooks Pfeiffer, *Frank Lloyd Wright Monograph 1924–1936* (Tokyo, 1985), 48–49. See also in the Frank Lloyd Wright Archives nos. 2801.0002 and 2801.003.

19. This text is written on the published drawing that illustrates the other variant, indicated in the previous note.

20. Luigi Zuccoli, *Quindici anni di vita e di lavoro con l'amico e maestro architetto Giuseppe Terragni* (Como: Cesare Nani, 1981), 23.

21. See the three different projects by Limongelli, Baroni, and Enrico Griffini and Paolo Mezzanotte, respectively, in "Concorso per il monumento al Fante," *Architettura e Arti Decorative* 1 (July–August 1921), 197, 201, 204.

22. Etlin, *The Architecture of Death,* 255.

23. Bruce Brooks Pfeiffer, *Drawings,* 98.

24. Handwritten note signed "FLW" on drawing 3710.001, Frank Lloyd Wright Memorial Foundation Archives, Taliesin West, Scottsdale, Arizona.

25. Bruce Brooks Pfeiffer, "'Memorial to the Soil,' Chapel for Southern Wisconsin, 1937," in *Treasures of Taliesin: Seventy-Six Unbuilt Designs* (Fresno: California State University Press; and Carbondale and Edwardsville: Southern Illinois University Press, 1985), item 21.

26. Pfeiffer, "'Memorial,'" in *Treasures,* item 21; and Wright, *An Autobiography,* 16–45, 61.

27. Pfeiffer, "'Memorial,'" in *Treasures,* item 21.

28. For other illustrations of this project by Samonà as well as the sources for the text that follows, see *Il nuovo stile Littorio: I progetti per il Palazzo del Littorio*

e della Mostra della Rivoluzione Fascista in via dell'Impero (Milan and Rome, 1936), 79–84; "Concorso per il Palazzo del Littorio" (fascicolo speciale con 43 progetti e 390 illustrazioni), *Architettura* 13 (1934), 10–11.

29. See Richard A. Etlin, *Modernism in Italian Architecture*, 413–415.

30. Etienne-Louis Boullée, *Architecture, essai sur l'art*, 136–137 (fol. 126): "Me trouvant à la campagne, j'y côtoyais un bois au clair de la lune. Mon effigie produite par la lumière excita mon attention (assurément, ce n'était pas une nouveauté pour moi). Par une disposition d'esprit particulière, l'effet de ce simulacre me parut d'une tristesse extrême. Les arbres dessinés sur la terre par leurs ombres me firent la plus profonde impression. Ce tableau s'agrandissait par mon imagination. J'aperçus alors tout ce qu'il y a de plus sombre dans la nature. Qu'y voyais-je? La masse des objets se détachant en noir sur une lumière d'une pâleur extrême. La nature semblait s'offrir, en deuil, à mes regards. Frappé des sentiments que j'éprouvais, je m'occupai, dès ce moment, d'en faire une application particulière à l'architecture."

INDEX